# *Fortuitous Event*

## ALSO BY MICHAEL O'CONNOR

# *Fortuitous Event*

## Michael O'Connor

*To those we meet along the way; the rich and complicated lives of those who came before us.*

# CONTENTS

## Preamble: *Stuttering Man*

The Stuttering Man

At Yerba Buena center

Lives between towers


Reaffirmation

Appears to have been received

Becomes a mandate


Were more noble

Resulting from peer review

Puts into practice


Reactively fair

Stems from a certain belief

Notably formal

With major advance

No limitations imposed

Reach for that exit

If one overlaps

Those limiting magnitudes

Pursuing subsides

Because this design

Cataloging his mission

Measures envision

Proceed on this base

Describe what is coming next

It is through stutters

Exercise they must

In response to some charter

Select that design

So fortuitous

Arts experimental cast

Does so with some depth


Extensive review

By those interested parties

Selection follows


The range of stutter

Intrinsic to this conflict

Propagate this scale


Very public review

Dynamic revolution

Determine its range


Formation is close

And disruptions dominate

As one can account

Even flow stutters

Could be seen to set limits

Works out to the few


The idea too

Measures the proper motions

Those facets of mass


So do assumptions

So dynamically inclined

To time fleshing out


Tourists face in spite

Calibrate by their distance

Remand attention


Put them on the spot

Keep these images at bay

Producing just one

Daunting it may seem

Small part on what can be done

To resolve this truth


That Stuttering Man

Why he is so flattering

And what should be done


When we quantify

With inherent example

Just one of the two


Distraction appeals

At irregular angles

Test all the facts


First the need to feel

Holds the promise of large gains

We drive to include

Fortuitous Event

Convince for so long

Those are compelling reasons

We must make this point


Our earnest to share

This community knowledge

Envelopes his path


We must not forget

Stuttering Men everywhere

Those events resolve

# Examination of Pleasure

Fortuitous Event

# Chapter One

## *Intersections in the Road*

THIS IS WHAT I CAME TO HEAR.   All around me sways constantly with the mild undulating currents as bits and pieces of organic material floats by in diagonal lines, then passing in symmetrical curves caused by the incoming and receding waves.  The rippled arcs on the surface of the water gradually intersect and the interference patterns are a marvel to look at; predictably some materials buoy to the surface while others sink in succession into the shallow depths of this naturally carved out waterway.

My movements are deliberately slow in the morning and silently in cold and blue gray waters because I do not want to cause any obvious disturbances with regard to the closest inhabitants of the rock wall I am currently mesmerized by.  The overall visibility is around thirty five feet in the earliest part of the mid week afternoon and mid month of non stormy weather.  Sea life is abundant as it collectively goes about its business of subsistence living on the steep walls.  Last night's moon was but a quarter sliver of silver and white gold hung directly above in a predominately clear sky.  It had been a star filled night and above the surface is very cold as a result.

These are the very important details I want to remember because I wanted to go free diving today without the usual weekend warriors—so astonished and marveling at the solo diver in the water—their banter as stifled because it is altogether nonexistent during the mid week. I wanted to avoid the churned debris in the water at slack tide that is comparatively murkier at the end of evening storms and as the day is breaking. This waterway is shimmering and it is clear fluid full of small particles of life but not abundant enough to diminish visibility. You might argue that I am a mid week warrior and my (current) world is cold and silent and I am as comfortable under its water line as I am on or near its cold surface. I am not uncomfortable and there is little chance that I am in any danger of drowning. Right now I am simply in a neutral buoyancy state.

I am supposed to hear the sounds of this underwater environment below the surface but I have managed to block it all out without trying hard. It is hypnotizing and I do not want to lose any of the power of this trance like behavior that I am exhibiting at the moment more than twelve feet down. I float easily from one yoga-like pose to the next and I am quite aware that these positions would be as harmful by a man of my stature if attempted on dry land instead of out at sea. I am not out of shape but I am cognizant of the fact that I do not bend easily. I did not realize just how flexible I could be in the water until now. I try several additional contorted positions and I am truly amazed that I have pulled them off. Namaste: it is all I can sense at the moment.

Turning one hundred and eighty degrees counter clockwise I am supported by the buoyancy of the long kelp beds that I have swam in to the middle of but I have nothing to fear, yet. My six to seven millimeter wetsuit—my outer skin—helps me slide away from the grabbing stalks and large leaves of this underwater kelp forest. I am cognizant of the knife on my forearm and the weight belt around my waist because I know that they can be hindrances to my fluid movements. I recognize that even my snorkel can be pulled out of my mouth at a most unfortunate moment if I am too reckless. I stop my accentuated movements and I regain a sense of calm that is required to keep me alive. I am one with the environment and I allow the weight of my belt counteract my buoyancy and sink to the bottom of this reef in this archipelago in the North Puget Sound. At the moment I do not need to take another breath of fresh air. I am on the bottom and I am better fit for it as a large surge just hit this passage. A boat must have passed through the outer channel.

Kicking off of the rock wall on a barren spot I move like a missile across an opening in the kelp forest which provides me with a new vantage point. I do not want to get crushed against rock on the next series of waves. I kick further down on a four degree gradient, hugging the bottom.

There is a small cave ahead and I have already spotter a wolf eel that has mistakenly poked its garish head out into the open. Perhaps it is hunting or maybe it really did spot me and wants to make it clear that this is an occupied territory. I do not immediately back off and I make ready my Hawaiian sling with a suitably mounted trident tip. I stop my descent and I do kick in less than powerful forward motion toward the surface with my

21

elongated flippers and soon I am taking in another blast of cold but fresh air, surveying my current position with regard to land fall, spin in a tight circle looking for any incoming crafts, and then proceed back down and back to that cave. I pick up where I left off. The wolf is still there and is as astonished with my disregard of its earlier warning. It lunges with mouth agape and I dodge with another fluid yoga movement. We stare it out for a longer moment but then it is time again for me to spend to the surface. He had won round two and I have finished exhaling and have managed to take in a mouth full of salty water. It is a more common occurrence than most divers want to admit.

This time I would allow the mid day slack tide send us both to neutral corners of this reef. The eel would retain its command of said cave at the approximate middle of the reef wall and I would glide over through a richly dense forest of deep green with purple streaks, past an open area of salt water and low waves and across to a flat outcropping of sandstone rock. The swim is smooth and very fast. My way was less invasive than that of the guarded wolf eel and its cavern full of small bones that it either excreted or regurgitated during recursive feedings. It was cleaner at my new location; I had wanted to explore the cleaner walls of the other side away from the annoyance of being bitten by that monsters head. I was right and I wanted to have the last round on my count; a simpler time at an easier location not out of laziness but more out of wanting that sense of relative calm.

The other side richly rewarded the victor. The walls were covered with patches of cold water corals, short and tight patches of vegetation and an abundance of grazers in not as muted colors as one would expect outside of a more tropical underwater environment. The proud achievement of this far north archipelago was that it mimicked the color palettes of at least a half a dozen well known artists. This place was an exhibition of subdued browns and greens, spotted with streaks and dots of blues, pinks, oranges and lucid purples. For some reason I thought of this as more an exploration of triptychs in any one of Seattle's art museums, inclusive of *Chihuly* and his bright colored glass crowd. The palettes shimmered and were bright and smooth by the constant washing of the strong tides, and it was a still even more resounding experienced when some of it moved under their own respective locomotion. This was art: ancient and modern at the same time. This was life, another kind of art form.

Respective of the massive collectives of marine biology and oceanographically captured archaeology I swam before these large sandstone formations and made my own population assessment of the general area. By my count there are well over eight dozen species of plants and mobile animals just within the one square yard directly in front of me. This place is swarming by snail trail, by jets of water, the hoppers are in abundance, and the many types of fins used for maintaining momentum are more than abundant without embellishment of cumulative number. If you were down here this would be self evident. This was and still is a diver's paradise notwithstanding the native inhabitants to this ecological niche and their getting here first. I am apparently the only one who does not logically belong in this place. But I am staying all the same simply because I can for as long as my lungs can hold me at this location.

Why am I invading this place at this time? I mentioned earlier that the details are important. I am suited up appropriately enough to go hunting for a client. This client misplaced something and I have been hired to put together a trail of clues as to what happened, and where, and most important when it happened. There is a recession going on. I am employed and I plan on earning every pay check. The more salient point of detail is that I am under no circumstance to retrieve this lost item. The client just wants the lead up to the loss. All else will be forgotten with respect to my participation.

I took the job because I like being paid on time. This particular client's task is not unique with regard to my specific area of expertise. The only really unusual aspect of this particular series of tasks is that I am to actually be paid in full not to take the task to its logical conclusion. But I do not care. I am quite comfortable operating within the confines and operational definition of the job at hand. There is no need to question it, yet.

The rewards of this kind of lifestyle are sufficient and might even be considered somewhat excessive considering that all I have to do is look for clues and report in summary and I'll be on my way. The payoff will keep me happy and solvent for the next several years and provide a means of rewarding myself with several new toys along the way. I am happily employed—so self employed and keeping my own hours and playing in an environment I probably would have been in had I any more free time at this time in my life.

I am thinking hard about all of the clues thus far but a playful seal has happened into the area and I am losing my train of thought watching its carefree yet willful athleticism. The trail I was following so diligently is lost in the same span of time. I am as easily entertained by this sea mammal as it is by my more restrictive movements.  But I do not mean to be waxing in the anthropomorphic: I swim slower and I have to surface more often and I am definitely far less aerobatic.  Does this magnificent creature really know the difference? You tell me.

Enough playtimes—back to work at hand—I have surfaced and dove below for what I hope is the last time in this specific area.  I have discovered what I have been looking for and it is the absence of clues below a thick blanket of kelp that acts as a ceiling preventing my quick exit.  This is not the area I need to be spending my time in for more than one reason alone.  The survey is quickly ended and I swim underwater and back to another point of potential exit.  I am exhausted by the time I reach the sea wall of sandstone with a suitable means of escape.  My body feels like it is draped in heavy weights.  This is primarily due to the fatigue of being in very cold water for one hour.  This makes my muscles heavy and my movements over the rocks must look ridiculous; not standing but inching along on mostly elbows and knees until I reach a suitable ledge which is utilized as a stabilizing platform.  I am upright again.

It is time to walk away from this place and toward my original encampment.  I see the red and yellow of two watercraft strapped to a full sized white pickup truck with matching shell.  I stare at the twenty-five foot travel trailer that is also white and attached o the back of the truck.  The trailer is stenciled with the silhouette of a fox.

This is a very neat campground.  It is part of a park system that is very well maintained.  It is on an island. The island is mostly flat and I can see across the far north tip even at this close to sea level elevation.  I am not the only occupant, but still, judging by the astonished looks I am apparently the only one who is dressed to be submerged in the cold waters which surround this not too busy playground. Most of them carry cameras and I am sure that I am already in someone's collection: that strange guy dressed in dark gray-to-black, carrying the spear.

No, this has not been a complete waste of my time. I did spend a lot of time in the water and what I did not find was the real prize after all. It is a clue in of itself and this time it meant that someone has held back pertinent information about this particular point of my search. But I kind of already knew that; information that is left out is not always intentional. It simply meant that I would have to ask more meaningful questions in out next interaction.

At the moment I only had one other goal. I wanted to strip away from this cumbersome attire, take a hot shower outside of the trailer, and then proceed into the trailer for a blast of heat and a bottle of wine to clear my mouth and throat of sea water brine. It was a good goal that I would meet in due time. The insistent ringing of the phone would have to be dealt with first.

"Hello, yes I just got out of the water. You gave me bad clues. This is not a good place to start as discussed earlier. Do you want to do this over the phone or meet in person?"

Well, first things first. I did manage to open that bottle of wine while I listened and pretended to be more patient than I actually was at the moment. It was a fair turn of events, however. I was giving the caller another opportunity to do the right thing.

"Well, I will not be able to make the ferry until tomorrow."

This was a bit of a miss truth but I claimed it already. I was downing my first glass of Shiraz and I liked the way the spice finish tingled the back of my throat thinking about my life well into my fifth decade and I liked it. It was probably a good thing that my client was two decades older. I could attribute his misdirection as a slight oversight given his age if I wanted to; a far better cry than he was a bit of a flake.

"Oh, I know you meant well. But now we have to clear the air and get this thing back on track. It was your time table but I'll be dammed if I miss that last payment because of mistakes made outside the locus of my control. Ok then, I will see you tomorrow morning. Bye."

If my cell phone could have been slammed down without shattering I think I would have attempted it. They had attempted to blame me for the misstep. That was not only an oversight on their part; it was damn foolish game they decided to play. I already had too much information from them to let me walk away.

Having had just stepped away—from the phone still intact; entering the inside shower and stepping into the rich reward of a hot stream. Closing the wrap around door I shut my eyes and let the hot stream wash over my hair and my face and savored the heat over my shoulders and down the middle of my back. I felt the water cross the small of my back and swirl around my thighs and lower legs and I stood still as though the world had simply stopped sans this enclosed environment. I stood there and did not make any move until the hot water had run out.

Fortuitous Event

I could hear the water heater working overtime but it unfortunately was two steps behind maintaining the real kind of temperature that I had wanted. I was finished: the shampoo was run off, the soap rinsed from smooth skin and I was left tingling and in want of another sip of my wine so I exited and toweled dry. This afternoon was still mine. Stepping out of the trailer wearing only a pair of faded jeans I walked over to and slumped into a favorite canvas chair and let the sun finish off the drying while I continued to enjoy my wine.

# Chapter Two

## *Free Diving has its Costs*

IT WOULD HAVE BEEN PERFECT except for the crowds. That was what was going through my mind the day I had to rescue Roxanne and George. At the time they were just dating and had both graduated from a Masters program at Stanford University. I was just out of high school and had hitched hiked down the California Coast Highway to around central state as a graduation present to myself. That was all we would have in common at the time.

Actually that is not completely true. As it was in reality it was kind of a dual rescue mission. A close high school associate—a buddy—had dropped out one month before he was suppose to graduate and ended up hitching a ride to a place called Salmon Creek just south of Big Sur. His on and off again girlfriend; let's call her Bobbi; had talked me into heading south for a kind of intervention: a rescue of another kind. She was heartbroken of course by the loss, but she had already started sleeping with me during her recovery schedule (her words not mine) and used the most intimate moment to ask me to go on this humanitarian mission. Bobbi, at the time, could be very persuasive.

My arrival south of Big Sur was non exemplary. I recall I made it to Monterey on the first ride, and then to Salmon Creek on the second and sort of talked my way down to further latitude. I encouraged them to talk their ears off; explain to me a set purpose in life and I will have you talking overtime as well.

When the van's side door opened after we stopped I lingered a bit to hear the last stanzas of the last song of Workingman's Dead while climbing out with a completely over flowing back pack just in time to see the crowd heading over across the highway and over to a devilishly steep drop. The view of the Pacific Ocean was spectacular but man was it steep and a long way down.

The milling crowd was at a very excited state and I was literally pulled over to one side by a young man with very long and thick hair. He must have thought I was supposed to be participating. I had just arrived and all I wanted to do was head inward and in an opposite direction to reach a well discussed base of a waterfall. My goal was now pulled away and I was across the highway with the rest of this excited body of mixed aged people.

The man pulling me was deliberately hiding his face. Ok, I'll play along for the moment so long as you do not drag me over the side. When he looked up I recognized my friend from school. He was grinning from ear to ear and lifted me off of the ground to perhaps give me one more reason to give in to his asserted control.

"So what's this all about?" I wanted to get to the heart of the matter before he pulled me over the side in his own impishly and excited state.

"Some chick and her old man just drove over the side:"

"On purpose," I said rather than asked as I steadied myself over a brush covered ledge that would allow stability and viewing all at the same time. His hair was longer than I remembered. The fishtail tire marks in the dirt expressed acceleration rather than skidding.

Craig had been holding onto my arm. He was still quite fit in a natural way. He abhorred organized sports but invested himself in every other kind of individual competition. His grip was severe but at the time I would make no mention of it. I had wanted to lean over anyway, why not by brute force.

The VW bug was pancake onto the top of a coastal rock outcropping several feet above the water line, but at least fifty-five feet below our current position. Although I did not have an ideal vantage point I could still see some movement by the driver, but less so with regard to the passenger. And on top of this cliff side the crowd was now sitting and talking, several large bottles of cheap red wine were being passed around and there was the distinct smell of pot every time the summer breeze blew in our general direction. I looked up at Craig and it was very clear that he was already quite stoned.

"So this is what you do down here. Stand around getting high and watching the manic antics of a chosen few. This is a strange place indeed."

"Oh, do not be so melodramatic, man. Look out at that surf. Tell me you wouldn't want to be out there right now." Craig's suggestion really hit home. I was seeing some very interesting coastline and marvelous conditions. The coastal smells were overwhelming and I was immediately hypnotized by this location.

I started surfing the summer before so I was the first in the sober crowd that noticed the suppression of the dense kelp forest that floated in this small cove and redirected the surging waves towards that same out-cropping that was no so ornate I suppose my first thought was of a sculpture. The surf in this area had a beautiful undulating feel to it even at this elevation. I am up on this high cliff and all I really want to do is go down and feel the sea spray on my face. I am standing here without a board of any sort. Scanning the crowd which has split into two parties I can see that I am the only one thinking about going in and I am sure that there is no one I can ask to borrow a board. It's a look—so I can tell—who is who in this non water sports crowd. No one looks fit.

Was I going in? I had too; it was that dad transference thing that was now going through my head. I thought about what he would do in this situation and came to the only logical conclusion. I was shedding the back pack and stripping down to the gym shorts that I had wisely put on under my jeans. I was going to do a dad thing.

The good news about the coast line in and around Big Sur is that it is stepped. The bad news of course is that it is challenging steep and only the most experienced fool should attempt this drop down. I had trained as a high schooled outdoorsman at a place called Devil's Slide just south of San Francisco. We transverse the cliff only to get to some very attractive neighboring beaches. We lowered our play toys gingerly, and then followed the same path down and skipped across yellow sand to the water's edge. Back then we did not even appreciate just how much of a hunting ground this stretch of beach was for great white sharks.

When we weren't cliff climbing on the coast we were up at Yosemite National Park climbing seemingly impossible rocks better known as rock face walls. It was only a side interest and was a useful practice for scaling and transverse impossible entry places to pop a small raft into. And I thought about this as I was now attempting to transverse another type of insane incline but this time without all of the appropriate equipment. Not much difference here than Devil's Slide. We were always just short of the most appropriate equipment but when we were young we did not care.

The root systems and branches of the coastal flora are designed by nature to support the average weight of an eighteen year old male. It had passed the test of time and I have not had it backfire on me even as an adult carrying those few extra pounds. The rock formations of the California coast are deadly loose in composition and are just as unreeling when considering them as a life support system given their propensity to slide with or without heavy rains. To say the least this was a very troublesome and not well planned out repel. But I made it to the astonishment of the mostly wacked out crowd above and their giggles and not too stifled cries of encouragement were oddly encouraging.

Already at the bottom of the cliff I was beginning to appreciate the new perspective. The waves that I had judged as being two to three feet were now more likely four. I counted the incoming sessions—so there were seven. It was what we paddlers train ourselves to do always: count the waves and plan your attack; don't forget to monitor the outgoing.

So far so good; the VW's back bumper was solidly in hand. I could feel the vehicle shudder with each incoming, crashing succession of waves. I watched and marveled at this raw power as it took several tons of dark green kelp several yards out with each outgoing pull. How would the occupants survive trapped inside of this bug?

In between the next volley of surging waves I literally danced around to the driver's side of the car and yanked the door open. The woman at the wheel was fully cognizant of my position and greeted as best she could.

"Hey man, can you get us the fuck out of here? I can't feel my legs."

She was right about the numbing sensation. This was a typical VW Bug collision; all was collapsed inward and the frame under the dashboard was pressed tightly on top of her legs. I leaned down and grabbed hold of her ankle tightly. I could feel the pulse and this was a good sign for the time being. I would move her first.

I used an exit for my entrance. That is to say that I used the sun roof in a mostly untypical way draping in over the front windshield and reaching down I grabbed hold of the dash rim and pulled up using my torso. The metal groaned but gave way up into my chest. My shoulders were burning with the resistance and when I relaxed them the metal only returned to its half way mark. It would be enough to free her so I climbed down, dodged a five foot rogue wave and slipped my arms around her waist and pulled her out of the momentarily buoyant automobile. The car had slipped and was now hanging at an impossible twenty degree incline.

"What's your guy's name?" I called out to the woman as she held onto my legs and begged me not to let her go.

"George, his name is George. He's my old man. Can you get to him? Put me down, will you. I want to help."

She had collapsed. Her legs had not returned to the strength required to stand up let alone pair up in this rescue. The next volley of ways was heading in and for some reason the mass of floating kelp bulbs had taken that exact moment to part in the middle of that cove.

When the first wave hit it washed over the top of the vehicle. The next one shoved it clearly over the side and I heard the all too distinct screams of the members of the sobering crowd up above. Someone was yelling down at me and when I looked up a heavy loop of rope hit me right in the left shoulder almost toppling me into the ocean. The thick rope led back to a man in uniform and I was being told to tie it to any part of the car I could reach. So I dove into the very cold waters that most definitely warranted a wet suit. I would have less than ten minutes to loop and dash and hopefully retain the strength it would take to climb back out. I was still counting the incoming waves when I surfaced and coughed out several mouthfuls of salt water. I had duck dived under the last volley and I was still counting. Now it was time to climb out.

Signaling the uniform up above I heard the rope stretch to its manufactured limit and probably beyond. It held and the Bug was pulled up to a safer yet still semi submerged level. People at the top were holding onto the rope for dear life but it was the powerful might of the California Highway Patrol truck that winched up the VW onto its temporary platform. All I had to do at this point was pull the passenger from the other side of the vehicle. I sped to the task. But let me first explain what that means in real life. My body was stiff with cold from being in the ocean, my hands raw from the climb down and I was fighting what seemed to be dead weight. The man I was pulling; who became George at the same moment was not fighting back.

At the next instance I came to know the woman as Roxanne. She had been calling out his name over and over again and seemed intent to remind this unconscious body that it was her that was calling out his current plight in vivid detail.

"George, if you don't help I will fucking leave you. You have to help. It's Roxanne. Why don't you do something George?"

Her appeals were genuine and I found myself smiling as I turned over the body. Now it was my turn to become intimate with her old man. I kissed him. No not really; it was the start of what I remembered about CPR. Get air into the lungs first, a Red Cross instructor had literally drummed this into my head as I now repeated the measure.

No, it should have been getting the sea out of his chest cavity first. All right, I got there in time I supposed. He was draining and I flopped his body back in to a more helpful position to restart the procedure. One breath followed by seven pumps to the sternum. George was coughing to life and I could imagine my dad beaming with intense pride.

"Oh, I fucking love you." This is what she really said and then she pulled me into the longest kiss that any high school aged male has been faced with by an older woman.

This was the reward. This woman—once a stranger— was now slipping her mouth all over mine and at one point her warm tongue was probing the insides of my mouth. Everything tasted like sea water. George was breathing and I was making out with his significant other—his old lady. I hope Craig had caught it all. I could use this as leverage later on after all.

The crowd above was cheering us all on. George had rolled onto his side around the time I felt the metal rim of the rescue basket hit my leg. It was dangling by several repelled ropes and I was being instructed to stop fucking around and getting George into the basket. It was good direction. Apparently George really couldn't move much beyond his first roll.

There were several park rangers on the middle ledge now and they were pulling along with the Highway Patrol and the basket was steadied below by Roxanne and me. It was quite the team effort. Once George was topside a harness was sent down for Roxanne. We got her just high enough for me to start my ascent holding on to the back of her harness. I was told not to let go under any circumstances. I was the always dutiful student. I did not let go until I was on top of this world and back onto the edge of the highway.

Now my dad would have exclaimed pride in his son had he been with this crowd. Some of the others cheered me own as well as Roxanne and I felt many hardy slaps on the back followed by the stereotypical exclamation, "Far out man." But the looks I received by the rangers and at least one of the onsite officers told a different story. I was being admonished.

"Do you have any ID.?" The officer was all too close and his manner was not too friendly. So I complied after fetching my blue jeans, the wallet and remained in close proximity to my back pack.

One of the rangers came to our side. "I want him sited."

Now that was my misuse of the term. I misunderstood; at least at first. What he wanted was for me to be issued a citation for willfully ignoring the posted signs: *NO CLIMBNING ALLOWED*.

"Look, I witnessed a car over the side. I happened to be the first one to go down to see if the occupants were alive. I didn't intend to break the law."

Interestingly enough most of the crowd had slipped back across the highway and were making way into the woods. Most were either too drunk or stoned to be of any help anyway. But nonetheless I had Roxanne on my side and she was giving the officer a lung full. This woman was a pre law student, she told the officer in so many words and I was a young hero in her eyes. I was to be congratulated and certainly not to be issued any citation. She would see to that, she completed her rap. And it worked.

So this was my first encounter with Roxanne and my last with George. They did separate six months later and three months after that I would have my second encounter—so with her and without him our saga begins.

## Before Mavericks became Mavericks

What leads any of us to believe that anything in life is preordained? I truly think that most paths are made on purpose, out of spite and of course simply by accident. In respect to the latest of the three I confess to the following. A bunch of us had dads. This in itself is not resounding news. But what was the fact of the times was that my dad and several other dads living just south of San Francisco had a penchant for ocean water sports, friendly competition and passing this along to their offspring, respectively me.

My dad was a champion ocean swimmer. This was a guy that would jump into the San Francisco Bay and swim across not only on a bet, but because someone had brought it up in a conversation. This was also the guy that loved to bring his oldest son on these often excessive journeys. I say excessive because there was this pact between us that I could never reveal the details of these feats to my mom under penalty of death. He was using the phrase, "I'll take you out and bring in another one just like you," long before it became a joking mantra used by Bill Cosby. But don't tell your mother. My dad actually meant it all. So my punishment when I misbehaved was typically another journey with my dad into what is commonly referred to as hell week by Special Forces personnel in the varied U.S. Armed Forces. If I fucked up he took me out on one of his grand outdoors adventures to straighten me out.

One relevant point of conversation was when I was caught smoking at a campus rally while in high school. I was suspended for three days as a result because I was caught red handed by the VP of Boys at the school and I knew he was personally out to get me. I was more fearful of coming home that day than any other day of offsetting news. The result of this particular episode was that my father took me paddle swimming on the coast. Typically this meant the awful rip tide shoreline of Ocean Beach and speeding inward on four-foot body boards. They were always home made. My dad made me my first skateboard. Back then they were all long boards with metal roller skate wheels. Some dad's take their sons to ball games. Mine guided me not always gently me toward the water.

On this occasion he had something else in mind. He wants to paddle swim at a location one quarter of a mile off of Pillar Point, just north of Half Moon Bay. And he had borrowed two sixteen foot paddleboards from our next door neighbor who was high up in the Red Cross San Francisco Bay Area Chapter. They were officially rescue boards but now we were intended to use them for another father-son outing.

Ok, I was thinking hard about this excursion as we drove over the San Mateo Mountain Pacific Range over to the coast with these two large boards lashed to the roof rack of the family station wagon. The site was still a private installation—a military base with one enormous satellite for coastal watch. My dad had a friend that was in charge of security on the base perimeter and this was our way through the armed guard that waved us through. The beach was a very steep drop off and our target destination was only a scant one quarter mile off shore.

How hard could this be; having done three to six times worse by distance alone on earlier occasions—not always accompanied by trouble and a lesions learned aftermath. I stood up on a high ridge and looked down and out at the waves. They were far larger than I had ever experienced.

Well, it turns out that I was being brought out here because this place had another name. It was also called Mavericks by the locals. Yes, that Mavericks; before it was that Mavericks. And were entered the water in swim trunks and booties and that was all. I would have water borne lesson and stared at the back end of my dad's board as he crashed through an early set of waves. For heaven's sake, it was only a cigarette.

Unless you have actually seen Mavericks I will skip the pretence. If you've been there you know what kind of punishment I was about to receive. The conditions that day admittedly were somewhat less than the multi-storied building sized waves that many well known surfers ride in more contemporary times—without their dads. But it was a particularly ugly day nonetheless. The only saving grace was the fact that the man I was with had the opportunity to save me from drowning before. Why should I expect anything different this tale comes around? He used to smoke when he was young.

The simple summary is that I survived this round well on my own. Yes he was out there with me but at no time did I cry out for an assist. When I made it back to shore I found him already on the beach and he was beaming proud. I was just frozen and looking up at the cliff and wondering how I would muster up the strength needed to get this sixty-five pound board up that cliff.

"Next time out we should bring smaller boards. A big board will do just fine, but I want to come back with smaller boards. You did well today son. Do well in school. Don't waste their time."

I remember only smoking off campus after that day. We did come back with smaller boards and thankfully hit it on a much calmer day. I do remember sitting out on the water one quarter of a mile out that original moment and looking back at that massive satellite dish on top of those black cliffs. It was a wonderful sight. I wondered how many other people had witnessed this view. It would have been a shame to have missed this opportunity. I got my dad's whole point.

So how does this tie into Roxanne you might ask? Well over one half year after our meeting south of Big Sur I was hitching a ride back over the mountain to the Peninsula. I had this enormous homemade (built in wood shop actually) paddle board with me and I was not having much luck getting picked up. Perhaps it was the fact that I was garbed in a dark gray wet suit and not quite dry yet. The board was fourteen feet long and had a long pintail and a fairly oversized large fin. It must have looked imposing to even to the hippest vans that seemed to speed up after slowing down when checking me out. I was not so ride worthy. And that was when I noticed a very cherry dark brown Nomad sliding to a stop in the loose gravel along side of the intersection of HWY 1 and the road to the Peninsula.

The woman behind the wheel of the Nomad was wearing a long flowing white and very thin dress. She had the dressed pulled high and her tanned legs and thighs were exposed. One supposes that the face was familiar but I had not looked up from her lower torso just yet. I was smiling when I did and I suppose that her returned grin was not one of self flattery but rather an "Oh, shit I know you," kind of response.

I hoped in after lashing my large board to the roof rack and did not say a word. She just glanced at me and smiled and offered me the joint that she had been smoking. Declining yes—so not for the reasons you might guess—but for the daring position of simply saying no. I did not want to partake in any other substance than the sheer thrill of running into Roxanne again; under these specific circumstances I was aroused enough without an artificial stimulant.

"Man, you look great. How have you been?" I was starting off excitedly but cautiously all the same. My decline of the smoke caused no undue alarm and she simply went on driving and smoking and talking in short sentences until we were fairly caught up.

"So I am a free woman and I am thinking of dropping out of Law School and moving to Europe." She was laughing somewhat hysterically at this point and I must say I was disappointed at being left on the outskirts of this joke.

We drove on together in more or less short spurts of sentences until she suddenly takes the next side road off of the main highway. The Nomad bounced wildly across the rain rutted gravel and mostly dirt road and we continue without talking for the next fifteen minutes because the jarring was that bad. And then as suddenly we turned into a steep driveway with a six degree incline lined with tall eucalyptus trees and drove across a bridge just large enough to allow us to accomplish the task. The wagon was halted in front of an old barn several hundred yards from a main house. It looked occupied and I really did hope that Roxanne knew who lived here.

Walking past one barking and free roaming German Sheppard it became a fact that she and the dogs were on a familiar plane. The dog started to race and dance around us as we headed into the old barn. The structure is enormous enough when looking straight up but then she swings one door open and I am being led by this impishly grinning mad woman down a long and steep flight of stairs in near darkness until a row of overhead light is thrown on. We are now in what appears to be an underground cavern.

"Is this the most far out place you have ever seen? Watch your step, some of the pavers move."

This was an understatement as many of them slid under her weight and my weight alone. The dog seemed to be fine and centered its attention to the food bowls at the very far wall. It ate and we were apparently here to raid someone's wine cellar in what was later described as a bomb shelter designed to survive the impact of the on-going Cold War. I recall that the area used to be fondly referred to as ground zero.

The door to another room reveals an extensive collection. Roxanne selects two bottle of wine and then has the decency to leave a note on an enormous black board covered in graffiti. Most of the statements were from well wishers exclaiming their deepest feeling of love and other such poetry in the event of a coastal invasion.

We left another kind of message: *"Taking two—I love you—see you soon, Roxy."*

Somehow a bottle opener magically appears in her other hand as we close up shop and are heading back up and out to the car. The engine is raced and we leave probably as quietly as we had arrived. No one is disturbed by our departure with the possible exception of the dog. It is racing ahead and then when it falls behind it simply sits down in the middle of that dirt road with its large mouth agape and a heavy tongue hanging down. Roxanne is waiving to the dog when we head out of sight and make it back to the highway with our internal organs well shaken but not too damaged by the rutted escape path.

"Pick one and open it. There are tumblers behind your seat." This is a command to me and I comply not wanting to upset the impending direction of this strange adventure. Apparently the pot was not enough for Roxanne.

We have finished the first bottle and are stopping along side of Black Mountain Road when the conversation and the real points of this diatribe are discovered. She begins to make her real point here and now. We have large scale houses on one side of us and a game reserve on the other side. I am mixed on which direction I want to look.

"When I returned to the Bay Area from my accident in Big Sur I told my father about you and how you rescued us—George and me. Wait let me finish."

Roxanne takes the second bottle and hands it to me. She is shaking her head as though she has made up her mind. I am supposed to guess this next gesture.

"That was my father's place we just visited. He is a mathematics professor at Stanford. Now he is the head of a department, actually. I want to offer you this other bottle as a gift. This is all quite on the fly, mind you. But the bottle usually sells in the hundreds. You have a very nice evening ahead of you if you just hear me out."

Roxanne is moving closer to me across the tuck and roll leather bench seat. She touches my arm and begins to lay out a rather dubious tale. It involves her father and at the time it seemed rather wrong. My expression was plain enough to read.

"You want me to paddle out to a houseboat in Richardson Bay and retrieve an item your father lost to an old friend during a chess match. Is that a pretty clean summary?" I was not relieved when she answered in the affirmative.

"Look, this thing is personal with my father. He is the rightful owner—that is not in question because he feels that his friend had cheated that day. But the circumstances prescribe this kind of covert approach. He does not want his friend to know that he was caught cheating. No feelings are to be hurt. He does want the item returned, however. Will you at least think about it?"

She finishes up with a warm embrace and we leaned into each other and kiss. I now have possession of an older and expensive bottle of wine and an equally expensive relationship with an older woman. All I have to do now is think about it.

This woman is half way through Law School and I am barely out of High School and we are enabling each other as equal adults. It was new for me and I didn't want to appear too awkward or youthfully shy. I met her gaze, her embrace and the series of lingering kisses that told me that I was definitely trending on new ground. My dad had not prepared me for this—did he?

"And he will be out of town?" I am on a fishing expedition. "You say he was definitely cheated and this is nothing more than a once friendly rivalry?"

She answers in the affirmative. The professor across the Bay and in tenure in the Anthropology Department at U.C. Berkeley has complete disregard for alarms let alone locking his premises and commonly allows his house boat to be used by numerous grad students. Roxanne thinks that this will be a piece of cake. I am thinking maybe a mud cake.

So here and again I entertain other things as crazy as Mavericks. And why am I doing this at all. Well because Roxanne is really exciting and I like the feel of his seemingly just cause.

This caper was short and sweet. The following week I launched into an early day paddle over to Angle Island on a fourteen foot paddleboard. I caught the current back out toward the Golden Gate Bridge in the early afternoon and then cut south and rode a very smooth tide into the heart of Richardson Bay and into the middle of House Boat row just outside of Sausalito. The place was wide open as Roxanne said it would be. Three people were partying on the back deck of the floating home when I just walked in, found the disputed object, grabbed a Coke from the refrigerator, and paddled away with the strange looking marble sculpture tied to the top of the board.

I had to look at the butt end of this thing the whole way back to Baker Beach, by-the-by. If my board had tipped that day this seemingly priceless object would have been permanently entombed under the thick silt of the San Francisco Bay.

I felt really unnerved. Once before this I had shoplifted something cheap and obscure; something I didn't even need, on a dare. Now I was graduating to this, only justified by a long standing friendship between two professors that had gone somewhat astray. But Roxanne had been so sweet when I placed it onto its original stand in her father's house and we had been so busy making out that we did not see her dad walk in the door well after the fact.

He stood before us slowly stroking his white beard and his eyes were wide open. Mine were squinting back judging this scene with severe prejudgment.

"Young man, you have engaged in a truly good deed. I am indebted to you and I want you to know that this day will be forever remembered. Take your time here. I am heading out to an evening social. Roxy, why don't you cook this young man a fine meal? Pick any wines you wish. I won't be home until very late in the evening if at all."

I had lost my edge. He was approaching me and I simply shrank into the couch wondering why I did not stand up or move Roxanne's hand from my legs.

We take turns staring at one another. He is smiling in a way that makes anything I do an impossible task.

He bends over and takes my hand in his and shook it slowly and stares deeply into my face. At one point I thought he might kiss me as well, but in the end it was only a polite way for him to say he was very happy. He walked out that night and I would not see him again for another full three years. I wasn't sure then but I am now. I was more afraid of this guy than I was of my dad given that both gave me equally difficult tasks, and a learning experience should have been the common denominator.

Roxanne finished her Law degree one year later and began a practice in Palo Alto, managing Intellectual Property lawsuits for high technology inventers. She was too busy then and just slipped away from me. There was so more I had wanted to learn from our experiences together.

I was just returning from a short trip far up north and was contemplating on going into the Navy to sharpen my skills. In between those times my dad and I got into several other water borne contests including snorkeling and then the start of scuba diving. It was that very different kind of start to a cunningly linked sequence of events that brought me eventually to Lopez Island today, here in the Pacific Northwest. I was simply marking my time leading up to my next encounter with this other perplexing task at hand: find it, trace it back in time, but do little to disturb it in the interim.

# Fortuitous Event

# Chapter Three

## *Meeting of the Minds*

THE MEETING WITH MY CLIENT TOOK PLACE at a very scenic location on the bay south of my current home. We were meeting at Taylor Seafood and I was looking forward to slurping icy cold oysters and washing it down with a bottle of cool and crisp white wine that I had brought for the occasion. I was managing this image of pleasure before business and I thought that I was ready for just about any curve this client would throw me. But today he has the upper hand and I am flummoxed and nearly dropping my wonderful bottle of wine on the new dock.

I could see that he was not alone and that the other party was female. Perhaps I should have expected it at some point given that this client and I had at one time a more mutually shared connection. Recovering quickly I avoided stumbling onto the scene like a complete fool and instead opened sun warmed arms to greet this surprise guest.

"When I was driving down I kind of expected this surprise. Your father is not so good at hiding all of the details of his trade."

My comment was guarded but well played. I had wanted to show off a little and also send him a clear message that he had not played this one well at all. It always seemed like this old man was immersed in his damn chess tournaments. He was a world recognized chess master; this I would discover over a longer span of time supporting this theory including news blurbs, publicly known titles, and a multitude of magazine articles published in at least two countries. I should have been quite out of my league but took the job anyway.

"Roxanne, it has been a number of years, hasn't it?" Why was I being so curt? I really loved this woman and she had aged beautifully into the start of her sixth decade.

"Good to see you again." Her hands signaled that a less formal embrace was warranted. I held onto her for a longer than expected time.

She was warmed by the sun and her scent is just as arousing as it was when I was just out of High School. Now I am practiced; a Master's Degree under my belt; and I wanted to share all of this with her had her father not been standing nearby and staring off over the bay.

"Well should we make this a less formal meeting given your heart warming reunion?"

Her father—the Professor, the Chess Master—had played another round so well. I let her go and I sat down on the hard wood of the picnic bench and stared out across the bay as well. Was he seeing something I should have foreseen? The refinery across this bay is back on line again after a long rehab period. There had been a fire during peak traveling season and it became one other excuse in a long series of price escalation the previous year. Why was he looking at the long streams of white steam that exhausted from the taller stacks, seen at even this distance? Did the sea water trail hold a hint of some detail that was lost on me?

Why was Roxanne back in front of me now? Her father could be so impossibly cruel at times and she had explained this so many times long before this afternoon's meet. I thought that I could handle this client at long or short distances. And now he had just brought me to my knees—so figuratively of course.

Would I recover in time? Should I recover at all as I sit and turn and see them engaged in a long ago lost conversation that shouldn't include me? I used to engage my dad this way long before he died when we went out onto another more distant Bay, fishing for sharks under the heaving swells of the north tower of the Golden Gate Bridge. Then we were at the center of attention of the native and non native travelers high above walking and riding across that magnificent Bridge, looking straight down at a open cockpit boat bobbing in the surf, on their way to the Marin Highlands. He and I would fish and only sometimes talk but mostly about the waves the inbound tanker would make as it passed our inner position to the rocky sea wall around the point from Baker Beach.

I tried to suppress all of these memories when I watched Roxanne talk with her father. They had picked up on some key and salient point of a long previous conversation and the time lost between them didn't seem to matter. It only mattered to me and it was an imaginary theme. I had no earthly idea as to the topic of conversation until it had been readdressed to me. I was now the center of their attention.

"Why don't we get back to the bad direction you started me off on, shall we professor?" My intended demeanor was not mean but far less casual than the surroundings warranted.

Why should they stop what they were in the middle of just to stroke me unnecessarily with regard to my knowledge of tidal current predictions in this area? To predict the direction and speed of the tidal current was now as simple as clicking on the right URL. They didn't really need me out here to remind me of that. I was needed for some other minor detail and al I was waiting on now was for one of them to spring it on me.

"Oh my good man," he started off kindly enough. "There is time for all of that. But let's have a bite to eat and some of that wine you are coveting by your side. Is it a good one? You know I only drink good wines, don't you."

Yes, he was making fun of me. Perhaps I deserved it. I needed to be chilled just like the bottle I was expertly opening and pouring into the glass tumblers I had brought along. Be a good scout—so come ever so prepared—I had learned this well from my dad.

Yes we broached the subject of peace and more meaningful dialog over the next forty-five minutes. Roxanne had remembered to bring along two bottle of red and we managed to drink the entire contents of the three bottles, shared two dozen medium-sized oysters and scooped up their juices with the loaf of sour dough bread we had purchased at Taylor's Dock. And all the while the dialog was friendly and I caught myself laughing and quietly recalling the numerous times my dad had taken me to Fisherman's Warf in San Francisco to scarf Dungeness crab paired with authentic sour dough bread. Then we sat quietly and listened to the parade of barking seals and laughing tourists.

Was that was this all about—my mournful mood swing—watching her engage in deep conversation while I mused about the meaningful silence of my own relationship down by another waterside decades ago. I only wished that the professor would get to the point of why we were here now.

"You see my friend; patience always pays off with regard to life's elements of surprise. I insisted that Roxanne be here today because I wanted to offer you a common denominator. She is our bridge. I gave you deliberate misdirection because time had passed by and I did not know if I could trust you in the same manner as before. You were so much younger then and did not take things with such a degree of seriousness."

"At first I was ticked off. Now I am mellowed under the pretense of this surprise reunion and a suitable amount of wine to soften the blow. But can we please get this task back on track. I do have other clients as you may well know. There are other places I could be but without the obvious promise."

Roxanne let out a yell. She had been stung by one of the yellow jackets that had been coming on to this feast. At least two were on the edges of spent oyster shells and the third had found her exposed and tan arm as fragrant as the lotion she must have rubbed on her skin hours ago.

"I can smell the fragrance, Roxanne. Here wipe it off with some water. They will leave you alone. Professor, please sit down. Let me clear the table."

My offer was a peace sign. It would be a not so insignificant move in net next few moments. I was insistent to do all of the work necessary to clear this place and it left them unsure in the resulting calm. A fine breeze was blowing in from the west and it cooled all of our skin dispositions in one fell swoop.

"So go on; let's have the real starting point." I edged him on and gave Roxanne a playful kick under the table.

"Now we should do just that. I have this map you see; coming so prepared as well as you. This is where you need to start." He was laying out the previously folded and stiff map designed to serve small boaters of this section of North Puget Sound. Although they were easily available from local retails in the marine business this one had markings that were quite different. This one had an over lay of utility cables and piping. No one outside of the industry was supposed to have access to this material. I said as much out loud.

The older man had punctuated the last remark and had jammed his fingers onto the open map. I knew the island as well as the small bay he was indicating continuously under the pressure of his fingers. This was not the frail man in his twilight years. He was tough and he was now more exact and determined to put me on the next track.

The origins of the map, usually printed out on the bottom right hand corner of this kind of document, were clearly blacked out. I did however see the faded stamp of

Stanford University on the other side before he had flipped it over. I was supposed to see it, now wasn't I?

"Ok, I will start there. However, we need to negotiate a new timeline. I cannot get to this straight away. My other client has priority now." I folding the map and placing it in my soft sided cooler. I did this slowly emphasizing each and every movement. I had a point to make.

The point was undone. The document was retrieved.

"Yes, but I am offering you something of far greater interest than the money of your other client. Do you want to get rich or perhaps avoid some boredom? You choose and you will let me know today. I do not have as much time on my hands as your other client. Is this not true?"

He was moving the marine map back into his very old brown leather briefcase and snapping the fastener shut. His gin was displeasing and his teeth were slightly yellow.

"The difference is that he wants me to complete a task. You just want me to open some previous dead end. Is that not true?" I thought this was an improved move. Roxanne shot me a smile which supported this theory.

"Perhaps you have a very good point. I do not want the task taken any further than we had originally discussed. But I will make you a promise. If you do mine first Roxanne will accompany you to the given state, and then take over herself. Is this Ok?"

Fuck me running. This guy had all of the moves planned out well in advance of the first. It was no wonder that he was once a Chess Master; this Doctor and Professor and author of *The Mathematical Theory of Algorithmic Diagnostics.* I was dealing with this badly. I did not have to beat him at a game I could not play well. I just had to bring something refreshingly new to the table. So I did so without signaling his daughter under this old and weathered bench.

"Ok, you have a deal. Roxanne, if you are ready I have a boat waiting in Anacortes. Professor, you can see how quickly I am able to jump to this task. I am taking your daughter with me now. Do you know your way back?"

Yes, the last part was a departing slam. But we were all moving off to our vehicles with iced spare food in tow and icy and prolonged stare carried out to the dirt road.

It was mutually discovered that all parties were less than pleased with the sudden outcome and we left in opposite direction in two separate vehicles: Roxanne in mine and the professor driving off on his own accord. The daughter was laughing much later along the way as we moved onto flat land and an abundance of small farms. When we drove at a snail's pace through the winding streets of Edison she told me he would be fuming all the way back to his hotel in Fairhaven. He did not often leave a play so open on the table. He would be mad, and that in it made me so happy— notwithstanding the quick and essential reunion with this woman that I had known off and on since I became a young man.

I had made a final move and now I had my starting point. Was this one of the lesions that I was prepared for by my dad yesteryear? For the moment I tied the two together; this fortuitous event. And for the record she was still as fond of me as I was with her the last time we accidently met. Her skin was as finely smooth and clean as I embellished a bit with regard to our first encounter. Her face was once again cheerful and her stare as penetrating as it had been when I rescued her decades ago.

I had meant to see if the sweetness of her general person matched that of a deep seeded memory of sea mist and sweat during that time of terror in her life. In her mind's eye I was still the hero that risked life and limb to come to her aid and that of her ex partner. I wondered about George but only for the briefest moment. I could not even recall what his face looked like or the taste of his mouth; discovery holds much promise during rescue—so her father never brought this name up during the latest encounter. Or did he?

Taylor's dock was no place to make this kind of lock step comparison, though, and I as quickly dismissed the notion that all had stayed the same. Something may have been a bit off—that prevailing reason why I was thinking in this manner in the first place. Perhaps it was me that was off their game. Did I smell or taste the same. That much I would not know until I was with her alone and with suitable time to bring such a subject up. The sun was going down and these days were shrinking by approximately one minute. Should I spend my time with Roxanne reminiscing a short past, or was this an opportunity to promote a probable future? My life was not meant to be analyzed column by column. I was an entire block: screen it, challenge it or rebuild it from scratch.

Fortuitous Event

# Chapter Four

## *Nothing is Left to Chance*

THERE ARE SUBJECTS COVERING THINGS that I will only discuss in private. With that in mind there are topics about certain items that I will keep close to heart, resolve only in the inner chambers of my mind, and keep all else at bay. I want to stay on target for a moment. The Professor's latest clues shared only with me have already been exhausted and I am entirely pleased that they have mostly played out as he challenged me that they would.

I am resting on top of the sling netting of a medium-sized Hobie Cat in the very small bay of Clark Island. This is a beautiful, wondrous place and although it is usually frequented by much larger water borne craft during this time of year it is eerily vacant today. I seem to have the entire place to myself and have dubbed it my island.

Clark Island is approximately 1.8 nautical miles north of Orcas Island. Most people know about the later of the two because it is the predominant island within a chain generically referred to as San Juan Islands. Where Orcas' topology is enormously vast and varied, Clark Island makes its claim to fame by sheer simplistic beauty. It is small—no compact—and it is a jewel in my eyes and now I have this small dot of paradise to myself.

The clues led me at least thirty yards from shore and near the south east side of the island. I was relaxing on top of the Hobie Cat that was drag anchored into a soft bottom and submerged rock formations in between the closer formations of Lone Tree Island and the Sisters. I was about to enter into the very cold waters when I was interrupted by a pair of nesting bald eagles who were intent on screaming their displeasure with my solo invasion of their domain. The two soaring birds of prey maintained a high altitude above me and made closer loops and called out with piercing accuracy.

"We own this island," they seemed to say challenging my earlier claim.

This pair was displeased. The only path of recourse was for me to dive over the side and into the safer depths of the outer bay and minimally expose myself to the sometimes swifter currents on the inside passage between the islands and the mainland to the east. I was only wearing eleven pounds of counter buoyancy and it seemed to do the trick. This was a free diving exploration to recapture an earlier path exploited by whatever the Professor wanted me to discover but leave entirely alone. I was quick to the task and submerged and had become deaf to the air bound ruckus above the mildly undulating surface.

Four meters feet down I retraced the less than obvious clues that had been left behind. It appeared to be not too recognizable to anyone on traveling through by boat. But I was down just right through the only thermo cline, deployed with prescription dive mask and visually amplified by the properties of being underwater. There was no double jeopardy here and I had all of the advantage of preliminary detail from the Professor; desirably so but with no direct ties to my off beat mentor. If what I found appeared to be personally shocking news I could only fathom what it would mean if my actions were mistaken by someone such as the Coast Guard who regularly patrol the Strait of Georgia.

Thus far I was protected from the strong currents and well out of direct line of sight by the security tugs that stood vigilantly overseeing the areas surrounding our sole shipping terminal. I surmised the clues and jotted them down mentally. There would be no records kept at this juncture.

I wanted it to make it look as though this was a solo pleasure trip. But the depths exposed something so troubling. I had to surface to gulp in an ample supply of replenished oxygen and to shake myself from the shock impact of capturing it live. I had discovered something that guaranteed that I would not share the discovery with anyone else but the professor. But then he knew this all along.

I had been beaten at this game one more time. These were no counter moves as my mind races through one hundred scenarios and plausible outcomes. There was never a time in my life when I simply wanted to give up the ghost, so to speak, without prolonging the greater tug and pull it takes to reset a drag anchor. I returned the Hobie-Cat to a free floating platform as I made another pass through the mental check list—so it was in order I jotted down a sort of pictorial and encrypted sequence of events leaving out the pertinent details of these exact coordinates, if there were a later need to recreate this exact scenario.

What then would be my plan? What indeed.

There were always contingencies. Never leave home without at least one. Here it was, just past late day but early enough in the evening and I was still strangely alone. I sat on the tide rocking boat and became hypnotized by the views around me as I began to drift without the aid of sails. I was tucked inside and safe from the severe tide rips, around the shallow reefs and shoals to the north. I gazed across the waters and marveled at the height of the single mountain that made up the north east side of Orcas and followed the topology to the shoreline of Lawrence Point.

Ok, why was I out here alone? I had ditched Roxanne during a routine errand and did so within the range and scope of plausible deniability. She made me promise to stick to the original plan and make sure that she was part of the discovery. But this voice kept penetrating through and I clearly began to imagine that something was amiss. My tact: it is easier to beg for forgiveness than it is to ask for permission. My coming out here would become an oversight, my dear Roxanne. And I have managed to do so with the stipulation that you will have nothing to report back to your father without looking like a complete ass.

Poor Roxanne, will she still love me so when I come skimming back to the point of departure with nothing to show but a strange tale of getting swept up in the unforgiveable currents that are renowned for in this area. Will she begin to contest her own research as discovered early on in the game and so self declared apprehension of doing so in a light but super efficient Hobie-Cat. She showed fear and I took that as a sign to go through with it anyway—so I capitalized on her exhibited weakness. Hell, I've done this track on a sit-on-top kayak and a long paddleboard.

The Cat was a true luxury in my eyes. I was there in half the time—perhaps one third—and returned in as little time given that I had firsthand knowledge of the three o'clock winds that pick up favorably for the return track around the north tip of Lummi Island and through and across Hale Passage. Then you turn.

I made it past Portage Island and then engaged in an eastern heading back into Bellingham Bay. I wanted to drop something off before I then headed back out exiting the Bay and hugging the sandstone cliffs past Chuckanut Bay, through major pastures of eel grass, across the dangerous mud sloughs around Samish Island and eventually back down toward but stopping short of Anacortes.

It took me most of the remaining late afternoon and the early evening. I was sure she would not have waited and took the short ferry ride back from Guemes Island back to Anacortes on foot power and the energy of her anger and perhaps heightened disappointment alone.

This was not to be meant as a devious ploy on my part with regard to the upper hand that her father seemed intent to maintain. I was simply reliving a tip my dad had instilled in me when under the spell of strong currents and mighty contesting winds. Go with the flow, son—so go with the flow I did. Not out of spite but because I could. I needed to do so and rationalized these points as I went over the data I had collected on her father's behalf as I waited for the last ferry of the evening to transport my trailer bound Cat back to the Anacortes terminal. The summary was maddening but happily the terminal was empty and uneventful on my return.

To predict the direction and speed of the tidal current first obtain an appropriate reference point. It was a simple maxim to follow if one knew where and when to start, calculated in the same manner to predict where one wants to end. It was unfortunate that Roxanne and I would not have this spellbinding reunion after all. We missed our connection and I could not be more pleased.

Sometimes only the briefest glimpse of a whale out on the water is the prudent reward we have coming here in the first place. However, in this area if you see whales in route keep out of the whale's path. I understand this and Roxanne for the time being had not gotten this last clue.

By the time I made it back to Bellingham is was close to midnight; having stopped at a favorite eatery I accompanied this good fortune with a good bottle of wine and sufficient off road time to reach a more sober state to drive. I skipped the anticipated displeasure of seeing her father shake his head in mournful disappointment had we met at another designated location on time. He would be long asleep now in the comfort of his hotel and most likely dreaming of his next dozen moves in advance.

My victory would be brief. The things we know for sure.

**Chess in the New World**

A major advantage in the preparation of the trip was the inevitable exposure to the collective wisdom of those who sail here—that repeated usage of the North Puget Sound—and whose good council has served so many of us so well in execution of said trips. Over the years of living here I have benefited immeasurably from the suggestions as well as the challenges offered by private and governmental individual and groups, who so graciously served as a continuous source of information in solving the problems of full utilization of this watery playground for adults. It would be well justified to include the younger fare of this geographic location, but truth be known most of the people I see at the furthest reaches of this place are in my age group. It is a simple fact that most of the younger population is land bound, and truthfully, this is a wonderful discovery. I like being around people my own age.

Having been part of the generation that designed and implemented the marvelous network of communications infrastructure we enjoy worldwide, it is not so farfetched to say that the young simply are up to the task of sharing content via social networks. So much of what we have now at our fingertips is a culmination of the ages, abounding on line by obsessive users of handhelds. This is not new or unique technology. Most of what they hold in their hands and the methodology they use for access are simply over-hyped marketing driven fantasy. Texting: give me a break it's been around for well over a century. There are those suspected exceptions that so fascinate me; the first generation that gets to recreate the lost Libraries of Alexandria wins all. Recall that even Jules Verne wrote about vast interactive social networking in *Paris in the*

*Twentieth Century* at the close of the eighteenth century.

That said I am always cautiously drawn to the fact that many aboriginal people hold their collective histories close to their already ancient hearts. The tribal lust for story telling is mostly reserved to the eldest of their respective tribes and they have been the last population to want to see this archived on line, simply because he off spring generations wanted something more contemporary to go after socially. I could see where this notion might be taking me with respect to the two chess pieces on the table before me—so figuratively speaking of course.

I asked myself what do two professors living and studying on opposite sides of the San Francisco Bay—campuses away from each—have in common. At first the answer seemed rather innocuous. They liked to play a mental form of chess. Each one anticipating the others moves twenty paces ahead and in hindsight. I originally thought that I was simply a passive observer. This was my only interesting insight. As it turns out I have allowed myself to become a major object on the interactive board and I have been used quite viciously by these two opposing characters.

Prior to my latest exposure, and many decades ago I had returned from time in the Navy and back to my place of origin in the San Francisco Bay Area. I was indigenous to the area you might say and I knew a lot of the inner nooks and crannies that make up that vast place. One of the favorite haunts of my post military stay was exploring a place called Half Moon Bay.

Half Moon Bay in the mid seventies was clearly left behind. Most of its inhabitants were old. Some were really old. Its latest generation had rushed over the Pacific Mountain range that separated the Pacific coastline from that of the San Francisco Bay, to openly embrace the promise of a growing industry inclusive of advanced computer and network technology. That place in quick summary became to be known as Silicon Valley.

I would end up as a participant in the whirlwind growth of the Valley. But that is not part of this diatribe. My point is this: having enrolled in a community college that emphasized the study of local history, I fell into a crowd of students and we were obsessed with all things associated with the study of Anthropology.

I had two favorite instructors at this Community College. One was a Logic and Reason instructor who was of Chinese origin. He looked the part and was small, slim but very powerful in both mind and body. He had this way of constantly stroking his long dark yet wispy chin hairs like a number of like characters represented across time on popular television programs including *Kung Fu*. But this guys mind and propositional use of logic truth trees to understand the messaging of contemporary history pulled me in like a perfect vacuum, had this been physically possible on the surface of the planet Earth.

My second favorite instructor at the time was a (Caucasian) professor of Anthropology with a more European family lineage. He at once leaned into me during one of his most memorable lectures and challenged me to understand the web of cultural influences to my Irish heritage after I had made this fact known aloud. I had not meant to show off in class because I claimed to be pure Irish: living as a citizen in my place of birth, the United States. I was only sharing the fact that my dad's parents had originated from Ireland, and that my mom was raised in Ireland. But then he connected the historic dots of Ireland (across thousands of years) to the Moors, the French and the Vikings and I became much more of a mutt.

The real point of this was that between the two I had taken the task of defining and playing back what I had learned and had made my way by less than accidental exposure to in the coastal town of Half Moon Bay. I was looking for a person to study the theories I had been exposed to. And as a result I serendipitously discovered the perfect host.

Zigzagging through the back streets of Half Moon Bay I came upon a man of Chinese origin who was sitting on a bench in the sunny yard of this eldest child. This guy was easily in his late eighties and smiles and then waves as I was driving by at five miles per hour on a rutted gravel road.

What I consider most fortunate about this chance discovery was that he had a reasonable command of the English language. Later I would discover that he had mastered three languages outside of his own, and spoke twelve distinct Chinese dialects. He had been a scholar in mainland China and had escaped with his very young children and made way into the United States at the end of the late 1800's. His journey from China's already well developed and populated east coast was partially captured by me on analog cassette tape (high tech at the time) and we became fast friends. In short, I came to know this man and his offspring as one of the earlier Chinese families to permanently reside in this coastal berg.

With all such tales there is good news and there is bad. The good news is that I was able to capture much of his fascinating story and had made a transcript of it as a final assignment for both of my favorite instructors. I had received an A for both papers; similar but presented with an angle tweaked for a Logic and Cultural Anthropology class, respectively. The bad news is that I was not able to carry on the interactions with my new friend because he had passed away from natural causes. He was really quite old at the time.

So where is the connection? As my latest research panned out, the oldest daughter of the old man had a son close to my age and he was an undergraduate student at UC Berkeley during the same time span. His mother had presented him with a copy of my paper and he had used this in a research project with guess who? Yes, that was too easy. What about the other half of the equation?

The Stanford professor had an offspring. I met her in Big Sur, as previously discussed. Somehow the two of them completed the circle and I ended up paddling across the San Francisco Bay with a disputed sculpture that now had much more meaning than it ever had before.

This of course will lead us to my next accidental encounter with Roxanne. But first we will establish another operation definition to the phrase 'accidental encounter'. Let us for the moment redefine it as a 'fortuitous event'. Then let us continue to discover how it applies to the mastery of the game of Chess played out by two old madmen with a shared grudge and a very strange end game.

# Chapter Five

## *Where did I Leave Off*

THIS AFTERNOON WAS STILL MINE. I had stepped out of the trailer wearing only a pair of faded jeans I walked over to and slumped into a favorite canvas chair and let the sun finish off the drying while I continued to enjoy my wine.

The sun went down earlier as it is now officially the start of fall. My intent on coming here was the driving purpose to chase the sun. As it was I was not ready to give up and allow myself to be fooled by the incremental abandoning summer sun. We are losing the high arc in the sky; the bright ball filters through tall pine trees and the shadows are elongated by one minute per day. Soon I will be drinking my wine in the dusk light shirtless and shoeless and other campers will be walking by in down vests, jackets and heavier shoes and wondering who the madman must be dressed for a day at the beach.

My position is far from the fire pits that are already being lit in other sites and I am deliberate in my avoiding them, although I do find a bit of satisfaction when a slight breeze waifs a slender stream in my direction. I like the smell of campfires so long as it is only a hint of one. I do not appreciate it when it clings to my clothes or when it lingers inside of the trailer. Right now I am satisfied that all of the windows and doors at my site are tightly shut. I do return the occasional scans of my position by interested parties across the way. This is not a hermitage but I am using the trip to clear my head and imagine a simpler time in between visits and the persistent images that have returned from my past.

The more predominate image at this specific moment is one where I have taken a fishing trip with my dad. We have traveled up north to a place outside of Redding—the six hour drive from the San Francisco Bay Area up north—within a screams length from the base of Mt. Shasta and it's larger lake. I am in my last year of High School and my dad took me out of school for this trip.

We are far in the woods to the west and have just finished a day of fishing at Wiskeytown Lake. It is the same time of day and I am quite young but I am allowed to stand by the roaring camp fire and drink my one allotted beer with dad and two of his friends who are in an adjoining camp site. I did not know this at the time but I was brought to this place to be shared. This is why I was pulled out of school.

The other two men have sons. Their sons are in the Armed Forces and are currently serving in Vietnam. One of them had just written home and he lets it slip out with accidental deliberation that he has been wounded and that his close friend has been killed. The other man's son has been missing in action for well over one year. There is a lot of talk about this over beer, the promise of roasted trout and thick masses of smoke that fills this campground from time to time as the wind kicks up and the orange-flamed embers flair from the dried and crackling pine limbs that we had gathered for the occasion.

I am here and I have become the center of attention. The three older men I am with are veterans of a previous war. They recall events specific to heroics and stupidity, as well as a shared lighthearted reminiscence of why they wore uniforms at all. It is very hard to understand some of what they are saying but it become clear to me that I am seeing three grown men close to or already in tears. This is a painful night for the quad and we take turns blaming it on the smoke.

I am already eighteen and it was not too long ago that my father escorted me to a place that registered the next generation of eligibility with regard to the ongoing War in the Jewell of the East. I was tugged and pulled into that building not only by a badgering and caring parent, but I also felt the patriotic calling and if gave me fits of sleepless nights prior to the actual act. My dad at the time had taken me on another kind of swim for some mischievous act I did not recall perpetrating but I would be called on soon enough.

But I did this act—yes on my own accord. And now I was explaining my feelings on the matter through the blur of that one beer that turned into another, followed but yet another. This was another lesson delivered to me on that night by my dad. I was becoming a man at the same time I saw grown men standing around this camp fire and releasing all of those tears that they had managed to choke back for so long. I was now the center of attention but for many of the reasons that conflicted with patriotism.

What had happened that night was never shared with any of my friends. It was something that I wanted to own and hold onto for a very long time. That mix; whatever I could glean from it I would not be willing to share for one reason alone because it empowered me at the time.

I was thinking about it now, taking another sip of my wine, recalling the day I actually went into service and saw the large gray steel ship and its welcoming gangway. I was carrying an absurdly large duffel bag on one shoulder and that large official yellow envelope under the other arm, summonsing up the next stage of my life—asking for permission to come aboard.

This was not the lesson of what was patriotic, or carrying on the legacy of the dad's I had met around a previous campfire. This became something I needed to do—so lost was I at this time in my life I sought out the rigidity of Navy life and the expectation that I would finally understand a bit more about the necessary lessons in life having received those succession of hints from my dad, and after hitchhiking across several countries. I was simply making way for my own way.

The Navy became one of the easiest clues in the puzzle of life. Not long after I was at another kind of fishing expedition. This time I had just finished up spear fishing hammerhead sharks with two shipmates and we were on our fourth or fifth round of beers stoking up a campfire of palm branches and coconut husks. We are back from a tour in Vietnam, followed by a tour in the Philippines. We are at the edge of a private beach belonging to another one of the Armed Forces on the island of Oahu. All that stands between us and the powerful blue ocean are one half dozen long and colorful surfboards.

The other sides of this campsite are the telling signs of razor barbwire and jeeps full of young men much like us guarding this military installation for those who may soon depart to another place in conflict. The jeep men are fully armed and glare at us not in anger but in pure jealousy. They know that they do not have to be wary about an ocean borne invasion at this time because Navy is on the beach. They on the other hand will be flown off of this island paradise and sent to the other side of the world someday. Our end is their beginning and they show us that they know it before they drive off.

So compare and contrast if you will the center of attention always seems to be that campfire. What does it really do to us and how will it reassemble each time?

Although I have consumed one bottle of wine now, I feel that my senses are razor sharp. I know I want to get to the bottom of why I have been pulled into this shadowy area by the Professor and Roxanne. I have used my arsenal of things learned from the past to plan out my only path to the future. I need to lean into to that fanned notion of what it really means to be patriotic. I know that I cannot or should not make a go of this alone so I am going to reach out cautiously and bring in reinforcements, after refreshments. I head out to the reservoir for a well deserved evening paddle.

In the morning I am already hitched up and heading west. I am going to drop off most of my gear and head to the airport. It is time I confronted this daemon with a visit to the PhD.

It had been half a decade since I was in the Bay Area. I still know my way around and by memory alone I am able to find my way back to that side road on the way to Half Moon Bay. Now the road is paved and it is rather too smooth. The old world bridge is standing but it looks as though it has been reinforced many times. The old framework of the barn is still there but it too has received a replenishment of new panels which appear to have received a new coat of paint within the last year or so. I remind myself to raid that underground wine cellar if the opportunity presents itself one more time. Just one or two bottles would suffice.

There are two new automobiles and one old truck in the circular driveway. The expected German Sheppard does not intercept this time, as one fully expects. It might have sired offspring but all is lost on the quiet that surrounds this estate tonight. There is no sign of Roxanne, but then why should there have been. The old man is sitting in an oversized chair with a thick wool Indian blanket over his knees when I am escorted in.

"Dr. this one says that you are expecting him." The woman is most likely from Mexico and has been in his employ for as long as anyone can remember.

"Oh, well this is a surprise, but then everything is a surprise in this time of my life. Please join me. Sit down here," he gestures and bows and is unashamed as I am by the intrusion.

I am offered a late night glass of something but I decline in favor of a pot of Earl Gray tea. I want to be clear headed because I have other people counting on it at this juncture. I tell him what I was doing when I had my change of heart. I provide the detailed wisdom I have received from the outdoors and those who I have shared it with including his daughter.

"Yes, this is precisely so. I know about your other interactions with Roxanne. She mentioned that the two of you had stumbled into each other outside of Amsterdam. It was in the late eighties was it not?"

The old chess master and I traded barbs, as expected. I was ready for the confrontation.

"As Roxanne explained it she found you in a busy café in the middle of a large number of university students and you were the only American in the crowd, but had managed to blend in. She did not recognize you at first. But then when you had trouble ordering she stepped forward to assist you, did she not?"

I took a sip of my tea and tried to hide my excitement and my shock that he could draw forward with such vivid detail, of a meeting he heard of second hand. When I did encounter Roxanne she helped me and then I rescued her again. But why bring this up now? Should I hold onto this other piece until I saw his next move? We sipped our beverages and circled each other cunningly—mentally.

"Here is the part that I do not understand still. She happened onto that place to score a night's worth of junk. Are you surprised that she told me this? Roxanne tells me everything." He smiled and sipped and tilted his head away from my view. I thought he was going to make another one of his key and salient points.

This man was not as cleaver as he thought. I could see the wet around his eyes as he pretended to cough and then wipe his whole face with a fresh white handkerchief. He had held back to hide his tears.

"Then she told you that I sat up with her all weekend to get through a much longer and maddening nightmare. One that had lasted through two summers away in Europe; trips you encouraged her to take."

"My good man, it would do you good to respectfully hear another side of this woeful tale. I sent her to Europe because she was a junkie. The awful quality of stuff she had in America. It made me sick. So I sent her to a place where the quality and accessibility would at least let her to survive. I could not protect her here. I simply would not tolerate the shadowed and the oppressive people she brought into her life—our lives. No I sent her to a place where she had better odds of survival—improved probability."

The tea was not good for the moment. It was leaving a very bitter taste in my mouth along with his need to express an algorithm to justify the cost. I put it aside for the moment. Standing up I walked over to the large bay windows and stared out into the darkening sky. I wondered at what point I stop this challenge and turn to his side and offer him the forgiveness of an off and on again family friend. But my reflection in the large panes of glass reminded me that the image that played back was not that gullible. I had to move forward if anything to prove this last point.

"I have witnessed substance abuse by members in my own family, and my dad's family. I will not suggest that there is more you could have done at the time because that would make me a hypocrite. I stayed for additional time in Europe at risk to my job and to my mental health.

Amsterdam was not the safe and secure environment you thought it was at the time. But I stayed. Did she tell you that?"

"Oh, this is news to me. At the time I thought you only helped her through one fit. It was all she had conveyed at the time. I am not surprised by this late disclosure but I am acknowledging surprise and perhaps anger that you had abandoned her now. Please let me finish."

He was taking his time and standing up on his own accord. Watching him walk across the room was scornful. I was certain he was admonishing me and would simply exit from the room and leaving me standing there until I had the courage to follow him. That was when he turned and spoke very loudly.

"In my life I have lost more often than you think. Please accompany me now and I will show you something that will perhaps change your attitude toward me. Please, come along now."

We walked almost together through the house until we entered another study. Across the room I could already see that damned sculpture that I had reclaimed for him when I was barely beyond my teens. It was on a platform on its own and I could tell it was in a place of honor. This old man was about to pull out another grand move.

"Look carefully at this piece. Tell me what you see?"

There was more than a gesture in his grand manner. This was more of a demand. I circled and studied the object and came to no useful conclusion at first. That is until I saw the original one on another mantle.

"It is a lost wax cast off done in modern bronze. The original one is over here." I was beaming unnecessarily.

"Yes, but you did not have the opportunity to guess this decades ago. When I play other chess masters I cannot hide or obscure any details because they are supposed to know as much about all of the possible permutations as I do. One of us will win, but it will be based on a mix of time, circumstance, and understanding the cultural significance of our surroundings. This is why I never played on line. It is always live."

"Those things that are weighed so heavily are usually so close at hand."

"You are precisely right. So let me tell you about the origin of this piece. It is aboriginal in origin. They could call themselves a First Nation but their history is far more complex than it is over here. I am a scientist and not a politician. I deal with history when all else is stripped away. I deal with probabilities and do not promote possibilities. Do you understand what I am saying?"

"I do most of the time." He was acknowledging my joke. It was satisfying that this man was taking me on. My dad had done this and when he did I felt stronger most of the time.

"When my wife passed away I had only a fragment of life shared with her. The original came into our family by her work. She was an Anthropologist. Did Roxanne mention this?"

"No, I am quite sure she never mentioned her mother."

"Well I will tell you why not.  Her mother spent little time with her daughter.  She wanted to express herself in the field.  She loved discovery: the appealing surprises, the next piece of the puzzle she never wanted to be completely finished.  So she stayed and searched out there and Roxanne suffered as a result."

"Do you think this is why she had plunged into drugs?  Is this why you are so protective of her?"  I was making a strange point here and wanted to force him to disclose why he pushed his offspring into the path of this moving freight train.

"This is why you will always be one play behind, my dear man.  Roxanne died in Europe long after you rescued her for the second time.  She fell so fast I could not get to her in time.  Time is one of the key elements to play.  Remember this always."

"Then who did I leave behind in Anacortes?"  Ok, I was not even willing to play around his last surprise move.  Was I actually in shock?

"Yes, it is a surprise isn't it.  When I went to Europe to collect the remains of my daughter I met one of her friends.  She was so helpful at the time, but I had to acknowledge that she had fallen into the same traps as my beloved daughter.  So I am surprised as to how much she reminds me of Roxanne, and I offered her a new life. I did not want to come back to my home alone."

We have taken the moment to sit down and acknowledge one of many photographs which line this room.  It is indeed a new face that is smiling back.  I admonish myself for not knowing the difference.  Would it have made any impact at all? Of course it would. I felt cheated and very sad.

"And do you know what she does to reward me? She becomes healthy; goes back to school and get a degree from one of my peers in the Anthropology Department at Berkeley. That is why the sculpture has become a centerpiece. This is precisely why I had to hold it back."

"Tell me about the original?" I was not exhausted yet but I was slumping in this chair. There was something else missing and I was willing to wait this one out as I dealt with the sting of having been with two Roxanne's.

"The original was brought out of mainland China by my wife. It is part of a circle of pieces that were used to tell a story about a family's migration from the border now called Vietnam. It tells about the feuding lords that commanded all within the lands and how mere peasants slowly stripped them of their all encompassing power and control. It was humbling and although they showed no humility they protected these family story pieces in great museums during later raids by the mighty Japan. My wife brought several of these pieces to here so that she and her graduate students could unravel how they accomplished such an unexpected task."

"And the lost wax cast off?"

"That was my idea. I had wanted to have the pieces cast for a chess set. My wife, you see, was so much wiser than I. She wanted to explore the puzzle and I wanted to turn these same pieces into a game."

"Sorry for all of the questions, but why did one of the originals remain here?"

We were being served another fresh pot of tea. This time I sweetened mine with agave nectar. His house attendant was very happy when I requested a sweetener from her place of origin. Simple signals, symbols and noise entertain us all.

"It is the last original piece outside of China. I have been offered a trade for its safe return. It has remained a private matter until now because they did not want to announce to their people that they had not been diligent in having so important part of their collective history remain under the most stringent control."

"So it has been turned into a chess match."

"Oh do not be so pained by this. It is well looked after. But I am afraid that you are now part of the reason it remains in this room. Your task was so simple—a simple move even a novice could have completed. Why did you not complete the task? Why did you abandon Roxanne again?"

It was interesting that he would use the thunder of his fist on top of the table to emphasize so weak a point. Although it was not the first time I caught him using theatrics it was just as amusing as the last time. The professor caught me smiling.

"Is that her real name?"

"Yes, of course it is now. She was willing to make the necessary transition. She had a new life—so why not a new name. Why are you focused on such a detail?"

"Why indeed. I took my discovery to the Coast Guard. That is why I left Roxanne behind. For now you and she are not part of their ongoing investigation. Do you want that to change?  Let's assume for the moment that I am not a known entity to your counterparts in China.  I can simply walk away tonight.  What will you do?"

He looked stunned.  Really, did I just throw this intellectual maniac a curve?  I was really not ready for his reaction.  Then again I was definitely not ready to back down.

The Professor had no way of knowing what I really did—now did he?  That is where I wanted to leave it.  This is where I turned against his tug and pull went back home.

# Chapter Six

## *The Secret Society*

WHY INDEED DO WE TAKE ON a secret life?  It is not always to deceive others but to survive.  My dealing with the Professor was one of survival.  I needed to review my options and perhaps take enough time to review an important component of my past.

My interactions with the old man in Half Moon Bay taught me a valuable lesson about the extremes people will go to when in pure survival mode.  His story of intent to educate me as a privileged member of society was genuine; my luck and continued fortune of being a naturalized citizen was in stark contrast to his.  He was a member of a hidden society; one of great political interests every four years but not so much afterward the latest election.

The old man came into the country by the tried and true means of the times at the end of the eighteen hundreds and promoted himself as a natural during his reign in the first three quarters of the next century.  He was able to do so because his skills were in much demand at the time by our agricultural business.  He had the necessary skills to turn nothing into something which was divided into two principal camps: one figurative and one literal.

On the first of the two he aided farmers in the country to tame the harsh climate and soil of the Pacific coast. He helped them grow artichokes by the acre and successfully—progressively—each new year. At a time when a growing nation wanted no more or no less than to feed itself he provided technique and socially inherited knowledge of ensuring that certain species of plants could embrace the sea salt which permeated the air and earth in such dense quantity as it did on the mid California coast up through the northern patches of land after the sea but before the first mountain ranges. It was an enormous undertaking but his efforts richly rewarded an untellable land and the soon to be more prosperous land owners.

Now there was the exclusion—so literal. This old man could never by a prosperous land owner of the land he made work. His plight was to be blessed with the necessary knowledge but not the usefulness of birth place and birth right to reward his herculean efforts. He was part of our invisible society which preempted the rich debates which call for immigration reform after the fact—so after the land works well. He was then and he remains today a member of a once secret society.

This society as I came to know them included a population of just over one hundred members. They lived in a hidden valley just over a mountain range that would grow into the lion that roared called Silicon Valley. At a time where the foremost goal and gain was to grow micro circuits in the most pristine conditions, a previous generation did the same with vegetables over that mountain range and once lived in a valley that was transitioned into the aftermath of a succeeding and messier generation.

This valley of the old man and his contemporaries was once fertile and tilled and housed a generation of experts. This valley is now literally gone because its history had been backfilled with the garbage of replacement experts. This is a strange transition. Here is what he recalled and passed on during these interviews.

They collectively mastered an agricultural belt and Half Moon Bay grew with the addition of farming families and their offspring. This population included the original migrant families of Chinese, who were eventually succeeded by families from Mexico and further south.

The valley they had once lived in was purchased in the late 1970s by a central county in conjunction with the only sanitation company in existence at the time. There was a growing need on the west side of the San Francisco Bay area for additional land fill. The Bay itself was as backfilled as possible. Places like Foster City and Redwood Shores—now the homes of thousands of highly sought after new immigrants—were literally the previous generation's dumping grounds for household garbage. So a new place to backfill was purchased.

People are transitioned all the time in a busy nation. So were the inhabitants of this valley. They were moved and the clean and tidy rows of shacks that made up this hidden society were buried under garbage for two additional decades. A first disclaimer is this: it is not a cynical time. It is a time of growth, a time of abundance, and a time of enormous waste byproduct as a result. I was a direct beneficiary of this time of growth. We had built an empire that spanned the globe—literally so.

When I met the old man; having recorded all of his history; I met the valley's inhabitants. I hiked in and wandered around for several weeks and marveled at this encampment—so hidden from view of the growing masses. I watched a valley become a plane and then grow to a much higher elevation above the sea level just twelve minutes from their front doors. And now that valley no longer exists. One hilltop has enjoined another and the nonstop succession of eighteen wheelers continue to dump their loads and enormous tractors move it and level it and join those hilltops until they are no longer distinguishable from the once varied topology of the area.

Before the old man passed away he portended to be not bitter at all. After all he had helped cause this transition. It was that dubious double-edged sword that we all subscribe to and pass on to the next generation who forgets its merits and its origins and pronounces and decry its outcome skipping several generations of collected knowledge as we pealed each leaf from that artichoke and dipped it into garlicky oil and devoured it with such delight. And so then we vote with limited understanding of what the immigrant provided for us in abundance still.

My dad confessed to understand this and attempted to pass such perplexing histories along to me. He spoke of a generation of immigrants who once owned the east side of those mountains and most of both sides of the Bay. They were from Japan, however, and the story was as similar as mine; perhaps connected. The similarities are land bound. Theirs was lost as an outcome of the investment into a Second World War. It went from farm land to steel structures in the following decades, just as the coast transitioned from farm land to golf courses for the new inhabitants that drove over that Pacific range every morning to occupy the desks of companies who fought so hard for yet another generation of immigrants and their coveted H1B visas.

What is lost and what is gained from these hidden societies—perhaps now just another move on a much larger chess board. Not an indictment of a growing society, but an acknowledgement that there will always be those players who can see the next twenty or so moves before you know it. Did I relish the same?

I knew that I wanted to understand the significance of the sculpture that I had moved from one side of the Bay to the other. I wanted to explore the possibility that something more interesting was buried in its rich history—so not the object unto its self. What warranted this curiosity was inherited socially as the other life's lesson picked up from my parents—one natural citizen and one immigrant. Could I see the future while looking under the murky rocks of my past? Would I find another once hidden treasure to prolong the story of an old Chinese man I hardly knew? It has become an ambition—this fortuitous event.

## What can you do with Knowledge

In reality I did not really want to know how to play chess. I had once shared this with the original Roxanne. This was not something that had passed onto the new Roxanne, obviously. Never having wanted to be anyone's apprentice I moved forward carefully with this in mind. I could trace the past to a point of origin but not to an ultimate end. I would keep my promise to the Professor of not taking a discovery to a logical next step.

Instead I worked steadily backward into a number of pasts, including one of my own doing.

When I came home from the Navy meeting the real Roxanne again by chance on the highway was a good starting point. I had been living in Redwood City at the time with the son of a Japanese family. As history will show his father and mother had once owned a significant portion of land on the west side of the Bay Area all the way down to its flooded end. The stretch of land had been magically transformed from vast orchards from Stanford into San Jose. Like the Chinese the Japanese had the knowledge to transform harsh and barren lands into rich agriculture. But the times were quite different. A Second World War had broken out and the parents of my roommate had all of their lands taken just before they were sent off to Internment camps.

A second disclaimer: this is not a judgment. I can only peer out at the past because I did not exist back then. I can only wonder how the similarities of the immigrants of these two separate cultures are joined at the hip through the eyes of the amateur Cultural Anthropologist. I observe but never interact. I can recall interviewing my roommate's parents and using the tools I had been trained on by my favorite Chinese instructor (Logic and Reason) to try to shed some light on the past. I did the same with my favorite European instructor (Cultural Anthropology), long before I even entered the halls of several Universities trying to examine a possible future.

Having spent many nights playing Japanese poker with my roommate's parents, while consuming many bottles of Irish Whiskey, pieced the moments of their life into a more meaningful and descriptive picture of this life that my parents had brought me into—so compare and contrast. And I did the same with my taped conversations with the old man on the other side of the Pacific Mountains. I did so using observation and distance, as well as logic and reason. What is it about history that it fills in as many gaps as it creates between us all? This is why the Professor had nearly finished me off with so few moves. I could not take that leap of faith and create those next twenty moves to save my own butt.

My ride with the real Roxanne was an important event in my life with regard to this other worldly glass bead game. She had told me something about her father before we had raided his vast wine cellar. She had exposed a part of that underground place and revealed yet another hidden room. A place that was so dark and so recessed that we probed into its chest in complete darkness. We had entered into the heart of darkness and stepped into a room full of what I had then considered another junkyard.

When I close my eyes I can retrace the lines of every room I have ever lived in and relive those magnificent details. I am closing my eyes now and I am not just imagining the debris of this dusty and cob webbed place but its hidden treasures that now have more meaning after decades have passed. I remember a room of stoic figures designed by another culture of which I had little understanding at the time. I was only mildly impressed with what I saw because Roxanne had illuminated this chamber with a battery of lamps and I could see the illuminated silhouette of her body through the nearly transparent material of her dress. That was then and this is now. I am still mostly engrossed in this fantasy.

The length of her hair at the time is all I can focus on. I remembered that it covered her shoulders and her breasts and obstructed what I had really wanted to see at that time. I danced and I stumbled across the room over ancient artifacts, perhaps even damaging a few in pursuit of misplaced passions for the present just several hands away. I fantasized in the dark under the artificial light that was coming my way and we had embraced and merged exposed skin until we were one and the same. I had intercourse with the Professor's daughter just before we made off with two bottles of his wine. I did so recall this now to tell you just how close the truth of the past can continue to haunt us today.

So I go back so literally so (decades later) and I sneak into a place that is no longer filled with the clues I need to go on. The darkness aids me in discovering an empty chamber.

What can you do with knowledge? I can close my eyes and I can examine past dreams and make discoveries through the fragments of these examinations. I have the partial Libraries of Alexandria back on line as recollected by many other scholars who were able to close their eyes and recall scant details of the collective past and move them forward. The results are only a recollection and not really for fact. But it is enough to take on the Professor. I have my fragments of what I once so literally tripped over and I knew where to take them.

**Universal Truths and Accompanying Rivalry**

The only means I have of moving forward is to go to a football game. I head to the Peninsula and to the revamped Stanford Stadium and sit through Stanford versus UCB; red and green versus yellow and blue. I am here because my favorite part of the game is eating stadium hotdogs washed down with a cup full of icy cold Pepsi. Here is my one advertisement. I have mentioned one product and it is of course relevant.

I can spy several familiar faces in specific sections of the crowd because they are always here and they always sit there. This is not as hard as one would think. Some people are not designed to deviate from course. I make my match up as the game is already half way through its course. It is a mid game break and I do not remain in my seat for much longer. At this walking instance I can see the two scholars at opposite ends of the spectrum. And now I can see them in an attraction state like two electrons that have no likelihood of repelling each other because it was a fully expected state. They cannot change the nature of their being.

They do come together and I am observing them not far from a large ring that used to pierce the distant past of our universe—SLAC—to understand the present, and to predict the variances of outcome. The meeting of minds is profound to me because I can recognize what they share in the present. As they march toward each other—the half time stadium in between—I can see them talk to each other using the latest handhelds designed by the very people that are also in attendance at this game. It is a strange coincidence but fairly easy to predict the benefits of immigration.

With any certainty at all I follow the conversation I am supposed to hear. I listen in analog behind as the utterances are picked up and forwarded, translated to digital and then passed over several hundred yards, only to be converted back into analog again. When I think of the carbon footprint of their conversation I am dismayed. If they had only waited ten minutes longer I could have saved them from a lot of unnecessary resource utilization. What will they exchange here today that warrants the use of an iPhone? Yes, I have just mentioned another sponsor.

It is of course what I came to expect from their conversation. Two rivals now expose who is in position of the framed next move. It is something about their commitment to this game that was explained to me by Roxanne that I never quite understood until now. They are steeped in the ritual of exchange. I have my first appearance of an advanced move—so not the twenty moves I will need but the only one that will get me started in the right direction.

I am not a part of this ongoing rivalry so I so depart and make my way over the mountain, past the valley of the forgotten and across a revamped bridge. I park in front of the house in question and ponder the importance of my next decision. Will I go after the original or will I seek out another bottle of wine?

I pretend the two are meaningful together. I have an ancient piece from China and a younger vintage from France. I am not sure which I treasure more as I retrace my steps and seek out a place of neutrality.

My long but often sought after friends are always so surprised when I make my appearances. I am predictably unpredictable as I make my way in past the front door and cry out loud when I see the battery of picture frames of children now as adults. This offspring are now at favored universities across the land. The parents profess the difficulties of empty nest syndrome and I fake my way through the conversation as a sympathetic friend. We do this over a fine Bordeaux and I talk my way into their lives to access a piece of futuristic equipment.

My friends are still lost in the cause of the future and I meet one of them at a lab that can scan the truth of someone's past. The original piece I have in my hands is placed in the middle of a bank of scanning lasers and at long last I have a detailed picture of this object of exchange. I will no longer have to close my eyes to see its beauty. I take the resultant multidimensional digital files of this combination of the analog and the quantum world and I depart as suddenly as I may have appeared. I leave with both versions and return the more physical one back in its place of honor before the post game celebrations are concluded. I am off to the north with my digital files before the start of the next day and the next exchange.

The next step is easy. I go on line with my image and I compare and I contrast. I have found what I was looking forward to exploring and I go to the lamp of Aladdin for the next logical steps.

Fortuitous Event

# Chapter Seven

## *Those Special Expressions*

EVERYONE HAS ONE OF THOSE MOMENTS where they really connect with someone they are extremely close to and become them. There are times that I thought I knew a friend or a business associate so well that not only could I finish their sentences but I could append to them that what I felt most probable at that time. In the short time of span I knew the Professor I began to believe that he appended always. Perhaps he could no longer help himself, and it was here that I could have the advantage because of my intimate knowledge of the problem itself.

If we could play the emotions expressed by our body position the same way with numbers we could win the lottery time and time again. Haven't we all been there? We pick our parents birthdates, an anniversary, the first address, an old phone number or anything that might tip the scales in one favorable way over that of another when they have deep meaning and we regretfully promote them in body language even when just thinking about them. We wear them on our proverbial sleeves so to speak.

Numbers seem to have specific meaning and end up as expressions represented symbolically in art, military history, religion, and culture. To the superstitious and to the purely academic, we share them just the same: studied over time they retain their deep meaning always.

A case in point proves this point over the weekend.

As a fan of the arts I am drawn to gallery walks. I am fairly sure that it is one of the first things that I do when traveling to population centers around the world. I seek them out by scouring the local newspapers, scanning storefront windows for posters, and following up on line for cross correlation and grid mapping of the places I am visiting. Thanks to the abundance of data and explicit detailing in the on line mapping of downtown areas, I have my grid coordinates for this weekend in final minutes before I head out the door. It is already dark outside as the door is latched and I head to the car stepping over the abundance of fallen leaves, bright red and edged with brown from my two marvelous Japanese maple trees. Before long they will be stripped bare, as silhouette stick figures in the night, victims of the winds.

Although there were cries of wet and cold weather predicted for the area it was dry, far less overcast and comfortably warm to shed the rain coat I brought along. The downtown streets were busy with people seeking out art; not for art's sake alone but because it was a great means of coming across those familiar faces that warranted catching up.

Another crowd fills the entrance and the glass wrapped chamber of a popular cluster of galleries both new and old. There has been a changing of the guard on the anchor gallery and that has drawn my attention tonight.

Edging in through the double swinging doors I am confronted with a mix of young students from the local university, and the older crowd who dress and mix as one. It is possible that the most common denominators have become the adornment of wickedly strange knit hats during the early winter nights and the constant hum of excited conversations held via cell phones. When I see my reflection in the large glass panels I am pleased that I am not one of them.

I do profess that the notion that one cannot mingle and embrace oneself with art in this crowded room without overhearing cell phone conversations every two feet is troubling. I am witness to more backs and shoulders coupling small plastic devices that will most likely be in someone else's landfill before next summer. I am here to screen canvas, shaped steel and glass works; as it is more probable with regard to my earlier train of thought that I can finish their phone conversations for most of them without having been tied to the other end. For this I am quite certain is not a demanding task.

I see many faces I had not run across since the summertime—midsummer to be exact. We caught up to each other with casual glances, polite reflections of the most recent political event—another election come and gone—and we are as quickly separated by the flow of bodies moving in and out of the restrictive rooms as expected. There were new comers who wanted my attention. We do not turn away but engage, and then we separate because this cycle will go on throughout the night. It is what we are expected to do and this is not an indictment of social predisposition. It is however more out of habit. Habits can be broken.

I have finally met a pair of eyes that return my gleeful stare and we are drawn together for a very short reunion before heading upstairs to his gallery up on the second level. This is more than a casual reunion because he is a deeply interesting fellow and has obtained information about the scanned images that I had shared with him earlier. His news is startling both in regard to content and source.

"I was at my alumni party in the Bay Area and I was introduced to a very useful fellow at this planned event. He is a Doctor of Anthropology at the University of Santa Barbara. He is a specialist in the study of numerology; looking at numbers and the role they played for early dynasties in mainland China more specifically. He also looks at how numbers and their special meaning were incorporated into art pieces to be precise."

"So you showed him the scanned images?" I asked and answered this more than astute fellow.

"Well that was part of your plan was it not? I see that look on your face. It is a sign of weariness, yes?"

"More like I am getting over a cold; the large crowd below." I answered truthfully.

"Well I dare say that the images struck a nerve. He had this look in his eyes that he recognized something special. We had met the next day at his lab and he threw the images up on a wall with a very high end projector, allowing us to see more details than before. He recognized the characters blended well into the splendid details all around the object."

For a moment we share common phenomena as we stare up at an image projected my mindset. We then reengage.

"Did he know what the characters represented?"

"Oh, he did indeed. The numbers represented dates of importance to the carver. He must have been somewhat of a historian; by hobby or by trade, who knows. The good Doctor finishes off his discovery with a good many questions of his own. It appears that this is one piece out of a set. A set that at one time was used as a game to teach history. And he wants to know—so a demand really—where the scanned images originated."

"You were hesitant to tell him." I appended nicely.

"Well, yes, I was hesitant to tell him at first. Because he went to so much trouble to identify the numbers when I asked him for more specifics. Your piece represents an event that happened in 1122. The other previously hidden symbols represented an exploratory journey taken by the nephew of a great dynasty leader in mainland China, which so happened to border what is now Vietnam."

"Did you provide him with the missing link?" I knew the rest.

My friend sees the smirk on my face. I could never play poker with him because I cannot hide my expressions. It is some else I inherited socially from my dad. When it was coming from him I could recognize the impending impact immediately. Now I wore the same face. Could my friend now do the same?

"Why do I feel that I was so used?"

His reaction is soured and I quickly attempt to clear up the misunderstanding. Although I do feel that I have spun a reasonably well thought out story for his part, he insinuates that he is feeling naked on stage in front of his peers. We begin to address this reaction but are disturbed by yet another pair of female acquaintances of his that have just walked into his open studio. I am introduced with some reluctance as a long time friend. I am astonished that my earlier misgivings about strange knit hats are being strongly reinforced as the pair saunter quite close, asking questions about my point of origin.

So I stretched the truth for a moment and say that I am on my way out. I bid my closer friend goodbye and he in return assures me that the matter is far from closed.

I am not sure I care as the next move is clearly mine. The mantra of all Universities is published or perished. The fact that those two PhDs had not written about the significance of the argued over item is to my benefit. Opportunity denotes task and I was driven by the one at hand. But I would have to clear the decks, if you will, of all other extraneous information. I needed to stay focused.

Why they fought over the sculpture like a child's game across the span of several decades was anyone's guess. It did seem important but not enough to pull me in. I would have to guess around this aspect of their relationship and project one of my own. The intent was part of the original task, and if I focused on what I was not supposed to take to its logical end I would in fact stumble upon the next and most important move. The art walk and the necessary acquaintances came to a close and I went home to sleep on it.

That night I dreamed about discovery. The following morning I drove over to the boat launch and suited up for the paddle and then the ultimate dive of a lifetime— so close to the mainland, yet worlds apart.

Fortuitous Event

# Chapter Eight

## *Natural and Cultural Resources*

WHAT CAN I SAY ABOUT THE NATURAL WORLD and the accompanying resources that we must abstract first to gain access. There is an abundance of public beaches available to the outside world when visiting the San Juan Islands. My favorites are typically also the most remote. I like to be private where I go public. With all of the push for privatization one the few acts at the federal level that I never oppose is public funding for the *Department of Natural Resources,* also known as *DNR.*

I am very respectful of the fact that the acronym can also be used to denote *Do Not Resuscitate*—to bring back to life. We see the 'all jokes aside' aspect of *DNR* propagated in movies and television shows. If you have had the chance to visit the Channel Islands down south on the Pacific side or up north on the Salish Sea you are appreciative of the role that *DNR* plays in these wonderland archipelagos.

The San Juan track of islands was last on my list of playgrounds. I was only introduced –in intimate terms— to this scattered group of islands in my mid fifties. It has somehow catapulted to the forefront as one of my favorite places to be when I am not exploring-exploiting on the mainland.

One of the most accessible islands to the west of my home is Lummi Island, named after the indigenous native group called the Lummi Nation. But here lies one strange aspect of this Island's namesake. The majority of stake holders living on Lummi Island are of Western European ancestry. Lummi Nation is across the way and oversees a very large Reservation and ferry dock which provides access to this island. As a matter of fact it is the only access to the island unless you travel by boat. It is a clever plan the Nation has with regard to the Casino nearby. They will use the profits, if any, to buy back the land and put it under their control. The Ferry Dock at the west point is up for grabs.

This morning I am on the Lummi Ferry after departing from Gooseberry Point at the far west end of the Reservation. It is a very smooth twelve minutes start-to-finish on a November morning that has beaten all of the odds. It is clear skies of rich, deep blue with very scattered clouds and there is only the slightest off shore breeze and the ferry rocks effortlessly as it makes way to the other side. We unload—seven vehicles start up and roar across the small dock; the north track is more popular than the south.

I am starting on the east side of the island and need to make my way to the west side. After a fifteen minute drive I am heading around to my target—one of three public access beaches. This one is accessed at the pleasure of the white bleached church, the dominate building on a large and flat parcel of land. This place welcomes all inside and out.

A large hollow and yellow shell is unloaded off of the truck and filled with all sorts of equipment. I can leave nothing behind, it seems, and some of the bundles seem extraneous to the small crowd of curiosity seekers which .extend as a semi-circle at a very safe distance. Only one approaches.

"So where are you off to?" The middle-aged woman asks by my side. She is slim and very pretty and her gray streaked hair is tied back in a ponytail. Her skin is tanned for November. I compliment her on her general health and she returns the same.

This is not flirting. I suppose this will influence my answer all the same.

"I am heading over towards Orcas Island." I have said simply enough. She continues to smile and then points to some of my equipment.

"Are you going diving?" This one asks observantly and spells out the almost too obvious.

"Well, to tell you the truth I am exploring a site to prove the possibility that it was the Chinese who first discovered the New World." I am answering her with little regret. There is no fear that she will carry this seemingly absurd notion forward.

"Sounds interesting, do you have any proof?"

Now I am not sure where the connection is going or coming from for that matter. I was that certain that not all actions correlate to an actual source of transportable proofs, but I would go along for the ride nonetheless. I was polite and firm with my answer. The woman appeared comfortable with my last retort and my next accomplished plea is that this is just for fun. Would that satisfy her inquisitive needs?

"I have snorkeling equipment. Can I accompany you to the dive site?"

She is smiling so hard and I cannot say no. I am that easy. It is a very nice day and she does seem connected somehow to this property. She did seem to hold the attention of the dispersing crowd.

We agree to meet up at a point further south. Her family has a place on the land's edge and it is not at all out of my way. If you know this area you will not be shocked that I barely had to put paddle to water as I headed down the rocky coastline across a small bay.

This is not rough current per se, on the west side of the island, but it does translates to a cautious but easy ride around a small grouping of fishing boats tied up to buoys. My big yellow kayak is being trailed by a big red paddleboard. Perhaps I have over packed for this excursion but I like to mix business with pleasure always. I like the look I am receiving from some of the fisher people aboard their boats as they unravel reef nets.

After coasting for another ten minutes I could see the woman waiving from the beach. She is not alone. There is an older man standing by her side and he is holding back a medium-sized dog that shows intent to board and chew on my legs. The father title is real enough, as it turns out just wanted to introduce himself as the head of the parish; the place of launch is under his dominion.

The Deacon, as it turns out, warns me and then her about the inherent dangers of diving in these currents and the massive amount of reef nets that have been cut away rather than being retrieved from underwater rock formations. Cutting away and leaving them behind is apparently less costly than their retrieval. I can see that by the labored looks aboard those boats.

"I will keep that in mind. Thank you." I am holding my kayak just out of reach of the lurching dog.

The woman wades across the shallow bay and launches her own kayak into the same stream. She straddles on board her craft and counter rows to signal to me that she is well off if left on her own. It only takes a minute or two but the point reaches a comforting place in my heart. If things were to become too apparent to fast I would not hesitate to leave her on her own accord. And now there is mutual agreement. The Deacon and the dog are already half way down a private beach.

The paddle will be another 1.82 nautical miles from this point forward. We cut across diagonally heading southwest to a very small dot called Clark Island. Our intent is not to go to Orcas, but to a midway spot and another *DNR* on this small dot of an island. It is a non eventful journey across and she and I are not fatigued after the first leg of the journey is complete.

Clark Island has a small bay as described much earlier. It is where the woman wants to snorkel. She now carries a name, having shared a good part of her history across the first and the largest channel.

"Will you join me after you are done?" Julia's plea is endearing. "I have a joint." Things have a tendency to happen quickly in the Pacific Northwest. I have gotten used to it.

I could argue, just as effectively, that I did not see this coming as she is the Deacon's wife. But then again extensions of spirituality are a mixed bag. My favorite way to get into my spiritual zone is a good bottle of wine. I have tried the other but it doesn't get me there in the same way. It just makes me lethargic. Perhaps today will be different. But then I remind myself of the rumored potency of the stuff up in the north.

"I will, and I have wine. I will be over by The Sisters. If you do make a surprise visit keep in mind that there is a severe rip in the center channel."

Wine on the beach—that will get me to my spiritual plane. I strike a balance in my modest proposal.

"Yes, I know. I am very familiar with this area. I will see you later then, at my dive location." She is kind of laughing—hopefully with me and not against me—and bids me along with a very friendly wave off.

I can tell that this was more of a day than I bargained for and I am happily paddling across a small channel. I am singing to myself. Soon the bay disappears and The Sisters appear in vivid detail. I am amazed that so few visit this place.

It was what I would have gone with as well given the tossup between getting to know her and approaching my task. I closed my eyes for just one minute and followed a point to her face and was not at all surprised that she was showing teeth. She loved to cap off each moment with an endearing smile; didn't she. I caught her husband doing this as well but not quite as effectively.

Julia is probably singing happily to herself as she paddles off in an opposite direction. The Deacon was doing this when he and the dog headed off across their small beach. Did they match each other blow-for-blow?

This I pretend that I did not know. I am paddling with my eyes shut for the moment. My other senses are not so stilled.

I open my eyes; the setting is still real. For the next moment I have a flash back to an earlier time in my life. It is my own family that comes to mind out here on the water.

When I was growing up I found that my dad had a keen sense of the song as well. At one point in time my dad was supposed to have pursued a career in song. He did opera, but was concerned that it would not carry him far enough, given his other desire to marry and raise a family of his own. Five offspring on the salary of a mid range opera singer did not stack up at the time and he had set out to find a more suitable means of employment. But all the while at home he sang.

I had stopped paddling to pay attention to this inside voice. I wanted to pull out a particular image while the sea water lapped onto the side of the kayak. I wanted to blend in a specific recollection with the vision of the small flock of sea birds that has just flown by and paid me scant attention as they head to another fishing ground—one that is perhaps less occupied. The salmon had stopped breaking the surface when I stopped paddling.

My most entertaining vision of my dad's secondary path to fulfilling his dreams was coming home in the mid afternoon and finding him in his starched white underwear. He was preparing to go to a job that started in the early evening. He was belting out loudly into a wired microphone that was hooked up to a half-inch reel-to-reel tape recorder. His face was beet red as he held the note for longer than intended. The music he was accompanying was a kind of a show tune but done to the fusion of jazz. He was thus engaged in the reenactment of Mario Lanza, an Italian-American tenor and ambassador of that age, in our family living room, dressed appropriately enough in white. The image is reserved in a special location in my brain and it is only pulled up in especially rare times as it was today.

I started paddling again and I have strength in the recollection and power across the next channel. It helps that I am also moving with the currents.

## This Place is not Devoid of Life

It has taken me at least three decades to get to the location and I immediately appreciate what exists on the bottom and what it must have meant to those who arrived well in advance of this day. I am not a great discoverer of this channel. Many have been here before me but most likely engaged in fishing, or perhaps even hunting. There is fur bearing seal which swim through this place after the more than occasional salmon. The history of the place is greater than the sum of its parts.

I enter the cold water and I am immediately exposed to the current and I roll off of the side of the kayak, careful not to disturb its anchor. It can be controlled with a minimum of effort right now. I am floating across between small outcroppings of semi-exposed rock formation and there is an abundance of life. I love this feeling of buoyancy as I am somersaulting in somewhat transparent water to show off to them as opposed to myself. They are watching I can sense it. I want to exhibit that I am almost their equal but the darting fish and small eels are able to exhibit showmanship that I pale by in comparison. The only other floating debris absorbs the light and the bottom seems to sparkle. I am equal in capacity and capability to the debris that floats by.

Occasionally I glance forward and witness the movement of tall eel grasses that make a grand habitat for the juvenile salmon. The grasses sway signifying another series of inbound waves. This is not a dangerous place per se for an adult human. However, that said if you do not pay close attention to what is around you that next rock formation will not be the one you were just looking at for fixing a location. The current has just taken you further than imagined in a split instance. The waves here are circling just like that previous place and for a moment the disorientation causes a mild sensation of panic.

I surfaced quickly at one point and when I searched for what I thought was a common rock it became clear that I had drifted far from my target destination. Now I see nothing of the familiar. What happened to my kayak and my paddleboard? I left them tied up and now they are nowhere in sight when I experience the next series of rolling waves breach the area. It is the rock that is lost.

Wait—there is something else there. I feel compelled to turn one hundred and eighty degrees and find another strangely familiar location. My confidence returns—so spurred on by the telltale yellow tip that is bobbing behind the formation in front of me. I am back on target. I dive down—self rescue.

Now I am suspended below in near silence. I have ample weight on my belt to provide buoyancy compensation at a maintained depth of twelve to fifteen feet. I see another cave and this one is large enough to swim into. I slide in cleanly. Every spot rubbed is someone's home. I am not a home wrecker and I am diligent as I slide through the entrance.

If my eyes saw nothing to begin with it was due to not adapting to my surrounding environment. I will not dismiss this place because I think that it will do for the time being. I look at my pressure gauges and I am well within the safety margins. I slide further in and there is slightly more than dimmed light from several sources-- directions.

The cave is exceptionally clear when I switch on my lantern to amplify the scene. My first submarine encounter is relived and I add to the bank of memories with all of the new details. The green eel grass and yellow and brown algae recess into the deep shadowed areas in the far recesses of the cave system. There are hints of orange and purple as well and some of it is moving. So what is this system? It has many chambers and hopefully more than one exit. They are all abundantly filled ecological niches.

Nothing is out of focus now that I have adapted. I am pushing my way through the submerged rock formations. My arms are mighty enough to move me and my hands are placed well. I do not want to be crushed, bitten or raked across rough edges for that matter. There is an upcoming gray and gentle slope and I am pulling myself along with only the occasional kick of my flipper extended feet across a higher than expected pile of sand and rubble.

This looks completely out of place. I dive closer to inspect the odd formation.

What were the things I looked for and what was I seeing now? It is a semi-covered grave of broken debris and semi-recognizable vessels encrusted enough to act as camouflage. The sight has held me in place as though I am too paralyzed to move. Several crabs move across this mound for me; giving me direction to that next big thing. No one is this lucky. I find three cups stacked in a smaller cave that I can only reach with one arm extended. They were not as disguised as the other human made materials.

My heart is pounding but I keep my head. I control my breathing because if I let it go I am dead—stuck forever in this cave. Did I mention that cave diving is one of the more dangerous activities know to humankind with regard to playtime activities in the sea. I have plenty of air left. I pull one cup up to my face and rub its sides with my thumb. My exhaust is sputtered as I read the inscription and place this item into my net bag; carefully it is wrapped first in yet another nylon bag. Then I am heading out and back to the surface. I think that I was actually slowly letting out my air all the way back to the entrance of the cave. I was stunned enough to not inhale to calm myself.

The entrance is just ahead. I am examining it and I am apprehensive and turn around again.

There was one more than one exit. This made it a cave system. I am outside. I am bobbing close to the top and I am now on snorkel power. The find is dizzying I extend my body in a stretched out position and unlock my web belt, swinging the weight over the side and onto the top deck of the kayak with a loud thud. I am much more careful with this other object found in the sea cave below.

Pull yourself on board. Just pull yourself on board—stay focused.

I am stretched out across the deck of the kayak and I am looking straight up at the sky while examining this found vessel. It holds sea water—the particular quality of the material with regard to osmosis is unknown. It is thick and very smooth after I have rubbed the grime away carefully with a sponge and mild cleaning solution.

Yes, I did pack everything. Well almost everything.

"Well I am going to go back to achieves to unravel this mystery." The remark stirred the curiosity of the company pulling along side. The vessel has been turned over to another set of eyes whose deftness carries the prize out across the water and under the distant blaze of a November sun.

"I did not set out looking for museum pieces. But this surprise discovery could be centuries old. The markings are ancient Chinese." I said this as though I was ruminating like a scholar of ancient things.

I wanted to ask Julia why she came to me. I recalled the deal was that I would seek her out. She had this look of expertise, but at what I didn't know for now.

"Well, this is evidence of something. But I would not be making any serious public declaration until you have this examined by a more serious archaeologist." Julia was rubbing the edges of the raised characters with her exposed fingernail.

"I know someone who can look at this for you." She added and was handing the object back across open waters.

"Who do you have in mind?" I was calmly wrapping the cup before putting it into the thick floatation bag that mimicked the color of the kayak.

"My husband spent a lot of time as a missionary in PRC. He is a trustworthy soul, I assure you. He was there long before we had met. I joined him at a conference in Hong Kong years after his journey and we started dating. The rest is history as they say."

How naïve this may sound now, but I enjoined her not out of hope that she was a useful add to discovering the point of origin of the object, but for her calming smiles. My breathing was normal. My hands were calmed even though the sea and the inside of the cave were mercilessly cold. I had no better recommendation at this time so I said an emphatic yes in approval to the offer. But first she wanted to show me something else. I was going to trust my treasure to a missionary—hopefully not a mercenary.

We paddled our two boats over to the outside of a cove that is used as a popular entrance to the only *DNR* campground on Clark Island. Stopping short of the protective bay for visiting boats she began pointing down.

"You want me to dive down there?" I was indicating the obvious.

Julia had rolled off of her kayak well ahead of my entering the cold water for another sea trial. It looked to be at least sixty feet down and I could just make out the object that captured her attention. She had drifted out of the bay while snorkeling. That roam took her over this area. I was somewhat detached from the impending task because we were dangerously close to another channel current. This one felt stronger.

"Look, I have an inner ear drum injury from the time I served in the Navy. I was an engineer and one of the ship's two designated divers. I was sixty feet down when I was overcome by a nagging smokers cough. I had to be carried back to the surface by two dive buddies."

I had accidently swallowed a mouthful of sea water and coughed for emphasis. I felt like a clown acting on suggestions from an audience.

"I'll act as your dive buddy today." Her attempt was pleasant enough. And it was accompanied by that arousing smile.

"Don't be so sure. Can I really count on you to snorkel down sixty feet if I get into trouble?" My tanks and vest had been removed before sliding over the side of my kayak. The water was smooth but did I mention that it was cold?

I was preparing for my free dive and beginning to manage my breathing in the same manner one might attempt a difficult yoga procedure. I was too focused to see her swim to my side but felt her touch on my arms.

"I think that I can manage in an emergency. I have lots of experience, remember?"

The voice in my head reminded me that this was a troubling undertaking. I would free dive to thirty feet just to make sure that this was not a dead end—literally. I was detached from the idea that she could rescue me and I headed down and leveled off with only a hand held counter weight. My other hand grasped the nylon strap that was tied topside onto the kayak. My first plunge forward was a worthy one.

On the surface I described what she had thought she saw and a place of reality. This was no aberration, but it was at a working depth just beyond the safety limit I had in mind. Luckily I had planned for this limit of safety and returned to the kayak and water tight bag and retrieved the camera. I did bring everything. Nothing was left to chance. I had to plan out a more logical attack.

Julia egged me one. She steadied my craft with her added weight and held onto the line that might save my life. For the next fifteen minutes I swam up and then down to take a series of close-ups with the telephoto lens.

Mission completed we were back on board and north. Several more strokes in complete silence and I would have enough time to go over the underwater images in my head.

We were back on shore now. We pushed the kayaks up onto the *DNR* beachhead and played back the photo session on a two inch by three inch LCD screen. Between the two dives I was tired and she knew it and tried to help me regain my energy with impassioned smile after smile and a lot of touching. It had a strange way of working out the day's kinks.

The lure of the object that had fetched our combined attention turns out to be more than recognizable. It is a roughly carved out circle of stone. I have seen this object before but up off of the north coast of California and Oregon waters. It was an anchor typically used by very early Japanese fishermen who explored across the great expanse of the Pacific Ocean chasing large schools of fish. Only this time I was hoping that it was Chinese by design and by nature of parallel development across cultures.

We stared at our find. Yes, I was willing to examine this in a sense of play fair and share the discovery with almost a complete stranger. It would not be the first time or the last, as we embraced across the sides of two kayaks; we pretended to be great salvage hunters, taking in the 2 by 3 inch views, the calmer than seasonal seas and the wonderful smell of salt in the air.

Around us sea gull cried out impassionedly to their mates or other such winged invaders. My greatest wish when bobbing along this far north is to see a low flying squadron of pelicans heading across a watery corridor in search of food or a place to land. For now I would enjoy the company of the gulls, and the salmon that broke the surface when they sensed the splash of our oars as we headed back to Lummi Island after drinking my bottle of wine, just short of anything else.

Right now I would enjoy just hearing the slap of water under the bow of my kayak and try to determine if it sounds different from my trip across the Sea of Cortez when I was tracking an enormous whale shark, six years prior to this trip. I also craved an accidental interaction with a pod of Orcas whales for that matter—taking the feelings closer to real time. Something bigger than us all, and possibly more profound than the underwater discovery we had just made shared this wider channel

We paddled furiously across the channel away from Orcas and toward Lummi. There were no other boats in the vicinity but there was a solo sail boat heading in the opposite direction from us perhaps twelve nautical miles away. I could not hear its sail over the din of her voice. But then even she grew quite. Just then all I could hear was the wind that was picking up as it typically did in mid to late afternoon in contrast to the steadied slap of flat paddle blades on the cold brine water.

This is what I wanted to hear. This is a favorite sound and even if I have let nature drown out the stream of thoughts expressed by my companion explorer; I kind of knew what she had to say without being tempted by the actual words. This was a woman who spent most of her younger years living on other continents and living in or around small villages. I had been around missionaries before and her dialog was not so unexpected—the stories she streamed around me. That is not by any way meant as a demeaning summation of her past, altogether recollected at a less than opportune moment. It's just that not all recognizable patterns of the human voice are enjoyable to me when I am focusing on the water. I like the strain of the different view, the changing horizon, surprising noise that emanates from natural sources of disclosure. I had no patience listening to her explain how one culture rescued another from itself through the introduction of a religion. They think that they are heroes—these missionaries. They are not *Doctors Without Borders*—the true saviors. The missionaries operate with a chief mission to convert.

I was thinking about this as I paddled because there was a disjointed connection. I thought about the ever changing people of China and the missionary efforts to convert them over the centuries. Was that how those fishermen ended up and over here—to drop their anchors to gain a moments peace from the incessant chatter of those who desired to save them? It was an interesting means of departure from the lectures they incurred in comparison to the one I was receiving now.

What other continent could I escape to now? The mainland in front of me would have to do.

"Julia, when we get back to your beach, what will you say to your husband?" I hammered back to force a change in the one sided conversation. It was a two headed jest.

"Well I hope to engage him in a dialog about an earlier dynasty in China. Perhaps he will put the task to some of his vast resources in the church in order to discover and timestamp your cup."

This was a troubling perspective. I did not want his vast resources anywhere near this find.

We were heading around the point that would lead us in toward the small bay owned by their parish. There was no one on the beach and I was hopeful for some additional time together with obvious intension. The tree line along the shore was not quite bear of its leaves and the intermingled pine trees gave off a warming hue of green. I stopped paddling and Julia did the same.

"What I meant was you got stoned and I am still feeling the effects of the wine. We flirted for quite awhile on the beach over there and I was just wondering if you are going to be able to pull this off without full disclosure to your mate."

Did my plea fell on deaf ears? She was not smiling and waived me on.

"Please paddle in with me and I will share something with you as you are loading your truck. I wanted to share this with you earlier but the time just didn't seem right."

We did as intended. My equipment was repacked on top of and inside of the truck and I assisted Julia pull off her wet suit. While she sprayed both of our wet suits with a stream of cold and fresh water we gave each other strange and lingering stares. The Deacon's dog joined us for only a brief moment and then something else caught its interest as it ran off toward a grouping of tall pine trees. I saw something dart across the parking lot and the dog was close behind it. A small patch of clouds hovered in above us and the wind was picking up strikingly. The day turned yellow and brown toward the small hills and valleys across the island; the waters were grayer than blue to the west—so lustrous scanning out to the horizon beyond the silhouettes of north Orcas and the southern tip of Vancouver Island, the sea ran forever.

"My husband and I have a strain in our relationship. He has recently accepted a transfer to Indonesia and I have elected to remain behind. There is plenty to do here during the transfer of the parish for the incoming Deacon; his wife and family have already arrived."

She looked so scornful at her predicament and stared down at the puddle created near the hanging suits. I did not think that she was going to shed tears as I stood by and listened to the impending chapter of her life unravel.

"I know today what I would like to do with my time until this can all be sorted out. Would you mind terribly if I traced the vessel and anchor and its place in time. I have plenty of resources I can tie into because of my earlier training, and I promise that I can do so discretely. I will not share any of this with my husband for the time being. He has enough on his plate with this upcoming move to yet another country."

"Do you have a place to stay?" I was not asking for that reason, but I wanted to know. Yes, we had our intimate flash but that is all it was—a day on the beach.

Julia's answer really did surprise me. But then everything about this day was shock and awe. She followed me over to the truck and stopped me from getting in.

"I have made friends on this island and I will be well cared for. We have a woman in our parish that lost her husband several years back. She and I grew very close; during her time of pain and recovery we grew too close. I have been invited to stay with her. She has this love for historical puzzles. I am sure she will be the right person to share our discovery. I do trust her—I have to trust her. She did something for me which warrants it"

I had swung into the cab of the truck and was about to start the engine. There was something else that spoke through her eyes but she wanted to hold back. Would I push or let it ride I just didn't know at the time.

"After I get settled in, will you come out and visit me? I might have new information for you by then." She was smiling again and I witness the full repression of her earlier mood. She was smiling again.

The dog was back in the parking lot and it had something in its mouth. We both looked on in discomfort but then dismissed the interruption. The animal headed around the back of the white washed church, crashing through a row of bushes on its way to devour whatever the meal might be.

It was after that point that she leaned in and we kissed not like new friends but as old lovers. She then kissed my forehead while holding onto my head with both hands. This had a double meaning I suppose. I had an aunt that used to do this during family reunions on special holidays. The things we flash back to.

What kind of friend did Julia want me to be? We already shared a grand secret. There was more than the close encounter we shared briefly on that small dot of an island. She had expressed a very intimate portrayal of an impending transition in her life and I barely shared anything about mine. What would a good friend do at this point? I had a hunch there was an underlying reason for her behavior, and my agenda centered on the kiss instead.

Driving back alone to my place was expectedly silent. The ferry ride was rocky on the return trip because the wind and the waves caused the current to roar. There were only two other trucks on deck heading in this eastern direction, but I could see an even dozen vehicles already queued up for the trip back over to the island.

I touch my camera repeatedly. I did not have any of the usual apprehension with regard to leaving the vessel behind. I had caught every angle on my data card. I was already making notes to return by boat to salvage the ancient stone anchor and I was sure that I would not seek out Julia at that point.

The drive home was gusty and I probably drove at a slower pace than warranted. I used the silence to flash back in time and revisit an earlier conversation. I wanted the time to rediscover any other hints that the Professor may have slip to me during our interactions over an extensive period of time. That was the old man's mode of operation. He was always dropping advanced hints, tempting his challengers while knowing the only probable moves.

I completed the execution of one of his anticipated moves. I was certain that he knew that I would ignore his pleas and take this task to a logical end. Was I also certain that the final warning I had received from Roxanne would be one of providence.

But just then I recalled that I had told him the story of my old friend in Half Moon Bay. The Professor listened keenly. Usually he wanted to talk. No, what was it that I said to make him take a keener interest? Did I say it in front of the latest Roxanne, and did she in turn react to it as well. The thought had me under its spell.

I touched home. I would unload tomorrow. I went inside and switched on a bank of computers to look at the discovery on several much larger screens. I was right to do so then. This was some find—this fortuitous event.

Fortuitous Event

# Chapter Nine

## *The Clock Starts Ticking*

THE EARLIER PART OF MY LIFE was really all about being on the water. I recall a day my dad comes into my room when I was listening to music—the kind he did not attempt to understand—I am in a groove. At the time I was listening to the Big Brother and the Holding Company and probably at an all too loud volume but now I am certain that was the point. It was a Saturday and I had developed that young teenage crusty edge and wasn't getting along with other family members as a result. My mom must have been fed up with my week's moodiness so the big guns were called in. I needed another life's lesson—a physical one.

The door to my room swung open with gale force winds. It was dad and he had this look on his face that said cooperate or die. So I jumped to my feet, shut down the stereo, put on a shirt and a pair of shoes and made sure I complied with his next directions diligently.

"Pack a bag; we're going on a road trip." The door stays open when he leaves the room. He never has to tell me anything twice.

I am lingering a bit too long with my canvas duffle bag strap slung over my shoulder. My hair at the time was shoulder length and it manages to get tangled in the strap. He helps me with it and yanks it free and tosses it in the back of the station wagon. The vehicle is moss green with fake wooden side panels and enormous headlights and tail lights trimmed in chrome. Most teenagers would have been devastated by riding in this car with their parents. I on the other hand was pleased. This thing was such a vision of suburban crude that it made it all the more cool in my eyes. I liked the truly obscure at the time.

Dressed in my mode of the time I came fashioned in really faded blue jeans and a t-shirt with a tight neck. Although it was a perfect day weather-wise I wore thick Vibram soled hiking boots. The bag was packed light, per instructions received and I could already see the he had packed wet suits. We were going somewhere cold. No, I did not have a clue other than it was to be another lesson learned on the water.

We drive together toward the Golden Gate Bridge and my dad reminds me that his parents had walked him across when it first opened to the eagerly awaiting public. He had many marvelous treasures in his story book and they were relayed in stream as we passed Muir Woods, Stinson Beach, and on up the coast past one of my favorite places to go after abalone at Salt Point State Park. They would all carry a similar message as we continued to hug this expansive coastline.

At this point in my life I had a reasonable trust in what my dad was attempting to share with me. We had our on and off again trials, but when we headed to the water—the coast—there was another kind of bridge that was rebuilt between us. The stories at the time never got old and I sat in silence not just to the words that were being spoken, but the hypnotic space on this area of the California coast that was still scantily occupied. We were at long last in place called the Lost Coast.

The woody wagon was turned east onto a dirt road with clear enough markings. There were enough *No Trespassing* signs to wake up any adventurer to the impending dangers that must lie ahead. Someone was very serious about their privacy. The house ahead was three stories and had a top deck that visually cleared the tall strand of trees in between this place and the ocean shores. There was a solo figure up on the roof and he did not turn around when we skidded to a stop on the loose dirt and gravel driveway that semi-circled the house. The sound did however strike a chord to the three muscular dogs that made their way down off of the expansive redwood porch and launched to greet us.

Only my dad stepped out of the wagon and his voice seeped to appease the trio of dogs. Soon they were after his slaps on the back and the rough house petting; no doubt they were accustomed to it. They knew this man—I was that sure as I stepped out.

We are joined soon thereafter by the owner of the place. He tells us that his wife is at the market and that we have the afternoon to ourselves. After a brief introduction we are headed into a large standalone shed—also made entirely of redwood—and I am stunned when the large double doors are swung open revealing a beautiful array of paddle boards of all shapes and sizes.

I do not count the boards but I am convinced that the number comes close to one and a half dozen. This friend of my dad is already stripping down to his boxer shorts as he and my dad—doing the same—catch up like long lost brothers. This man is a second cousin to my dad's family. At one time I was told that we have two hundred relatives living in California.

It has been one year since they last embraced and it is truly an eye opener to see the two men happily embrace while stripped down to their underwear. But then I am doing the same, sans all the hugging. We are a fine trio of parading males.

The lesson evolves and we are pulling a small buckboard down a steep path behind an all terrain vehicle that looks like a leftover from World War II. The flat wagon we are pulling is loaded up to its side edges with a variety of boards, some exceeding sixteen feet. Most are fiber glassed but there are a couple of long boards that are wooden planks (strips rather) with a sheen epoxy seal. They are all finned and we come to find out that he has designed and constructed all but three. One of the long and wide wooden boards was a gift from a friend who died shortly after the Korean War.

This is the initial connection between the two men. They served together aboard a Merchant Marine cargo ship during the war. Like many men of their generation they never lost touch. I think they are the last generation to say 'let's keep in touch' and put it into long lasting practice. As I fast forward in age I will come to find that I did not retain any connection with high school chums, people I served with during the Vietnam War, college friends and associates, but do stay kind of linked (virtually) with one dozen friends I worked with in Silicon Valley. Clever how time changes us, and the habits we hardly retained from our parents generation.

It is a beautiful day on this part of the California coast. It is overcast and with a suitable off shore breeze that shapes the waves in a most desirable way. The moon is in a quartered phase and the tide lines are higher today. Although I am not the first one in the water with board of choice I envy the two who duck dive through two series before I can catch up with them. I am out of breath but I am being treated to a valuable lesson. These two men are still in fine shape. I am being taught to share the moment because they often do not last as long as today. They stay within ear shot of each other and I am taking off through another salvo of oncoming waves.

The man who entertains us on this semi private section of the coast is dying of cancer. My dad shares this in at another time. He smoked all of his life but we do not see him light up the entire weekend. This old waterman glides over and along with powerful waves with the grace of a much younger man with perfect lung capacity—that would be me. My father points this out even though it is entirely obvious. I get it then, and now, because he has to reinforce this now connected series of lessons.

At the end of two days of paddling and surfing in near perfect conditions our visit comes to a close. His wife does not surf but stays close to him every waking and sleeping hour. She knows that the moment is close and she has the staying power needed to get through this tougher part of time. I never see her without a smile on her face, but the worry lines are clear enough to read across the room. We only had one private conversation when my dad and his fried go off to hunt on this expansive property.

"Are you close to your father?" She asks a question that I suppose is the common link to these outstanding lessons. We share a small round table and are having tea and a bite to eat.

"We have our ups and downs, I suppose," I murmured between bites. Is this a show down with another adult?

"I never lose track of time—it is that precious. We are here for a shorter period of time than most youngsters think. I see the look you just gave me—so I gave one to my mother at one time. Stay focused on the things that really matter and stretch that limiting time. That is all I have to say to you. No more lectures, I promise."

The woman keeps her promise and we separate as expected as I go down to the shore to take one more look. Her words drum inside of my head. But instead of being mesmerized by the sound I turn toward the bluff that looks out over the Pacific and I take in all of the sights shared on that late afternoon. These sights and sounds carry me forward. I am too young to think about loss the way she describes it and I am more interested in the lessons of earlier in the day. I close my eyes and all I can see is my father and his friend straddling their boards on the outside of the break and engage in deeply prolonged conversation. There is some laughing and there is a distant perceived seriousness to the exchange.

This is what I came to hear now. The sound of the wind has picked up and a grouping of darker clouds has floated in above. I am not certain what occurred on the hunt as far as my dad and his friend is concerned. I remember that my dad sauntered back into the house alone. He is silent and our eyes do not meet. He does share a prolonged look with the other man's wife and she begins to smile. Then she turns and walks away out of her own home.

After that my dad explains that I can pick out the board of my choice from the large shed. I am told that this is a parting gift from his friend and that he was thrilled with the two days we spent out on the water. My dad never explained why the man did not join us in our departure. He and the man's wife share a long goodbye and make promises to stay in touch. I am sure they did.

Heading south we have made it to the north end of the Golden Gate Bridge and we barely shared a word during the long drive. I could tell my dad did not want to talk on the trip back. As we turned off of the bridge we headed west again and hugged the coastal highway even though it would take us out of our way. I am excited when we pass Devil's slide and the patches of fog break for a moment to allow me to see the beaches far below.

We stop for something to eat outside of Half Moon Bay. It is a pizza dive that is very popular with the surfing crowd who share this place with us. I am listening to my dad over the rowdy din.

"Son, you picked out a good board. Did you see the inscription on the tail?"

My dad is finally talking to me and we are smiling because he knows that I get it; between bites of pizza, washed down with ice cold Pepsi I am drawn in to his every word. I am thinking about the answer I want to give him.

"Yes, it is 1959. Is that when he got the board?" I was in between bites when he lets me have the real news.

"No, it is the year when he first found out about his condition. The date was added to the board because he wanted to remind himself why he was taking in everyday as the best day in his life." He looks as though he wants to say something else but then decides not to. I think it is enough.

We are finished eating and I am taking another long look at the lines of my new board before entering the fake woody. As we drive over the hill and back down into the Bay Area my dad looks over at me and starts in again.

"I would appreciate it if you did not tell your mother about the end of the trip. Just say we had a grand time and it was the perfect road trip between a father and his son."

That was it. Those were the final words of the trip until we pulled into the driveway. We were home.

I unloaded my fine gift with the help of my dad and stacked it carefully into the back of the garage. We silently climb the back stairs and crept into the family room to join those who were watching television. The show was interesting enough so no one asked us questions when we entered. It was a family affair, no matter how urbane we shared this night together as millions across the country do, and it was I who was most satisfied. I had my next lesson and another board to show off to my closest high school buddies. I was giddy with excitement and I did not stop to think of the real circumstances of my inheritance.

Later on that night I am listening to my music. I have CSNY on and I have the volume turned way down. I can hear the creeks of the hallway outside of my door. It opens and my dad pos his head in.

"Is everything Ok?"

"Yes, we're good." I am sharing the only answer in retrospect to the lesson learned. Keep it short but keep it on target.

The following weekend I do take the board out to this place called Maverick's. The waves are low and I am more interested in paddling this enormous board than I am surfing. I am not alone this time and there are several surfers paddling over to see my adult-sized toy. One is a young man and the other is old enough to be his father. We share a few experiences about the waves and we are acknowledging why we are out here in the first place. The older man comments on the inscription on the tail of the board I am laying down on.

"It is the year when the board was built." I tell him this straight enough. He is satisfied with my answer and soon he and the younger one paddle off to intercept the only fine waves of the day.

I choose to lie back on my board with my head propped on top of my arms. I am satisfied just to watch and hopefully to learn from this duo. It is obvious that they have been at this for a much longer period than I have and I am in awe at their polished skills. They are popping over the waves instead of paddling furiously in front when the current set breaks. I have not seen this method before but I know now that I will have to attempt the seemingly backwards approach.

I will attempt it some other day on my board; having been created in 1959. This is now my belief as well and I will carry this forward. The memory of the inheritance of this board never really fades too far away.

The decades have speed by. I no longer have the water toys I had in my more youthful period. The new boards I enjoy now are a combination of fabricated by friends, found and purchased in less than usual spots, and one that I built modeled off of the one board I loved more than the others. I have not inscribed anything on the tail because I am not sure I have a right to yet. Perhaps I will some day.

Another day: my interest flags because the telephone is ringing and I wait for the caller to go to voicemail. The screen is lit and I retrieve the deliberately passed call. It is Roxanne—the mock wood sided panel version. It is strange, but as I listen to the *please let's get together soon'* in her call I am forced right back to the day when my dad took me up the coast to visit his friend. I tie the two events together.

Call this intuition or whatever you like but there is something in the tone of her voice that leads me to this link of my past. I'll return the call; I will do so tomorrow. Right now all I want to do is grab one of my old boards and head to a nearby lake for a much needed paddle.

# Chapter Ten

## *One Sovereign Domain*

WHAT IS IT THAT WE THINK we see when we hear what we thought was originally happening. The fact is apparent to my senses and now I needed to appraise the circumstances of this surprise discovery. I now had scientific proof with regard to my hunch and the experiences incurred freeing the anchor from the enveloping silt bottom of the channel—the centuries of surreptitious cover below the waterline has passed. The object was real, the date of origin kind of known, but the circumstances of it being here apparently died with the last sailor in good standing—all withstanding the obvious fact that it had be so literally thrown overboard to hold fast an inanimate invading species.

It is most fortunate that I had a friend who was a geologist. Actually he is in the petroleum business but has access to a lab full of people who know rock and stone like nobody else on this section of the coast. The appraisal takes several weeks, then retested for almost another month, but the conclusion was surreal even when I received the feedback in first person.

I was standing around the table along with a bank of specialists and engineers who all offered hunch as well as hypothesis as to the circumstances of this two thousand pound anchor. Someone had tossed it overboard and had left it behind. Only this happened centuries ago.

The heavy and dense material has been tested using the latest dating techniques. The chiseling technique was been compared to a specific circa and it falls comfortably back to the early 1100s. When it is x-rayed the scientists could no longer ignore the subtle markings along one particular edge that prove to be proverbs. It is in a poem sort of arrangement and it spells out the relationship of their land to the soon to be discovered. It is reverent to the depleting resources of their time and makes comment about the future and need rather than desire during feudal times. This is some find, many around the table agree. It should be in a museum others argue with intense emphasis.

I am not sure what to do with all of the data returned along with the stone object of great heft. It is returned of course because the powers that lurk above this crowd of engineers and scientists can never know the extent of the valuable resources that were used for this task; well out of the definition of real work in their industry from any perspective. It was a challenge to this group and that was the primary reason they ran with it. It only started out as a favor and then it morphed into a greater puzzle that demands resolve. And now I was indebted to these fellows and I had the fully laden pallet loaded onto the flatbed of a borrowed truck laying in wait outside the door of the test lab. I have accessed everything in kind and I made promises to return the favor. Take the piece to a museum was a parting plea and a promise made in return.

When I pulled the flatbed onto another friends property we used a hay bailer to lift it into the top section of his drying barn and it retained a place of endeared history behind several other bales of equal to and exceeding its height and girth. When we closed up the barn we popped open the two beers brought out by his daughter and we toasted our hidden treasure until sunset. My friend explained that it wasn't the most unusual thing he hid in his barn over the ages, and then promptly asked his daughter not to spill the beans to his wife. His pleas echoed another incident quite like this one still dancing in my head.

The anchor was left in peace and I drove off after begging off dinner. I had somewhere else to be after all.

Roxanne was already sitting on my front porch when I turned into the driveway. She was smiling in a most pleasant way when her head turns to greet my entry and then exit from the large flatbed truck. She is bearing gifts apparently, and I am ushering her along just before the downpour. She asks if I am entered into another industry altogether.

I am happy for the rain outside not only because of its refreshing drops washes my exposed skin, but because the torrents that follow will clean the bed of the borrowed truck. She now know that it has been borrowed but not for what intention.

What is it about the truth we seek to wash away rather than retain to close today? No, this was not deception on my end but rather controlled disclosure. I did not want to give Roxanne too much before I heard what she had to say. Wine was of utmost importance for my guest, and then I took leave for a much needed shower.

I did smell like a hayloft and it would be too hard to explain away.

The water of my showerhead is like a strong waterfall. I am disclosing this because it explains my long departure from my guest in the kitchen. I could hear her pulling open drawers and rustling around the cupboards and while I showered I assumed that she was making something to eat. It was hopefully a counter to her wanting to go out for dinner.

I think I must have slipped in and out of consciousness because I was still under the still warm torrents when she entered the bathroom. She was sitting on the toilet seat and apparently taking care of business when I stepped out to towel off. Some might have faked a modicum of modesty under the circumstances but this guest continued as though we were long lost lovers. The flush was followed by a determined stance with pants around her ankles and she laughed at my surprise.

"Actually I was about to join you in the shower. My drive up from Seattle was exhausting and I think that I smell, well, not fresh. May I?"

"So disclosed, so welcome I assure you." I think I may have finished this off with a little bow.

Roxanne completed her non teasing strip and talked to me for several moments before stepping behind the smoked glass door. She looked quite good as a woman can well into her forties. I continued to stand and call out several items of appeal until she was rinsed off and drying in front of me. I never left the room to get dressed. I had lingered in the room and before a full length mirror to remind myself that I was reasonable in stature for a man well into his fifties.

This is not narcissism by the way. I just do not like to make a fool of myself so I do take note from time to time. Time in reflection one supposes. Between biking and paddling I retain a properly oriented sense of self esteem. Enough said?

Yes, we did so embrace when she was out and drying and I was so aroused that there was no clear way to disguise it. Her intent may have been to fain shock. There was a real sense of closeness—catching up—as we made way to another room and spent time living beyond friendship.

Life was meant to be explored this way and I wanted to maintain that balance of give and take as we examined all of the possibilities of our moving forward in slow motion. Talk was countered with locomotion. As expected be went to that peak state and peered out from our surroundings two hours later to get something to eat.

I would need to shower for a second time that night. Perhaps this next time she would join me and we would have expected lathered fun in my stall.

The kitchen had been fully stocked and there was food well prepare on the tabletop when we arrived. Roxanne had seen to all of the details while I showered alone. It was a healthy feast of cut fruit and vegetables, finished off with of all things, pudding. I stood at the table with shock and awe as she brought to bubble the sugary top of this vanilla crème de la crème dessert. We ate that first and then munched lightly on the others.

"You are a lot like the Professor, you know." She was fawning with her fingers over the top of my hand as she spoke with soft intensity.

"And tell me how so?" Well what did you expect me to say? Most people like a good comparison.

"I can tell when he wants to avoid getting to the point. He used to treat me like his graduate student all the time. He would drop little hints and have this great expectation that I could run with it and profound him with my enlightenment. I never did really—he never did at all. I must have been a very disappointing substitute for his daughter."

"Oh, I do not think that was it. The first Roxanne once told me a similar tale. She would play back just as hard and more or less perplexed the old man rather than profound him with ongoing bullshit. She told me that he never could separate his private live from that of the academic one, so she more often played the role of a student instead of the role of offspring."

"Let's get straight to the point then?" She was opening up the package she had coveted thus far. It was the original statue and a mate. "Let's see what I learned."

I had received and handled both and caught the connection almost immediately. Did he have the entire set? How extensive was his hidden collection compared to what I saw in the museum of his? I wondered this out loud.

"Oh, his collection was quite extensive. But these are the only two he retained. He did make sure Stanford retained control of the remaining collection in his will.

Oh, did I mention that he passed away several months ago? Sorry, I was so sure that you already knew."

I had a sense that she was playing me. Did she want to think that I was caught up? I would answer as best I could and held back just a little. The evening droned on, not.

"That is the extent of my interest, actually. I did a favor for his real daughter and that was the only real appeal."

Her declaration was clear enough. I had made a gross misstep. Did she think that her investment in the Professor was just as real? What about mine?

"You know he was a real father to me. My parents did not give a shit about me after I became a junkie. The Professor forgave his daughter in adopting me. I do not expect you to understand this at all."

Yes, she was kind of crying but it was not out of hurt. There was little pain in her face—just discovery of a stopping point. I was not too thrilled with this outcome.

"How will you get by now that you are cut loose from all of this?" I wanted to push to the next level.

"What the school got were his treasures and an endowment for future graduate students. The estate closed quickly and I was left with a generous account and the cloths in my room and two very lovely and well maintained automobiles. The house and the wine collection were sold. I cannot and will not complain."

This was read plain enough in her eyes and her body position. She did seem satisfied for the moment. At this moment I was only thinking about myself and the current affairs. Did I have enough to go on and why were there more unanswered questions to go on. We both could have benefited from a little more closure.

"The Professor wanted you to have these two pieces. I know you did not honor his earlier request to leave well enough alone. Before he passed on he told me that he had been appraised with regard to the scanned files. At first I thought he was angry. But I know that look. I pushed him to tell me the rest. He said you did what he expected you to do—so checkmate."

Well this is about all I want to hear. The old man is still several moves ahead of me and he has died in the interim. Did I have a post op game, I wondered to myself. Some open thoughts just can't be explained. And well I thought that the woman in front of me really did not care anyway—I so rationalized to no avail.

The remainder of the evening was not so somber. I had placed the two sculptures on my office desk and made way back to the bedroom with this Roxanne. We talked, made close encounters and then fell fast asleep in our own corners of the bed. When I woke up in the morning I could hear her showering and lingering in the kitchen over a hot cup of coffee. One would normally see a guest to the door, I chose to lie in bed and think about where this left me. Thirty minutes later I hear the front door close and the start up of her rental.

She sped away. I got up and sauntered to the front wondering less about her speeding away than I was by the notepad on the front room table. I do not want to be unnecessarily cruel but then again I deplore messy goodbyes. I remind myself that I am not part of the 'let's stay in touch' generation. I picked up the letter she drafted and left behind on my table. It did not call me to tears but I now felt really saddened by the infliction of pain to those she felt had abandoned her.

*I am glad you chose to sleep in this morning. It will make what I have to say easier. You told me that I did not have to explain my relationship with the Professor. Now you have had a similar interaction with both of his daughters with the same name. My surprise did not add to your life the same way as his real daughter must have, this much I can feel. Last night you went through the motions as much as I. You had fallen in love with Roxanne and I did not plan on trying my luck with your emotions. The outcome would never be the same—it couldn't ever be the same. But all the same I am glad that we were able to meet and engage under this set of circumstances.*

*In the end we are to travel two separate paths. I will take mine back to Europe and hopefully make back the lost time with my friends; hopefully they are still alive. If I am now endowed to provide them a substitute from the drugged life they might still be living, then the Professor's money will be well spent. I do not need it for myself. I wanted nothing in return in the end.*

*Take care now and enjoy the statues. The Professor did not intend for their care to be left in your more than capable hands. He would be angry now. Perhaps you have finally beaten him at his own game of chess. There will be no rematch so use this final win wisely.*

*Yours with much love,*

*Roxanne (really)*

I did not expect to hear that her real name was Roxanne. I suppose it did not matter now. The truth always has as many facets but reflects little beyond what we wanted it to explain in the first place. It has continued to rain outside and surely this meant that her exiting trail would be covered or washed away forever. I was so sorry that I chose to sleep in.

The intensity of the message caused me to re-read the note several more times. Yes, I was looking for those subtle hints that might take the sting away. The sorrow I felt was not her disappearance as much as it was her discovery that reflections of the original Roxanne could be mimicked to anyone's perfection.

What is it about her initial appearance in my life, or the observed features of her facial expression this morning during her morning toilette? What did I witness this morning during my own prolonged reflection in the same mirror? Something else she would leave behind beyond this letter should have been a hint to shed reality from the things she chooses to leave behind. Was it the woman or the figures in my den I longed to fathom, I did not have a clue; perception versus sensation was the ongoing examination of this life. What was in my house that was so real in the first place?

The letter would gain a place of honor in the file cabinet in a folder marked *memorable occasions*. The sculptures would be left the same for the time being. There was no reason to place them into a more adorned position, and hiding them was out of the question, for now.

The rain had subsided a bit and I watch across my wet patio for the telltale signs of absorption. This place floods from time-to-time and I did not want another pre winter disaster to occur at this time. I watched the earth absorb the standing water in a reasonable timeline. I listened to my heartbeat and noted that I was still sane.

I had wanted—perhaps desired—some cooperation from the elements so that I could go and play outside—so no longer wanting to exist as an adult. Would I take the bike out to the waterfront or would I load up my favorite paddleboard onto the SUV and make way toward the same. The outcome was always the same. I would paddle my way to the next extreme point of exhaustion.

Are we fortunate when someone dies or is it that every death brings with it new discovery. I had an appreciation for the drama of exploration and the appreciation of just wanting to see what comes up next. I live in anticipation of what lies below me and my paddleboard as I make way across another channel and the chance that something floats by my way. The air is fresh and the waters are actually warmer in mid November. Sunny day frolickers only get half the picture. It is fortunate because they leave the rest of us alone during the late fall to early spring.

It is a quite sea I am paddling over now. I get to think about it, and much more without interruptions. I will not reveal too much detail now; having the proof with regard to my hunch and the experiences incurred freeing the anchor from the enveloping silt bottom of a neighboring channel. I do not know what has happened to me but I do know I will never be the same.

Fortuitous Event

# Chapter Eleven

## *Under the Leagues of the Sea*

UNDER THE DEPTHS OF THE SEA WE EXPLORE
with artificial work lights the extent of the cave system.
The fellow divers I am with are from a University across
the borders to the north. They are ocean Archaeology
graduate students from Simon Frasier University and I
am delighted they allowed me to squeeze into this cave
in my seven millimeter wet suit.

Western Washing University did not want to participate
when we attempted to access one of their experimental
submersibles. Perhaps we were too pushy, but then
again it had been explained away by budgetary
constraints. They could not afford to participate in this
fourth quarter.

The sun is out but there is not ample light below for two
reasons including the overcast expected in late
November and the fact that we are well within the
recesses of a cave sixteen feet below the surface. We
are thankfully working against a slack tide and this
minimized the blender effect we would have succumbed
to otherwise. A tranquil sea against menacingly sharp
rock formations is no picnic. There is only a slight surf
churning the kelp ceiling above and the light that does

trickle through paints the walls like a light show at an indoors rock concert.

Most of the divers are strapped with rebreathers rather than tanks. This affords us the luxury of working without the disturbing stream of exhausted air. The rebreathers are an enclosed and watertight, oxygen and carbon dioxide scrubbing apparatus, and we work leaving no overt trails.

The visuals are exceptionally good because it is a slack tide. We waited long enough for all of the churning and floating debris to sink to the bottom or cling to the rocks. Now it is food for the brave cleaners who scramble around feeding without so much as a hint of fear from their much larger counterparts. Humans are not a threat down here because we are not hunters of those who are too small to be devoured. I suck on my mouthpiece to test that air is flowing. I do not have the usual feedback sensations as I do when I am using air tanks, as I am paying out another taught length of our equipment rope and clipping on both weights and floats and additional under water lighting. I am also watching out for the numerous underwater video cameras that are being used to capture each and every moment.

Another wave washes in gently and washes over the gridlines inside of the cave. I am visually pulled into one area that has already been explored because I have spotted something new. I am nearing the bottom and I expressly waive away silt and eel grass from the point of discovery and I signal what this spot reveals. I was not to touch, but to explore and to discover.

One of the graduate students swims over to my find. We watch the non transparent plate extend out through the encasement of sandy muck. A pattern seems to appear as we examine this thing closer. We see the same raised lettering as we had seen on the original cup. As I watch the deftness of the experts I am witness to another great pattern of discovery, lifted out of a century's place hold and returned into the safety net that will carry it to the surface; fresh air that will not destroy. And I have the clarity to capture this shot with close-ups with the camera I brought to this dive site.

Something interesting was going on up above when the object is retrieved from the water. I followed the plate to the surface because I was also witness to the looks inside of their face masks and it dawn on me that these are not good poker players.

"Kelsey, move out of the picture, I want to get some details." I hear the voice of the expedition's leader crack out in the cold air topside as he circled with a digital video handheld.

"I'm taking a break. Can someone else watch the lines?" I am begging for relief and have already removed my heavier equipment not wanting to wait for the reply. A body splashes into the water by my side.

Climbing on board the research vessel I stand among the giants of Canada's west coast archeologists and listen in on their clamor. I am tolerated because it was originally my site. I am not being treated as an equal though because it was not a focused discovery of mine alone. It was just luck. I catch several of them looking at me and then again at Julia who stands across the deck looking equally proud. She is with her mentor and her roommate. I feel like a piece of a puzzle that has been placed but now all but forgotten. There are many pieces still to come.

This is both luck and fortune to be working with these not so tired hero's of academia. They are a rough and tumble group and are not at all feigned by hard work, muddy channels, long hours and miserable pay. Their discoveries and follow on papers are their payment in kind. No one but the administrators make great amounts of money in this area of endeavor. This is not gold or rare jewelry, or rare earth minerals that can be refined. We have found the words of a lost dynasty and by all rights this opens a new door to who really discovered this place; notwithstanding the bragging rights of First Nation or other aboriginal inhabitants. But it does continue to support that the notion that people have always been one of China's chief exports. This is still in good standing.

Someone on the deck calls out USC—the United States of China. There is a chuckle across the deck of the research vessel. I hope in part because of the novelty of their being mostly Canadian, and the continuing undertones of what China's enormous investment into the country's finances will do over the long term. Either way the forward march of China across long spans of time and wide oceans keeps knocking at the same door—the New World.

Over the next several clear days we make our final discoveries. No one from the media is on site because no one has told them about this adventure. The next public exposure to this site will be well into the next year as publish papers in a journal few will take the time to read. I have come to find out that all joking aside, no one is interested in rewriting who probably discovered

America. These folks are just interest in all of the rest. The world is already filled with flashing stories which are forgotten as fast as they are sounded. These folks are the true professionals. This story is just an indirect direct line to the next. Suddenly I understand one of the life lessons my father tried to expose me to.

We left this place on a fine day but a darkening afternoon. Passing over this place took careful work. We were at many times watched by the Coast Guard. Now there was a group that could keep a secret. I passed by their keen scrutiny because I was listed as only an accidental discoverer. I didn't mind because this is what the Professor had trained me for—to be glad to understand the next twenty moves without revealing that you can. I was left alone and as suddenly my relationship with Julia was taking a new shape.

We are alone and looking out over the coastline of Lummi Island. The horizon is not clear and the cloud banks above us are laden with snow soon to be released over the islands and the mainland. We have picked this place out because it is in front of a little bay; darkness looses out to the artificial light that bounces across the tips of the incoming waves across the bay. I am astounded by the adult salmon that still break across the not so stilled waters of the sea. Their silvery scales reflect the artificial light from a city across the way; they plunge back into the Sound and into its depths.

Anchored fishing boats are deadly quite all around the bay and the nets are left hanging to be washed by the next rains—I suppose. I cannot be enticed to go back out to the cave's entrance for a follow up night dive. When I tell this to Julia she laughs.

"Come on, just suit up with me one more time and let's jump into the sea. I want to keep turning back the pages until we reveal everything about those earlier visitors. My roommate reminds me daily that this is far from over. The pieces are spectacular: what we did not find calls me out to return to that place, as I intend to do so now."

We are walking along the shoreline and I sense that we are not alone. The night has a way of instilling a sense of fear that anything can be lurking about, ready to jump out in a split instant. In fact the most steadied activity is below the surface of the water, where at night, the hunters do reign. I do feel compelled to don my wetsuit and take that plunge into this bay rather than the cave system several kilometers away. I was concerned about this: the incoming storm might excite the bottom with effects from the pressure changes that would surely expose more. That place was all but picked clean by the underwater archeologists. It is a crapshoot.

But even they are susceptible to mistakes. It infuriated me that they did not care when we discovered an underlying cable system stretch out across the deepest part of the channel. No one spoke about that which existed outside of the laid out gridlines. The grid was the all encompassing definition of the research to be done. If it was outside it was also beyond the scope of discovery.

Focus is not always fun for the amateur. Julia had a point that there was something else that our one more dive might reveal. We just simply had to tempt fate and seek out that other answer.

"Look, we are not guided by the simple principles of research. We can stray if we want. I have watched that corner of the Sound for days now and even the Coast Guard is interested least of all. Let's find the answers to questions we do not even know to ask."

"I had a boss in my past that liked to exclaim 'what don't we know about what we don't know. Or something similar to that, I suppose." When I looked up Julia was approaching me with an arm full of flat rocks.

"Here is the deal. I will start tossing out rock and we will judge whose skips the furthest. The winner decides if we go back to the area for another series of dives. But we have to decide quickly. I am sure that you do not want to dive while it is snowing."

I attend to the task at hand and I am losing the contest—perhaps on purpose. That is all I will reveal. But the next night we went out with arm loads of equipment, filled them with water for counter buoyancy, and placed them at a spot below. I tied lines over several sides of our kayaks and we used them as guidelines of sorts as we scoured the bottom for new clues. We did this all in one trip and this included the thick underwater cable that was semi-submerged on the bottom and pointed well above the tip of Lummi and towards the mainland shore.

We ascended very slowly finding the most interesting thing of all. All of my life in technology I have thought it: who was listening to whom? All of the fish in the area swam across it, including the curious seals. But most of all it was the underwater disturbances of the mighty storm that passed over, that would reveal this at a just below average depth that could be reached by most well trained swimmers, or seen above by boaters.

There was something to find out here and Julia knew it; she relies on persistence to get me to the same place in time. The submerged cable has a jacket with a metal envelope containing a place of origin I suppose. It is poorly designed and has Chinese characters stenciled inside that have not been destroyed by the swells up above. This is a dangerous place to dive. The rips are notorious and that is why that cable lives outside of the shores of the bigger islands.

We manage to take an imprint of the etched stencil onto another material. Yes, we came prepared but no so thoughtfully for this—so lucky and so fortunate again. I boarded my kayak and waited for Julia to come upright on hers. We paddled with glove covered hands until our hollow plastic shells thumped broadside. Was an all important discovery now on the surface? We would have to research the true meaning of the characters—so we knew the likely origin of the cable stretching towards the opposite shores.

That is what we discovered before the first snows blanketed the shores and then melted just a fast. Nature covers and then reveals and sometimes the trail is lost. Then again we regain some hint of something which follows: who put this cable in and when?

# Chapter Twelve

## *What the Fishermen Seek*

FISH HUDDLE IN THE DARKEST PLACES on the bottom of the Salish Sea when the sun comes up. Fishermen (and fisherwomen) notice this and strike down with appropriately weighted lines, lures and fish food—real or synthetic. That said, we do not all rely on science and technology to remedy hard sought after game. Most of it comes from just trying, folklore examined as universal truths, and blindly going to locations by hunch or by habit.

The small fishing boat that approached me couldn't have been more attracted to the area where I was kayaking. They had stayed out of my way for as long as possible but had to move in before the high sun lowered their chances of netting salmon. As they approached my location I made ready and pointed out that there was a diver below via the handy red and white float and flag that called out the same. I cannot use the word obvious because a diver down below float and flag are more often ignored than paid attention to.

I am not always so observant. What I had failed to notice is that the fishermen—tribal cast—seemed to be herding a very small pod of orcas in my general direction. But as a matter of fact they were only enticing the pod to fish for salmon at a distant fishing ground. I just happened to be in the general line of fire today. What a treat.

It became clear that the boat was dragging a net as well. The net looked as though it was straining away from the rocky coastline and out of the shallows. The net tugged and pulled against the abundant eel grass in the wake of its path. The grass is cruel and grabs, weaves and pulls at the translucent netting material. The crew of the boat—three—lined the gunwale of the starboard side of the boat and monitored the progress of net to the aft and the orcas swimming forward of their horned bow. It was a methodical journey for all. The wet slick skin on the backs of this pod seemed to cast light instead of simply reflecting it each time they arched their backs out of the cold sea. When they submerge they pull down the surrounding water with a great sucking vacuum. Sea birds retain their height and glide on the updrafts and monitor the big water borne mammals as they progress north. The birds are waiting on the resultant scraps.

I had gained herculean strength on this approach and paddled with a single oar into a smallish cove, barely enough for my kayak let alone one of the younger and curious whales who attempted to follow suit. It bumped me gently into the overhanging sandstone cliff side and flipped its tail just out of harm's way. I got the message. My hope was that the diver below read all of these useful and natural signs as well, given that they made no attempt to surface to join in the wake left by the whales.

The day had brought many surprises. The first was Julia suddenly appearing on site in her rowing dory without the appearance of intuition, still having her diving gear readily available all the same. Her appearance on site made no demand on my day. I had already exited and maintained close vigilance over the artifacts I had brought to the surface. The prize materials held fast on the bobbing inflatable raft that was tied to the stern of my kayak.

"I thought you might be here. I left several messages on voicemail. You must have left quite early. It looks as though you are done for the day." She was excited and pulled in closer on her initial arrival.

"I smelled the ocean inland this morning and it drew my attention here. As it turns out it would be a good day to be on the water as well as in it. There is a pod in the area. The last time I looked it was just north of this location."

Without moving closer we both exchanged pertinent data within ear shot. I showed her my new underwater housing for the video camera and she produced a handful of bags containing samples from another site out to the west of her home base. She brought me up to date on the analysis compiled by her roommate and we concluded that at some point a more modern Chinese fishing fleet must have been busy here. The stenciled characters from the inside of the metal envelope were etched with modern means, and the words and phrases denoted contemporary use of the Chinese language regarding manufactured goods. The roommate had assured her that this was a thorough assessment but did not yield anything specific.

"It will be a struggle to connect the dots to a specific manufacturer with the limited data. She suggested that

163

we had to find more." Julia's report was unsettling. I had wanted more now.

"The research I found suggests a slightly different tact. For sixty or more years agencies have been trying to spot and get rid of undersea cables used for research. Apparently it was easier to leave them on the bottom instead of incurring the cost of retrieval." I was deliberately non opinioned in my summation.

"Another kind of pollution I suppose," Julia sighed and completed her outfitting to go down to the bottom at our site.

"It's more than that. Some of the research papers I discovered suggest that other countries including Russia first, followed by China, simply found a way to tap into the submerged cables and put them back to use. They had a highway of free cables to add their own communication equipment arsenal. This gives a whole new meaning to freeway."

Yes, I did get a laugh on this one. Julia composes herself and slips over the side of her dory and does a final check on her dive gear. She has to push away a small bunch of floating kelp kept high by the inflated bulbs that were too numerous to count. And then she disappeared below a stream of bubbles marking the direction of her first in a series of steadied descents into the slightly churned water.

Julia had wanted to see firsthand what had been discovered earlier in the day. When I first told her she thought I was joking. In a strange sort of way I wish that I was pulling a prank, but not so. The image down below fed another. It was like a small spun ball of yarn and it trailed directly into a sandstone cliff.

While she dove I watched and paddled out a bit to get a better view of what was on top of this steep cliff. I guessed I had to push out approximately three hundred yards before the enormous estate was visible from the waterline. It bears an off white in exterior that covered three stories and its architecture resembled the high end commercial building one finds in the downtown area of Los Angeles. Several load bearing walls towered around parts of the main structure and I could only imagine how they were able to truck that much concrete into the area. The estate was surrounded by a very mature forest and main house was pretty far in from the only highway that passed through this area.

Interestingly enough that highway was one of my favorite conduits for biking. I must have peddled that road at several dozen times during the late spring, throughout the summer, and during the early fall. During the winters this road is closed more often than it remains open due to the plentitude of mud and rock slide in the area. The last one took two weeks to clear by the massive road service equipment. And when it snows in the area: forget it.

One of the other really strange aspects of this road is it is dotted with only very large estates, with most of them literally built into the steep cliffs. But the maddest idea surrounding this lovely stretch of bay lined forest is that most if not all of the homes are populated by people so old that one can only wonder if they were completely senile when they made the decision to carve out nature for seven and eight thousand square feet palaces for two person occupancy. Notwithstanding the numerous slides and punishing approaches, the sun sets must be a delight.

My dive buddy is bobbing back on the surface and waiving me over to the Cliffside. I can't wait to get her view on what lurks below.

"It is a spectacular bottom; it is so populated—so fantastic." She is trying to clear her mouth of sea water and manages to sputter this out between gulps of air.

"I do suppose most would think we reached a proverbial end. However, I have a neighbor why has a device that can probe the entrance of the conduit and snake up for a better peak. It should be able to tell us direction and overall length." I was returning her impish grin.

"Oh, I do love a mystery. But you know where this is ending so why bother. I can see this estate from my island. It is massive and quite private."

"Tell me more." I was assisting her back into the dory.

"Well, I have gotten a clean line of site from the DNR campground on Lummi. We were out birding years ago and caught all of the gritty details with a pair of big eyes. Do you know what they are?" Julia was catching her breath and laughing at the same time. She started in again but started coughing.

"Yes, I used to be in the Navy, remember. One can't see this house from the road, so hiking without being discovered is out of the question. There is way too much land to pass across."

"Are you thinking of going in?"

She was truly shocked; at least I thought she was at the time. But then she was shrugging her shoulders when I had done the same, earlier.

"Sure, I'm in. But first I want to research the owners. I have a friend in real estate. She owes me one. Do you want to do any more diving?"

"No, I think we have enough for the day. Let's push out and drive down for some oysters."

It took us around one hour to pack up, load up and then drive south to Taylor's Seafood. The winds had picked up a lot and it was nice to see the resultant whitecaps from inside the cab of my truck. The drive was worth the effort and we consumed an even dozen shucked beauties and sopped up their juices with a loaf of sour dough bread. The crisp while wine I brought originated in Spain but was consumed here in the Pacific Norwest while looking out across the waters to the perfect vision of islands galore. Who said one has to travel to far away exotic places to witness the same.

Julia and I talked about our surroundings and the changes of lifestyles since landing here in paradise. I had been here for a little over five years and she was closer to twelve years. During one serious moment in the conversation she explained why her husband chose to move on. She also revealed her relationship with the other woman on Lummi whose residence she shared. Her friend was an Investigative Genealogist.

At the time I had given this all due consideration. It was a friend who provided her with a place to stay. Most friends would have done the same. Julia's husband, on the other hand was a whole different kind of character.

His was a life commitment to his church and she said she had gotten tired of sharing the same man with close neighbors and distant strangers alike. She had to move on beyond that lifestyle and find one of her own. This lifestyle had lasted decades, she explained, and she wanted a means of opting out of the prevailing message that the workings of the church were the only things that mattered. That was not the case for her any longer and she was actually happy when his transfer was announced. She felt free.

This is when the offer came to her via the friend. It was an offer of a place to chill out and to refocus on what she wanted to do next. This expressively uninteresting connection at the time might come back for a revisit some other day. No, I was not making some sort of prediction. It was just a feeling. I would go with it for now. It wasn't all that interesting.

# Chapter Thirteen

## *Acquaintances be Forgot*

WHEN I WAS FIFTEEN YEARS OLD my dad took me into Chinatown in San Francisco. Interestingly enough I did have this love for the older and more authentic schemes of the finely divided neighborhoods of San Francisco. We lived south in the suburbs which were not quite as varied so trips north to the City Center and outlying areas close to Ocean Beach were hot spots in time.

My dad was very cognizant of the fact that one of my favorite hangouts on the weekends was the closest neighbor to Chinatown, but he deliberately takes me there from the west end to avoid the confrontation. My choice to spend the day would have been just off Broadway and deep into the Beat section of the city, exploring funky independent bookstores (the norm in those days), dead end alleyways covered with art murals, and the smoky blues and jazz clubs which seemed to be populated twenty four hours a day.

It was a beautiful blue sky kind of day when we entered this metropolis with the ocean on one side of us and an enormous bay on the other side. We parked several block outside of Chinatown because there was simply nowhere to park within the area. Any emptied slot was hovered over by locals who held them forever for friends, family and commercial truck that were entering this area in streams to drop off or pick up merchandise and people. You could not argue over parking spaces in the same manner in this section because it always ended up with a yelling match in some Chinese dialect. If you were an outsider to the language and subtle mannerisms of dialog in this neighborhood you would not be taking that coveted spot.

Walking on the streets of Chinatown was especially exciting for me because it meant walking into a mass of people all conversing simultaneously. This meant you were tugged and often followed for blocks by nonstop pleas to do business at this store verses the one across the street. I was certain at the time that all of the stores carried similar if not identical product lines. Product pricing differed in the cents. The real differentiating factor was on the services end. Services really do make the difference when choosing between a generic shopping mall, and that of a 'local' market. Services did make a difference between storefronts and sides of streets in Chinatown.

It is interesting that several blocks away they have barkers who attempt to pull you into the red light district shops and theaters on and off Broadway (at the time). In Chinatown they were just as loud and exceedingly persistent but the virtue of being pulled into art shops, food markets, fish shops, junk stores eateries made this a much more pure shopping experience. They got abreast without exposing their breasts or the promise thereof. And the food: chopped and stirred, in cups or on plates, hanging upside down and dripping, and rooms full of steam filled almost every need. Nearly everyone made eye-to-eye contact even though we were not native to the neighborhood. We were welcomed shoppers and the services exhibited were near perfect in appeal.

The true point of the visit was in dad fashion. There was another life lesson to be learned and he was pulling on my arm and leading me into a deeply recessed series of interconnected alleyways without a map for guidance. The man seemed to know where to go.

The entrance to the back of the building was not distinct from any other but we had turned abruptly into a well lit hallway crammed with smiling faces. The noise was equivalent to a ballgame or late starting concert where the crowds self agitate into a working frenzy. Some of the faces showed more strain from the ruckus than others as we continued deeper into what I thought might be the center and lowest level of this particular building.

Suddenly the noise was pushed aside and a more tranquil feeling was felt as we entered a moderately filled room as large as the center of this commercial building. The place was filled with gamblers.

Now the interesting thing about this place is neither one of us ever gambled. It was thrust upon us to blend in so we milled in and out of the tables and chairs and monitored the facial twitching and extremities fluctuating, giving away the personas of the individuals flipping chips or cards. They were tells. And even I was able to read them as well as the dealers.

This was so noted but my dad wanted to linger at one particular table in front of two old men of Chinese origin. The two appeared to have a run of the place and their gazes were eagerly met by the other patrons who rubbernecked to watch their every move. I was mesmerized but oddly enough when someone shoved an overflowing beer glass into my hands the look from my dad's face was not one of protest.

I tipped the cold beverage and my eyes stayed glued on his to monitor any hint of change or demeanor. He only laughed and then took a drink of his own. It was not a beer, but it did signify that they knew the man well enough to not only serve his young son yet bring him a more appropriate cocktail of choice. My dad knew this place well and it showed in their faces.

After watching the older two men saunter away from the table with their winnings one of them turned to my dad and nodded to follow. My dad returned his stares to me and indicated that I was to stay where I was. His face denoted a stern 'do not move from this spot'. I would be more than compliant, I signaled him, because I had a beer and ample sights to still take in within this new place of fascination. My being here when he got back was all but guaranteed. Or so I thought.

I am a kid still subject to moments of youthful abandon and I saw no earthy reason why I should not join a group of younger people sitting in one far corner smoking and engaging in some wild and franticly loud dialog with another old man of their choosing. I sat down in the only empty chair. The semicircle grew very hushed as all eyes were turned on me, nursing a half empty beer glass and smiling back toward their empty stares. This moment was not lost on me. I had to hold my place. Was this the lesson?

Boredom enters this corner. Sooner or later silence was not the winner with this crowd and they returned their collective attention to the old man who looked unmoved by the entire incident. He dove back into what I could only decipher to be a story of some sort. There was this deep reverence of the crowd to this monologist. His legs never moved but his facial expressions and exacerbated hand and arm movements punctuating each carefully spoken phrase. I did not understand his language let alone the specific dialect he must have used. There were translations galore going on throughout this mesmerized group but not of it in English. I did not care.

Without a doubt the old soloist noticed and overtly directed his gaze to two young women sitting near me. With hushed tones they negotiated their way to either side of me all the while the orator did his thing. And when the two young women were in place she smiled and bowed his head to them—so begin.

The thing about near simultaneous translation is that it works best when it comes in a single stream. I was getting balanced stereo and it confounded more at first. The problem was we had not gotten our rhythm yet. Yet into the next topic of exchange I was being fed an alternating stream of translated words and embellished visuals that I immediately forgot that I could no longer understand the language of the original speech that left the man's lips and punctuated its way onto both of my ears in perfect mimicry of pitch and tone, as well as pure intention. I knew this man's subject well.

It was about then that I had remembered what my dad had asked without ever speaking. I knew it was certain that he would launch from the recesses of the building and scan for his offspring in one particular direction. The question was would his gaze get there first? I had to know and explained this to the translator on my immediate left. She giggled.

We had entered our own round table. The round lasted more than the old man could tolerate and he called for the other young woman to come to his side. Judging by the looks on his face: astonishment, laughter, and concern; the table turns and I am free to explore the possibilities. He addressed me directly in close to perfect Chinatown in the heart of the City English.

"You would like to please your father, yes?" It could have been a statement of fact rather than a question. I could go either way but sat fast and leaned into the two way dialog.

"I would like to please him, yes. He is expecting me to be on the other side of the room." My facts were in order.

"Then we should all do so."

Ok, I did not expect this heartwarming gesture on his part. But when he stood and turned his attention towards the center of the room everyone in this group mirrored his gestures in the most finite detail. This old guy had clout and I was more than curious as to why.

The group held together and we made way across the room and scattered the gamblers waiting their turn at the center tables. It was like the proverbial parting of the seas; all scampered back and then forward again like two waves of opposing force until we found a place to sit down. We were one when we sat. The old man resumes his story as though the activity was a necessary one to emphasize his last point. The group held steady with their stares and I was not the center of attention any longer.

So what was this story all about? It had simple scripting. Many people in his clan left China and made way over to the west coast of the New World in droves. They were tired of the feudal wars that left many of them with both emotional and physical scares. They ended up in a place that was not sure if they were welcome, but they stayed nonetheless and were rewarded for their courage and fortitude. There are several new generation who will only know the pain suffered by their parents at the hands of territorial lords who wanted all and left them nothing but the spirit their families could carry on their backs, across a disquieting sea. And there are new generations now who will only have to look across the street to see that this is a better place to be with the next string that unfolds.

It was a pretty simple keystone as far as stories go. But there was a finishing statement that must be made by the old man before the man emerging from a backroom comes to this place in the brightest corner of this enormous basement. He emphases that none of us should lose sight of that distant shore and what it has meant to him—this place of origin. The old man finishes off with a joke just before my dad makes his way to my side.

The joke emphasizes that there are always strings attached to everything we do. My dad only hears the Chinese original and is left to ponder why I am laughing out so loud along with the other members of the group native to this language. He signals me and soon we are gone out through the crowd, winding our way out through endless passages, up a flight of stairs leading to a labyrinth of alleyways and back onto the streets of San Francisco.

"Do you understand the Chinese language?"

My dad's manner is direct but I can tell he is baffled by the stern look on his face. We are waiting for the light to change.

"I knew enough to fill in the blanks."

I did not choose to tell him about the pair of attractive translators as we cross the busy streets which empty into this four way intersection. I find it useful if I can send him back a lesson of my own choosing every now and then.

I will see the two young women one more time. Both wanted to go to a beat poetry reading the following week and I was able to share the entire day with them in Golden Gate Park. We listened to an impromptu concert later in the day—twenty or so congas—and capped the early evening off with a bottle of cheap red wine and a mix of street vender food. They tell me a lot about the old man and why he had such a following.

But for now I am walking down the street with my dad and we stare at all of the variety of people out on the streets of the middle of the City. We take long pauses inside of the doorways of the Italian restaurants in the area and engage in long inhales. The smell of garlic entices us but we are not hungry enough to eat just yet. Instead we walked mostly in silence until we had reached the next busy intersection of Columbus and

Broadway. It was there that he turns and asks me a more troubling question. It is one I am not prepared for today.

"Have you ever had the interest in going into one of these places?"

He was pointing to the neon marquee titled *The Condor Club*. Even though it is still daylight the neon strobes rhythmically as we cross the busy intersection. It looked as though we are heading to the front door and within range of one of its obnoxious barkers straddling the entrance and the street. The corner is so crowded with people looking on from every walk of life. I am more interested in the activity outside of this place. No, there is not a hint of interest on my part or my dad's. It was just a question.

No, explaining if I was sexually active was not in today's lesson plan. I turned away first and we both headed up to the real target—*North Beach Pizza*, at the top of the next hill. This is where I breathe a sigh of relief. This is where we ate and drank our sodas in a deep booth and where he relayed why he had really brought me into Chinatown.

Intention and reaction are brought to the surface. All is laid out over the best slices of pizza in the whole of the City. Lessons were learned. I never felt like a more ready student of life. I finally shared my experience as well as we exited and when we drove back out to the suburbs richer in knowledge of what separates and then rejoins a father to his son (me in this case specifically, no slight to my sisters intended, disclaimer ended).

I learned why that day, that we had to retrace our steps more often than naught. We had to allot sufficient time to understand what makes us before we can embrace what we can become. This becomes the string that is often attached through the wisdom of storytellers. This helps us trace backwards and forwards again; who we have become is amplified by exposure to other people and cultures. It reinforces what we already know: we were always on the right track.

# Chapter Fourteen

## *Lights across the Bay*

JULIA CALLS ME NOT TOO LONG after we had traced the undersea cable into a solid wall of stone. Her real Estate buddy had come through and we were looking at the not too long history of the mansion across the Bay.

The place was built in the prior century. It has had only one owner and they still live there according to the public records. They are an elderly couple and the records list the ownership as two entities rather than one. There is no mention of their being husband and wife in the records which specifically calls out two business entities rather than a single domestic one. They both share the same last name.

This in itself is quite enticing. An additional trace has them both listed as U.S. citizens who emigrated from China seven decades ago. Ok, now this has really heightened my interest.

Standing high on a bluff overlooking the DNR campsite on Lummi Island we stare across the Bay with two powerful binoculars. The place appears as a fortress but in reality it is just a high tech design. The high walls never connect and from this distance seem to intersect with railings and window frames connecting the offset edges of the building. It appears to be for art's sake rather than security. It is a wonderful architecture on this second look. I propose that we get closer at some future date.

"So what do you propose," said Julia as we both relaxed our stealth poses and sat down on a flat surfaced boulder inside the edge of the cliff above the beach.

There was a three-quarter moon out even though it was not quite dusk. We stared at that for awhile and then I strung together my thoughts on the matter before us.

"Well, I think we should muster a way in."

"Do you mean break in?" Julia fawned over a small bush at her feet making it difficult to see her face. I wanted to know if she was alarmed.

"Oh, off course that's not what I meant. What I meant was that we should find a way to get introduced to the couple and warm our way into their abode. Perhaps then we could have a look around. Can your friend provide anything more intimate about this mystery couple?"

We had gotten up and were making way across a trail that would take us back to the road. Julia's car was at least on half mile away. It got dark fast and ye did not think to take flashlights. Stepping across the branches and root systems kept us both hyper focused for a period of time and we moved carefully and in silence.

I heard a loud snap and Julia went tumbling down an embankment, stopping hard at the bottom. Turing my attention to the task at hand I was able to lower myself to her position and reached out to the woman who was in pain.    She screamed out that something had punctured her side.

My hand felt the warm liquid that oozed from the wound. I could not clearly ascertain what caused it but I suspected a broken branch that extended out from the trunk of a downed tree.    It was too dark to get any additional information from the scene of the accident.    I lifted her up and across my shoulder as I apologized for the awkward positioning.    It was clear that she did not care.

"Just get me the fuck out of here, will you.    This really hurts.  My leg feels as though it is on fire."

I carried her in this position until I had reached the street and her automobile.    Draping her across the hood of the Jeep I fished for and retrieved her car keys and got her inside and laying across the back bed of the Jeep.    For some reason I kissed her forehead and told her everything was going to be fine.

We are in the driveway where she has been staying and I manage to get her inside without additional help.    The roommate is on the mainland and will not be back until tomorrow.  And this is where things come together.

Julia allows her attendant to strip her and assist her into a bathtub full of hot water.    This was after we had both attended to the wound—it was a simple puncture and it bled a lot.    She is bent over washing her leg and removing all traces of the dried blood.  I am washing her back with my hand.    Apparently I am too intimate with my attention drawn to a particular area.

I have backed off and sitting with my back braced to the tub wall and away from eye-to-eye contact. Perhaps this is a deliberate act and I feel somewhat cowardly. I listen to Julia stand and step out of the tub after a rather long pause.

"To my rescuer go the spoils." She has just shot me a very strange grin.

"I'm sorry. What did you say?"

"Help me out here. Hand me that towel, I want to dry off."

Ok, now I do have to turn around but only to look down and discover that the bandage is doing the trick. I am still refusing to meet her stare.

"What the hell is wrong with you?" She barks this out and heads into her bedroom leaving her towel on the bathroom floor.

I am sure I am confused. There is no avoiding the confrontation and I now have to follow suit and join her at her bedside. This time we are sitting next to each other and looking at each other's face with greater intensity than I can remember before this off put moment.

Julia leans in and takes my hand.

"I am kind of sorry. I over reacted a bit, but I did not invite you to touch me that way."

"If I say that I got lost in the moment will that help?" I was being sincere. I did not want to lose her friendship.

"Well, all that aside—I am inviting you. Yes, I am sure now. Please stay the night."

Call it a moment—so call this a span of time. There was a great chemistry shared that evening. Any more detail is not the point of this part of the tale. Let it be said that we grew closer and that her roommate came home the next morning and found us both still in bed, comfortably in each other's arms.

The roommate joined us for breakfast. As a matter of fact she made us breakfast and it was filling and led to additional details being shared about the old couple and their palatial estate across the Bay.

Mornings are fulfilling. The afternoon was spent on the mainland and we gravitated to a real solution to our dilemma. We concluded that they only way in was to provide a solution to a problem the older couple did not know they had yet. Time well spent at City Hall allowed us to discover a request for a permit for an external modification to an existing foundation. It seemed like the request had been put on hold for a longer than required time. This was fortunate enough for us and we found someone who could move it along. We were operating on the behalf of the estate, although is an exclusively beneficial manner.

Two day later we were inside the front gates of this fine estate. The couple was ecstatic to make our acquaintance and they shuffled us inside of their home for tea and refreshments, and then a tour of the ground level.

It became clear why the foundation had to be attended to. We found out later that the original contractor had simply abandoned the task for a larger and more profitable job. This was not untypical for work ethic in this area. Julia and I both had similar experiences and we were tightly bonded with the two after finding this common link.

The work would begin the following week. A plan was now in place.

## Repairing and then Binding Friendships

This is maybe one of the stranger things I have been involved with and it turns out that I am good. Julia and I negotiate the contract acting as project managers. We sub-contract out all of the actual labor and materials required to complete the retrofit. It was not a great stretch of the imagination, however, it was interesting and it brought us closer to the owners.

As it would turn out the owners had a very rich and familiar history. They had been educators in a major University in one of largest cities on the east coast of PRC, as it was called then. He was teaching the internal framework of large building complexes, and she was a biology teacher and graduate student working under agriculture grants from the main governing power at the time. They are brother and sister it turns out. The surprise findings on the property title were now becoming clear.

Their time in the upper crust of Chinese society was shortened by another family member—a first cousin. The cousin got involved in politics and the entire family clan's future was put into jeopardy. Their parents who were alive at the time were moved from the inner city out to a village in the center of China's great agricultural belt. They died two decades later in what is now a desert belt, which by the way is contributing to all of those enormous sand storms that now plague the east coast population centers twice a year.

The parents only two offspring—Zhao and Yuecan— received nonstop threats of forced relocation from the University and out to some mining town on the opposite side of China. They were not alone. There had been a massive relocation of elite educators at many universities out to menial jobs and horrific locations and there was only one possible way out. They were given the only other choice of leaving their homeland.

Now this is where the connection begins from our standpoint. Both Zhao and Yuecan had received funding from a secrete pool from the University to maintain explicit details of their journey to the New World. They had received detailed contact information regarding those that were forced to leave just before them, then again later, to maintain records of people who migrated afterwards. Since they were both gifted researchers this habit of maintaining and updating the chronological activities of those identified was a natural path.

Zhao was very polite when he asked us if we would like to see the results of their work over a multitude of decades and across several generations. Our tour resumed and we were taken down several flights of well lit passageways through a series of libraries, galleries and ultimately into a computer server room that would any networking nut drool with envy.

The computer room had two separate entrances. We went through two swinging double doors into a cavern of raised floors and rack after rack of blade servers and associated data farms.  At the center of the room was a row of access consoles and banks of flat screen monitors.  In the corners we could also see the predecessor equipment to what existed now.  All around are saw racks of older backup media: ½ inch reels, ¼ inch cartridge tapes, boxes of neat rows of floppies and CDs, and a new rack that secured several high banks of removable hard drives.

Now it was Yuecan's turn to show off.  She eagerly steps in front of one of the consoles and logs herself onto the network of servers, starts a small script and the genealogy records of well over two thousand families and their off spring appear as a graphical matrix.  She clicks on one particular family and the icon spawns off detailed family trees across four additional monitors. Each individual has an icon which when selected call up a spreadsheet of the details of where, when and why of their entire lives, pulled from a well designed and maintained database.

Julia and I are blown away when we are allowed to click on one particular family member and a succession of digital photographs appears in chronological order. They are complete and up to date histories of all willing participants.

"This was a condition of our being allowed to migrate, and a condition of the others who followed us.  We are not boat people," Yuecan continues to elaborate.  "We are willing subjects in this collaborative study.

"How many other studies are there across the United States?"

I had to ask even though I am nudged by my counterpart. I guess she thought these two should do all of the talking without unsavory prompting.

"In the United States and Canada I am aware of several dozen research centers." Zhao repeats this twice and looks to his sister for confirmation.

"We are assured that there are an equal number of such research projects in Europe as well. My friend has told me this." She returns this added bonus with a great, wide smile.

It was at that point that I felt the desire to exchange my experience with the old man in Half Moon Bay. The tact works because they immediately ask if they can have the data. There are notes of sorry when I inform them that the data is long lost. Then as immediate they move very close and almost at a whisper tell me that they can help me recreate the string of events if I would be so kind as to work with them.

"I would love to do this with you both." I counter with genuine regard. Julia is pleased with my narrowing down our next opportunity—she smiles.

As we maintain a suitable pace back up to the ground level we are offered one more parting cup of tea. We do not accept but do make plans to return in the very near future. Bows are exchanged followed by warm handshakes all around. Julia hugs the brother and sister and they are thrilled. A plan has been set for the next visit.

One the way back into town, carefully hugging the banked turns of Chuckanut Drive and adjusting to the thirty-five degree temperature outside, we review our experience. I am still overwhelmed with what we had stumbled onto. The road is dark and I manage to express two key points between upcoming tight curves.

"I spotted a bank of telecommunication hubs in the basement when we were touring. One of them was fed from a floor drain. Let's assume that is the one that comes in from the bay, far below their waterline. The others looked as though they we linked to the outside world. They were tied to Comcast broadband of all things."

"When she was giving her demonstration I saw dates sent on one of the spread sheets, followed by a confirmation dates received. Do you suppose their database is tied directly to something in China?" Julia was laughing when she finished her findings.

"I think we have to assume so, but not over broadband on the mainland. That would be too risky. Data would have to move through too many checkpoints. Even if it were encrypted the resource overhead would raise flags moving across Comcast's network. My guess is that they are utilizing the undersea cable for transmission to China."

I was certain but not positive at this point. If I could ring out the line using a noninvasive tap I could tell for sure. That much I could do under the cover of the Bay. Underwater tapping is not that difficult if one has the appropriate tools. I did not. Now that could be overcome with a little bit of sweat. But if I were not careful, just looking for a source would raise a whole bunch of flags.

"Do you have a plan?" This was a point of asked and answered between us. I did have a suitable plan and unraveled it as best as I could, up to the point of dropping Julia off at the Lummi Ferry.

"They did invite us back to rebuild a historical picture of my old friend in Half Moon Bay. I say we take them up on their kind offer and take a closer look at how their programs and database generates the trace."

"That would be genius, my dear." She kissed me before boarding the small ferry.

It lingered until I heard the blast of the horn and the ferry churned across the Strait. There was something else, but I just could not place it. The transport headed back across the channel and I simply drove away in an opposite direction. It was enough for today.

Fortuitous Event

# Chapter Fifteen

## *In the Spirit of Discovery*

JUST HOW MUCH ENERGY does a data center across the Bay produce? When I think about the earliest knowledge I gleaned from my start in advance technology expended energy was at the top of the information heap. Energy output was a double-edged sword.

For the first part it can denote total BTU output from the equipment in an enclosed structure and the resultant cooling requirements which must be met to maintain it at a nominal and then constant temperature. It was all number crunching with a little variance deployed. In the second part, the most complex, it is the fathomable accounting of the extended output over time infinitum.

Zhao and Yuecan were the finest representation of Chinese lineage. Maybe not from the standpoint of what we think of in terms of family genealogy from the perspective of the Mormons' and their massive computer center in Salt Lake City, but what we think in terms of traceability of output in general. Who holds the clearest memories, holds the most probable gateway to the future.

I was not the first one to suggest that China's greatest exports were people. In five words I can sum this up: we will be the world. It is like the first line in a Japanese Haiku: five syllables long and setting up the importance of the middle and to the end. It was a note of importance that Julia and I took with us when we revisited our newest acquaintances looking out over the Bay and recanted the following:

*We will be the world*

*Are we special not unique*

*Convincing proof how*

The entrance to this estate—a fortress really—was none too descript. It was a simple swinging metal gate that is operated from a panel inside of the house. The gate hangs between two very tall stone stanchions that connect too little else. The only thing this protects is the roadway itself. The cameras on either side however tell a different tale. The world of Zhao and Yuecan has been under surveillance for a countless number of decades. Later on we learned it was three.

To live in a place surrounded by surveillance cameras for three decades gives the notion of reality show a brand new definition. What yielded secrets of this span of existence produce that would have any real meaning. Perhaps this place was more like the reality shows than we originally think.

Yuecan met us in front of the house and she stepped forward to meet us with a deliberate bow and then a warm handshake. She was of course covering all bases. When the three of us entered the back living space we were offered refreshments. There seemed to be something amiss in this extended hospitality given that we appeared to be alone. We then had to coax out the real intent of this invitation if Zhao was not on campus, so to speak.

"My brother is traveling abroad." Yuecan started out in between what turns out to be three courses of refreshments; starting out as traditional Chinese and then transcending to contemporary cuisine.

"Oh, I suppose we guessed that we were not to have the pleasure of his company by now. Can you tell us where he is?" I spoke out for the two of us. Julia signaled that it was allowed.

"Yes, he is at a convention in Hong Kong. He will not be returning until the end of the month."

It was discoveries like this that makes one want to step back and start the whole conversation all over. But then how were discoveries like this an impediment to stop cold. In reflection to the disclosure I wanted to flee the place and regroup. However, with a bit of visual facial prodding by Julia I mustered up the strength to move forward with a much bolder plan. I used our understanding of the definition of Chinese connectivity to push on.

"I am so sorry hearing that Zhao could not join us. I was so excited to be able to restart my conversations with my old friend from the past. He was one of the earlier Chinese settlers to Half Moon Bay as you may remember from our earlier conversation. Zhao seemed very excited to attempt this as well."

Well laid out as intended, this did the trick. No sooner than I summed this point up Yuecan was on her feet and ushering us down the long descent to the basement of this industrial styled homestead. We were entering their underworld again and Yuecan made ready a console for Julia and me to get started. The training was scant yet unnecessary. This was such a well designed program that it was self guiding even though it was encapsulated in Chinese typescript. Ah, but did we come prepared?

When I pulled out my laptop I showed Yuecan the translation program I had installed prior to this visit. Preplanning had been made apparent the first go around. It was not difficult to pool my resources from around the industry and find friendly virtual faces that could help me out. No, I did not give them all of the pertinent details. This was one place I wanted to leave well enough alone; in the interim we dine and dance alone.

As I prepared my data Yuecan prepped us both and we had a marvelous time recreating the family histories of one of my favorite relationships in the past. The old man's family lineage flowed forward into the present like a three dimensional puzzle floating across two flat panel screens in high definition. I matched my data in regard to his grandson teaching at UC Berkeley and Santa Clara University. It was dead on to his last presentation on campus. We co-discovered that the grandson had an offspring. Little did we know at the start of this digital conversation just how powerful this database was, let alone how up to date it had become. The family track was damn near captured in real time.

Now I had brief exposure to the Salt Lake City data center for Genealogical Studies when a new generation of computers and high speed network hubs were being installed. Then I thought this was a start of the art environment for the Mormons', which is until they let me trace my dad's family back to his entrance on Ellis Island. Then is just becomes somewhat scary. It turns out their data center went well beyond the members of their own Church.

The Mormon environment produced results that were grainy, blurred images lacking much detail. The Zhao and Yuecan environment produced results with perfectly clear images that were overwhelming with detail.

When anyone asks me what do I think the primary goal of National Security should be in the 21$^{st}$ Century? I always give them the same answer. It is not the physical interruption that I would be most afraid of, but rather the intellectual disruption that would incur the longest set of resultant circumstances.

The questions I was left with after being exposed to this system were equally complex. Are we special or even unique? Is there room for variety, after all?

This left Julia and me with the next big move. Yuecan had left the room to go upstairs to receive a prearranged phone call from her brother. She thought she might be gone for over one hour. We were left to our own designs but with the full recognition that our every keystroke would be gathered at this point of entry. So we refrained from the obvious.

What we did do is survey the room. Julia looked for indicators of evolution: looking over the hoarded history of past computers and back up media that lined every wall to corner. Apparently this couple never discarded anything. My focus, on the other hand, was to surmise the extent of connectivity to the outside world. And I found the same.

The entire composition of racked blade computers and communication hubs were on a closed network. This is only kind of true. There did seem to be a way out. One high speed broadband path led me physically to a junction that fed a set of older coax cables. It was the only aspect of this enclosed environment that seemed out of spec. The bundled cables were simply labeled *THERE*.

The coax disappeared into a thick line of conduit as it snaked under the false floor and into the only floor drain. I did bring along a piece of really specialized equipment to test out a pet theory. I had managed to smuggle in a TDR.

Only people with a rich history of the network know what this equipment does well enough. Networks in the early days of computing had a more physical presence than today. Today most of the network's workings are deemed virtual. Today most of the emergent technology for connecting to and from the outside world is wireless in design and nature. A TDR provides for time domain reflective metering along physical media. It is a simple enough set of principles to grasp. If you send a signal down a physical trunk it will get to a terminal end. As a result some parts of the signal with reflect back to the point of origin. Using calculated measurements of time to reflect, based in part on the strength of the returned signal, you can create a pretty accurate picture of the length and general direction of the path under study.

The most efficient path should also be the least intrusive. I made a simple tap into the coax. I generated a signal and then I waited for its return from over *THERE*.

I took the measurement three times to create a statistical average. I had advanced knowledge of the type of materials used in this particular type of coax cable, and what that meant in terms of aging, impurities and signal attenuation. My knowledge and the sum accuracy of these measurements told me today that the information from this data center was heading towards the deep blue sea. We had our link to the outside world and we got closer to understanding *THERE*.

Yuecan returned one hour later as promised and we were escorted up the long and steep stairway compensating for her age. She was spry enough intellectually but no one can beat the physical aging process that impacts us all. Her labored movements were telling enough that a lifetime spent in the not small but surreal surroundings of this estate was beginning to take its toll.

"Our histories are steeped in historical constriction—my brother's and mine. But what we Chinese did lack in movement close to home, was not lack in terms of sprawl. Zhao and I are a mix of tradition in a modern context. We held on to the belief that the data we sent back to the mainland was necessary to carry on the history of our race and our nation. We did so through the notion of modern sprawl. Chinese just like us operated these genealogy centers across the United States, Canada and Europe. We in turn enable the blending of diverse cultures through the remodeling of the China global directive: spread the word. We are to ensure that we will all be one big happy family, after all."

Yuecan was close to being out of breath because she was in a fit of laughter. We sat down on comfortable chairs in the front area of her home and waited until her composure was regained. When we think about the marvels of modern communication we have to include the notion of surviving the environment. For the moment I was surviving theirs. The origin of source and the intended destination were not so clearly defined lines at all. What was so special about THERE anyway?

This is a splendid achievement of contemporary civilizations that pool human wisdom. This is how the design of this massive home blends so well with its outer laying property. It is all a matter of scale. The basement is a modest representation of other worldly data centers but a ramification of its content exceeds them all. This was another glorious chapter to classic Chinese history.

Undeterred by time alone, wait patiently and witness those changes which were propagated all around the globe. Was it not the theme of the most recent World Expo 2010 in China that the pronouncement of the best of Chinese ingenuity was a performance staged in everyday life. Zhao and Yuecan had a data center that would showcase this: fraternity in the face of adversity; the tireless efforts of generations to come home from across the waters.

"So what do you think you and Zhao have lent to this cause?" I was only beginning to understand.

"I think I can only answer for myself, and not my brother. I use this experience with respect to the inspiration I can draw from it. This is more than promoting an approach to development and expansion of a culture and a place that I chose never to revisit. But I believe that it is convincing proof that the Cultural Revolution we were all told to march in is still the driving force behind this social progress. In the end we were asked to leave it all behind physically, yet it lives on in our dreams. It is only my brother who desires to forgive and return to the land that we lost."

I am being nudged by my counterpart. Yuecan is closing in on tears. Her head is shaking and she is bowing it instead of letting us read her sorrow. But I want to continue to push.

"Convincing proof how?" I am adamant in my demeanor and receive a swift kick to the ankle from Julia. I start to settle down.

"The proof is this: productivity generated in the last one hundred years after the Industrial Revolution exceeds the total sum of productivity of all previous times. One can say that the last three decades in China accelerated this growth one hundred fold. China leads the course of industrial development for the world. We do not have to wait on the future because we now promote sustained recovery of the world's economy." She is smiling and wagging a knowing fist at Julia and me.

"So this is in the spirit of discovery 'there'. However, the thrill is not echoed around the world." I was steadfast in my answer, but it was of course after the fact.

That was about the time Yuecan stood up and opened her front door. She was gracious in her attention to the details of being the sole host and she made it know that we were invited back, when her brother returned from China's other small island (off the mainland). I turned and waved back for added good luck. I wanted to be able to return to continue this exploration with both of them. I smiled warmly and gave a moderate bow. I thought I would return the last gesture thinking ahead— to those next twenty moves.

But apparently that was not enough. Yuecan returns the bow, followed by an exuberant wave, and then addressed us once more from the top of the stairs. We were not quite finished from her point of view and she gestured us closer.

"I hope this will be a memorable experience for you as well. We seek out the histories of individuals and crowds. You and I are not so different in approach; just in scale. My brother can go back but I think that he will not be able to pick up where he left off. As for me: I know that I would find nothing there that I do not have here. I will not bother to return. It no longer makes me sad, just disappointed."

Julia and I waited patiently until Yuecan reopened her eyes and took in the panoramic view of where she left off. When she turned back into her concrete fortress Yuecan disappeared behind the thud of a splendid and solid wooden door. It was quiet now, with the exception of the wind that blew in from the Pacific Ocean; the abundantly tall trees on the Cliffside property absorb the flow and the sea becomes less of a roar of what lie ahead.

# Chapter Sixteen

## *Not According to Plan*

EVERY ONCE IN A WHILE life throws you for a loop. I know this is so because I had been well prepared. My biography of an old man in Half Moon Bay never became part of my completed list because he had finished with his life as an early pioneer in the New World. This was a fellow that had witnessed the cycle of several entire revolutions in his country of birth, and then again in his adopting a host country to wind things down and it took more than half a life time.

I was sitting at my breakfast table finishing off a plate of cut mini watermelon, two types of olives, and a helping of warm brie cheese on water crackers with sesame seed. Maybe I should be calling this brunch given the time of the day, afternoon. I had a new book started that was a measured mix of good news and not so good news. The good news of course was that it is new, it was very well written, covering a single man's life journeys as a vagabond. I had purchased it from a local, independent book store for twenty percent of its original value. If you are a published writer you have already guessed the not so good news. Someone's new release only commanded twenty percent of its list value just four seasons away from its original release. It was kind of a mixed reminder of a general state of a marketplace that I highly valued—the bookstore.

However, that said I am no wimp, and I purchased it not only for its far below release value, but I also did so with an in store coupon for an additional five percent off.

We appear to be our own worst enemies—so there is no doubt sometimes. I am equally sure that my cohorts in the music business feel the same pain, as do the film makers. The commoditization of low cost computers, post production tied to high speed broadband networks, have significantly impacted many industries above and beyond what entertains us. And that my friend is the good news: more is being written and published, more music is being composed and streamed, and more films are shot and viewed in close to real time—taken quicker to markets today than in the entire history of these once standalone industries.

I have no beef with this and I do benefit from it—my next disclosure. I love having access to the entire planet in close to real time. My phone rings and I see on the small display that it is someone familiar calling. I pick up the wireless handheld and I listen closely to the opening statement. I can tell that there is a blow to come. The digital stream carries with it news that we hope doesn't come so quickly. Someone has passed away.

When I hear that Zhao is not coming back from Hong Kong I am at first shocked because the news represents the loss of a new friend. I had already moved him out of the acquaintance category. If there are truly seven stages of grieve over the loss of someone close in your life I was moving from stage one to stage two in the same amount of time the voice stream bounced one full cycle. I had a feeling of loss, not to dissimilar from the one I am recalling from the passing of my old friend in Half Moon Bay. I forgive myself for the jump to the next stage and plunged into the already changing tempo of this phone call from Julia.

"How did you find out?" I asked this question with a soft and serene voice because it was normative for my culture. Like many other cultures we immediately reflect on the loss itself but then regain a sense of strength as we recapitulate of vision of what would have been a life well lived and an individual well loved and respected by his peers. In this case that would include most of the people I knew that came across in the later part of his life—that is, Julia and me.

Zhao was a kind of recluse. I learned this from Zhao so no one can accuse me of being too jaded. I heard this echoed in Yuecan reminiscing about their life after being forced from the University, and then driven from their homeland and into this new and strange world. It was said by both that he did not miss the outside world because he was so engrossed in the discovery of new inhabitants and organizing their lives neatly in chronological order on their enormous database of theirs. He spoke of this in first person, and Yuecan reinforced it in second person, while Julia and I struggle to finish each other's post partum sentences recalling it all across the distance of a phone call. Did we plug in any gaps?

Julia did hear about his passing directly from Yuecan. She dropped in by special invitation—a woman-to-woman moment of shared intimacy—minimizing the extraneous noise from the external world. That would include me.

I was now an outsider in Yuecan's eyes. She made it clear that Zhao and I shared a connection and it was not to be extended to her. Julia was her singular point of connection with the outside world and she included her in the planning for Zhao's remains. It would be a task that Julia herself admitted later that she had wanted no part in. But it was clear that she was committed to what she and I had started.

"Yuecan doesn't dislike you. That much is clear. She just does not see the importance of trying to rebuild the life of your friend. As a matter of fact she has decided to send the last down load to China, shut down her end of the project, and sell the equipment via auction."

"That is an enormous blow on two levels. I know you think that one is quite personal. I will not talk you out of that. However, the data farm they created and then mined has mindboggling ramifications if shut down. I am sure there are a lot of people who would love to see what they have done. I am at a loss for what this will mean in the long term. I am only focusing on the immediate impact." I said my piece and then I expressed my sorrow for his passing on.

"Well we have to come to grips with the fact that Yuecan is quite bitter about the whole thing. She had just lost her only connection with her world. She admitted that she spends very little time interacting with others. Her brother was the sum of her life—her words not mine."

"That's grief speaking. Given time something else will emerge out of the shadows. I'm sorry—did she give you any hint of the timeline?" I wanted to stay focused. I was that certain that Julia would understand.

I was standing by a large framed window and staring out across my backyard. I was not looking for anything in particular but I was scanning all the same. There was something out of place but it was not registering yet. Perhaps I needed to get back to this phone call and its resounding purpose.

Sitting back down at the breakfast table I began jotting down a list of things I think are necessary to bring this impending thing to a more logical close. I have about one dozen items and I am reciting them to my friend as she provides additional details to fill in the blanks.

"I'm sorry, what did you say?" It stopped me short.

"When I got Yuecan to settle down—over a nice pot of tea of course—I made a modest proposal. I asked her if I could continue to poke around the system. To get a more general feel of what it would take to get a dump of the framework. She said that would be impossible. She wanted to honor a promise made by her brother not to deviate from their arrangement with the homeland. Apparently all of this is tied to the University, and of course funded and closely monitored by the government."

"Yea, but that is not news. We suspected this connection all along. Were there any new curves thrown—given the fact that she reached out to you?" I had a hunch.

"Oh, there is one great big curve." Julia was stopped short for some reason but then so was I—that strange shadow across the utility pole.

I got up to have a closer look through my window and I was sure this would give my counterpart a moment to redress. I could see it now and I wondered how long it had been there. Moving out through the back door I walked deliberately out with the garbage from under my sink and made way to the trash bin to the right side of my property. There it was, almost as plain as day. It was hanging over my back yard.

Having been involved in photography for most of my life I can say that I have personally seen just about every kind of camera known to humankind. This is not meant as a boastful remark and I am keeping to the facts. I have seen this type of equipment before. Interestingly enough they are referred to as lipstick cameras and they now have tremendous capabilities in their miniature form.

Someone had installed a lipstick camera on a public utility light pole just outside of my property line. That would mean that it was not necessarily an invasion of my privacy. It seemed only kind of aimed in my general direction. The only way to know for sure is to hook something else to the device and have a look.

The first thing that runs through my head is my call with Julia. I want her dump but I do not necessarily want if filtered by this discovery. Sheepishly I start in on the interrupted conversation to learn that she is still only partially dressed and needs a few more minutes.

"Are we having a naked conversation?" I asked this not so sheepishly.

"Well I would assume it is one sided. There, I am finished now. Where did we leave off?" Julia was laughing on her end.

"You hinted of another thing to come." I was back inside my house and searching for a long enough cable.

"Oh, you want to hear about the next big discovery. It seems that they have equipment that could sense your tap. I do not think that they are willing to say it was us, so I pushed a bit. Hold on, let me zip my pants."

She had just finished this visual when I caught the audio end. I could hear the flush of her toilet. Some things cannot be disguised over the phone.

"I hope that was just a pee." It was my turn to laugh.

"Yep, I never do the doo during a phone call. So here is where she and I leave off. It is not the first time they captured a glitch to their network. There were previous interruptions. So a local equipment contact installed a piece of equipment that we did not see the day of our last visit. She calls it a *pinger*. She described it as a kind of router rooter electronic scope for looking at junctions added or removed. It picked up your tap."

I had gone to another room to retrieve an adapter box. I was making way back out to the pole with the long cable, the box and a small flat screen. It took me a few additional minutes to retrieve a tall ladder, place it gingerly against the pole so not to cause the odd shake in the resolution of the lipstick camera. It would be a tell if someone was monitoring the picture in real time.

"What are you up to? That is a lot of racket." Julia was making a distant recognition of a ladder being opened.

"Oh, something must have fallen onto my roof. I am just having a look. Please continue." I was holding onto the pole and the ladder and had the phone cradled under my chin.

"No you please continue. What are your thoughts on the matter?"

"Well I think that the earlier taps picked up by their equipment correlate to the second leg of the coax I discovered on my last dive."

"Oh, the one you failed to disclose to me." She said this in a bit of a huff.

"All things in good time—I was not about to speculate at the time. But now I will. Someone else has been linked into their network trunk to the outside world. I should have guessed given the Coast Guard ship that passed by on that one trip out. At first I thought it was coincidence given our proximity to the border and surrounding waters. But now I am certain that it was us that called them out to that particular location."

"Who would have tipped them off?" Julia had returned to a softer voice. There were no insinuating overtones and she sounded relaxed yet curious.

I was not at the highest foothold of my ladder. The lipstick camera was just within reach and I carefully added my tie to the second port. Most of these devices came with a second port. I was that well prepared as I fed the cable into my converter and then connected the flat screen and fired it all up.

There was a beautiful fish eye view of my garden and the entire back of my house. This was one nice piece of equipment. And of all things expected it had an asset tag. The number was insignificant, by-the-by. I just needed to know who at this point of the game.

This is where it gets kind of weird. I added my own digital recording devices at the opposite end of the garden back behind the garbage bins. I was out of the perceived line of sight of their equipment when I focused my end straight at the utility pole. It was a curiosity thing. I simply wanted a composition of who would return to scene to retrieve their equipment and when.

My task was done and Julia had completed hers. We exchange several more tidbits with regard to the next probable steps and I told her that I would meet her at the Lummi College campus the next day. The first thing I wanted to get to the bottom of was who was looking at whom.

**Make Way to the Reservation**

These are a number of very important details I want to remember as I headed out because I wanted to finish up the day diving in calm. Although it is not a well kept secret most ideal diving days in the Pacific Northwest are during the winter months. If one finds a suitable slot between storms one heads to the water ways—at least some of us with this all important knowledge. Without the usual eyes peering out across my bow—so astonished and marveling at the solo diver in the water—the usual surveillance no longer stifles because it is rendered to a minimalist population. If they are out here it's because they are subsistence fishermen who do not want to be bothered and only after tonight's meal. The one fishing season that is open is for crab, and they are as far south as I hope them to be at this time of year.

I wanted to avoid the churned debris in the water after the last storm. I am paddling in a slack tide that is comparatively murkier at the end of storm and as the day is breaking, but very clear toward the day's end. This waterway I am on is shimmering and it is clear. One might argue that my current location is as cold as it is silent but I am as comfortable under its water line as I am on or near its colder surface. I am in a full wet suit, and because of that I am comfortably warm and there is little chance that I am in any danger of drowning. This suit provides near perfect neutral buoyancy.

To get to this place in the North Sound I launched at Gooseberry Point on the Lummi Reservation. The folks working and living in the area are always nice and friendly and we maintain a stance of small talk when our paths do often cross. Kayaking in the winter is popular enough in the area so little of what I do arouses undue attention. Sometimes a resident of the Reservation will pull alongside me in a traditional dugout canoe, and we will share experiences about currents and tides in the surrounding area.

I must digress. Let's go back one step.

My original destination was Lummi College on the Reservation. I have a friend there on the staff that has allowed me to use their research facilities from time-to-time. I met him at several presentations about the Lummi College activity provided to the surrounding communities. I received an open invitation as a result. When we meet after these affairs we will drink beer and discuss history and current affairs.

Whenever we meet we each have a specific topic of interest that we explore over the first or second beer. Today it took three beers before we segued to a conversation focused on family tree databases. As it turns out they are in the infancy of creating a more formal way of managing the genealogy of Lummi and Nooksack families and he is particularly interested in hearing about my two previous experiences. I provided him the particulars of my experience in Salt Lake City, but I am obviously less specific on the most recent experience with Zhao and Yuecan. I cannot quite play that card yet—not a full disclosure anyway.

Without a doubt I have him hooked on the capabilities of the software Julia and I had the opportunity to use when we researched my old friend from Half Moon Bay. My new friend is interested in a trade, provided that no money is required. His program is at the bitter end of their last grant struggle and money is too tight to even suggest a proposal, which is a primary problem. A secondary problem is that even if they did create a proposal, their money comes from the Federal Indian Nations Program, and they would want to know all of the elemental details. First and foremost: Where did the code originate?

In short, this would put us at an impasse.

"But what about trade and barter," quickly shifting the conversation out of this impending dead end I tacked differentially.

"Oh, what did you have in mind?" My friend is smiling because he knows that he is being played. "Should I pop a couple more beers?

I lay out an 'on the spot' idea that fuels this interesting digression. My proposal is I get him access to a copy of a well thought out program, if he provides me with a history of the undersea cables that seem to lace this area of the Salish Sea.

"Certainly the native fishermen have noticed the strange cable trunks that are sometimes exposed during low and slack tides." I passed on the forth beer. I do have to dive later on in the afternoon. I do not want to do so with a buzz.

"Yes, they most certainly do and continue to be plagued by those damn cables. We have petitioned the State as well as the Coast Guard to help us remove them because we snag our nets on them from season to season. But do they want to do this? They have budget problems as well."

He is sipping his beer and is wiping his mouth but then stops me from replying. There must be more to his end.

"I do not want to reenter this ongoing battle. Last season the U.S. Navy did assist with the pulling of hundreds of tons of gill nets from the South and North Sound. Our tribes benefited from this clean up and they absorbed the majority of the cost of the clean up that our fisheries contributed to over the last one hundred years."

"I get that. I follow the local news as well. But there was never any mention of the nest of undersea cables."

I wished I had not turned him down for the other beer. I wanted this to be maintained as a social interchange, not an opportunity to bitch.

"Please continue," I said and gestured him to sit back down. I could see that this was a touchy area.

"We provided a map of where we thought the cables ran. The Navy guys took the data and said they would review it with the Coast Guard. That was several years ago. It became a dead end. At some point someone said that they not find anyone who was interested in financing the task. It was a dead ended project as far as we were concerned." I could see that he was cooling off.

"You indicate that maps were produced?"

"We now provide an overlay of where we should avoid getting snags, and our fishing fleets have made the necessary adaptations."

"Would you be willing to trade the overlays for the software?"

I leaned in for emphasis, and I am smiling. He returns both gestures and encourages me to continue.

"I'm interested in details in and around the north end of Orcas, Clark Island, The Sisters, and Lummi Island."

"Are you serious, bro?" He was still smiling and leaned in rather close to me. We were damn near nose-to-nose.

"Yes, I am quite certain this is where I want to go."

"No strings attached? How will you pursue the paths?"

"Well isn't that with strings attached?' I wanted this to be the last counter.

"It's done as far as I am concerned. The less people know about this the better. That being said, the Coast Guard has been paying closer attention to those areas lately. Tell me this isn't a coincidence."

"It is not, and that is all I can tell you."

My friend leaves the room and heads out across the campus to another smaller building. He had a slight weave and I trust that is due to the four beers. I hope that he was not trying to get someone's attention. I am alone in this section of the building. Yes, I do poke around a bit.

After a short span of time he has returned with several tube mailers under each arm and reenters the room and drops the tubes onto a table. One is opened and a Sea Trails Marine Map is pulled out. From a second can he produces detailed depth and current predictions—an underwater topology map of the same region labeled Washington State San Juan Islands 2009. This activity is followed by the third can with an overlay of undersea obstructions that align to the other two mapped regions.

The fourth can produces all of the areas to avoid gill netting and why. This list correlates by GPS values and how to get small boats in and out of the indicated areas if nets are being dragged. This final map also comes with a sticker labeled *Practice Minimal Impact Techniques.*

"Is this useful?" He says this and bends over the last overlay to try to figure out why I would be interested at all. "No one else fishes in these areas, bro."

"Who is my contact for the software?" I am helping him roll up the maps and stuffing them into the four tubes. There is an interest in wrapping this all up. I looked up at the clock on the wall. Too much time has passed.

"You can call me, and then I will get the right folks involved. Is anyone else going to be involved?"

"It is just you and me. Thank you, man."

I received the tubes and I am heading out. My friend is in a hurry to go to another meeting as well.

I will assume that our transaction will fall on other interest ears before the day is out. This does not bother me because I am heading into the water and hope to be far enough along before the sun begins to set. As I paddle south there are no fishing vessels along this area of the coast and I am absolutely certain that my activities will not warrant closer scrutiny. I prepare to cut in toward the tall sandstone cliffs and drop a drift anchor into the water. It is eerily calm and I am steadied in my movements as I exit my kayak.

It's just a guy in a kayak, after all. It is winter. It is very cold and I am that certain that no one cares that this paddler has just entered the water. I spin around and survey the area one last time before I submerge into the depths of the clearest waters this far north in the Sound.

Fortuitous Event

# Chapter Seventeen

## *We Live in a Parallel What*

THERE IS A UNIVERSALLY HELD THEORY in the science world that we exit in a parallel universe. There is matter; the things we can see through natural and artificial means and that which we can measure. It is a matter of course, of the ever churning universe that we are cognizant of and have proved to ourselves splendidly through repeated measure. Most if not all of us in the world of science and technology are so convinced that there are times when we discuss it out loud as a fact.

Recently scientists and technologists have come up with a way to measure matters counterparts as antimatter. Yes, we have theorized about antimatter for several centuries; our clearest recognitions so popularized in climatic scenarios survived by both Kirk and Picard. Now there is a real handle on our opposite and parallel worlds. A group of scientists have tested conclusively the existence of antimatter through repeated measure. Eureka, we have found it.

When the New World was discovered by the Chinese, Japanese, Irish, Italians, Portuguese and the Russians they must have had a difficult time explaining this to the native aboriginals. But through repeated measure the theories moved over to facts and we have a new continent; notwithstanding that all of the continents were joined at a point of time, well before our own histories provided credibility to the nature of existence.

Yes, it is all explainable through repeated measures. To compare and contrast parallel views.

My time in the water was well spent. It appears that almost as many countries were involved in exploring the nature of the extended archipelago which stretches its arms and legs from the southern to the northern ends of the Salish Sea. We find indicators and signs everywhere. And now we continue to find them on the bottom floor of Puget Sound and it is suspected that there are as many countries involved as there were centuries ago, so indicated by sunken vessels, drifting debris, particulate matters carried across by trade winds. Ship loads of household goods, and now through a complex maze of undersea cables.

One often argues that this New World is a melting pot. If we let the pot settle we can witness all of the layers that separate and those that continue to blend. We have become a fine stew; those who were invited to the party. This is the argument of late. Are we one big happy family?

I have traced the nest of coax as indicated on the 2009 overlay. However, I have only made the concerted effort in the north of Puget Sound. I have my biases too.

There is one particular trunk that I am keenly interested in, and two that are of minor concern. The big one of course is the cable that shoots through a wall of sandstone and connects the centuries of proof of existence of Chinese immigrants to the mother ship. It is here that I have added a tap—so not one but two because I too believe in repeated measures.

Accomplishing this task on dry land was routine. Attempting it successfully underwater was a test of faith. But I had faith and got it on the first try. I practiced in my bathtub at home. No I was not taking a bath at the time. That would have been rather strange. Besides the section of conduit covered coax that I had taken from another section of the undersea web displaced a majority of the water in my tub. To coexist in the same void would have been too problematic.

I was so excited that this was possible that I called an associate of mine and we compared notes. The measures we took were designed to parallel each other. Coax snaked out across two homes in two distant states and were connected by patch, splitter, and signal amplifiers into coax installed by our friendly broadband providers. We also snaked cable into signal converters and then into hubs and then into banks of laptops primarily for transportability. Our little test labs would have to be moved soon.

"Do you have the streams?" I asked him this the other day.

"Yea, I received them but this is only half the news. The encryption algorithm we deployed only added fifty-five percent overhead. We are definitely shy of the expected eighty." He was laughing because this inside joke would be funny only to a small pocket full of people.

The additional tests we ran over night and well into the next day confirmed our initial notion that we could mimic the overwhelming volume that would have been produced by someone streaming back-to-back movies using a common service. Of utmost importance was the notion that the activity coexist with the available bandwidth that was monitored for quality of use by an industry that measures everything. We were elated. We had our proof of concept.

Without going through a great deal of unnecessary detail we both knew that what we had accomplished was pretty trivial. But it did prove several key and salient points: it was done once, done twice, and the third run over an extended amount of time. Time was the most key element. We acknowledge the time we had to do the task with compounded and repeated measure. We could exist in a parallel universe.

"So where do you go from here? Your original approach suggested an enormous amount of encrypted data. What we just accomplished is trivial."

My friend had a valid point. What we tested was fairly trivial. It was a far cry from transporting the history of this segment of the world. This thing needed to scale.

"I do have something in mind, but it is not going to be easy to pull off. The expense of the thing is far beyond my reach. I need another partner. You my friend are too much in dept to be of any use."

We both had a good laugh over this last statement. My friend was a key member of the technical staff at a new company that had absorbed his old one. He's existing in a parallel universe, and had been told that he was unnecessarily redundant. He no longer mattered and he was let go. This was a onetime master of this craft and now he was ushered out with an insincere goodbye and into the lever extending line of the unemployed.

"I am not sure what I will do. I have a lot of time on my hands. What did you do?" He inquired not out of the blue.

"I started several hobbies. I stay incredibly busy." It was all together short and pat but to the point. I had a feeling it would resonate.

"Well, when you have completed your task you are going to need someone to decrypt all of that data and make sense of it. As it turns out I am available. That is if you will have me."

We both laughed. It really was funny and kind of reminiscent of the Y2K debacle. When they are backed into the proverbial corner they will seek us all out. History has a way of repeating itself—sometimes a great notion.

"I will, I promise. But first I have to seek out someone with more money than they know what to do with it."

"Is there any reality to go along with that?"

"There is indeed. I will call you in a couple of weeks. I need to pack for a trip overseas. Take care for now and thank you for helping with the proof of concept. I owe you one. Cheers."

## What do you think about when you Fly

When I arrived at my hotel I was so tired. All I wanted to do was head in and get several hours of sleep. I had been moved to a point of exhaustion by the plane full of overly excited youngsters who were coming to Europe for a field trip. I had also stayed awake racking my brain trying to figure out how kids could warrant a field trip of this magnitude. We had only been allowed cross city trips when I was their age. Several generations later, in a time of severe budgetary cuts that spanned across most segments of life, these fine youngsters were off to Europe to visit the museums of the past. I chastised myself for thinking that this wasn't fair and pushed my way through the revolving doors and into the lobby of my hotel.

I was moved through the line with expediency. The elevator that ran past the higher floors looked as though it was the first one built post World War Two. Everything was a marvel of older mechanics and the push button panel indicating the floors were my favorite part of the experience. With what little energy I had left in my head I reconstructed a three dimensional image of all the systems that would have been involved. I was satisfied with my image and my deep recall.

The room I entered was not worth describing with the possible exception that it included everything I had anticipated. It was a place to reside until I was able to track down my patron. I had with me several points or possibilities of beginning the journey through the avenue maze with street names I wouldn't be able to pronounce. It was not my first time here and I was certain that I could conjure up enough of my past; to migrate around the city grids in and around Munich was not trivial at all.

I slept, I showered, and then I stepped out into the night lights and ventured out for something to eat. I used a combination of GPS, dead reckoning and line of sight to move forward. The food I ate was heavier and I remembered the native diet was one I would not take back home. The buildings were mostly the same, and the series of parks along the major waterway I walk along are just as spectacular as the last time I was here.

I brought a physical map, and I compared that map to another loaded onto my laptop while I was in the restaurant. When I left I walked and studied the screen of my phone. I had a phone. It was called a smart phone but it did not live up to its proposed reputation because of the fact that I still relied on a keyboard and a ridiculously small screen to venture out across the crowded streets of Germany. I walked and I wished that a smart phone whose key purpose is voice centric, did not have to rely on a silly keyboard and finger tipped movements over the ridiculously small screen. My friends in Japan simply roll out a cloth that deploys a flat organic array of LEDS. I needed that now.

The storefronts were decorated with a predominant theme. It was almost Christmas and it was a commercial notion that was shared around the world. I put the phone in my pocket and pulled out the larger tablet. Although it too relied on a keyboard, albeit a simply overlay, it did come with a more reasonable sized screen. I continued to walk. This scenery could never be as enjoyable through the windows of a taxi.

Thank goodness for the back end systems— those are the life lines to this current generation of handhelds destined for landfill. This was not my sweet sentiment but one displayed across a giant LED marquee that amplified the message tenfold.   Siemens needed to remind us all of where the true necessities of life really reside.  They are in the background.

I crossed the next busy intersection and entered an office tower.  It was a twenty six story journey up in a modern marvel of elevator technology.  Its buttons were all flat screen, constantly blinking illuminations I intent and destiny.  I was not alone so I could not get more personal with the panel in front of me.  There were other travelers around me—so a physical presence—and several surveillance cameras with signs that reminded us all that they were here for our safety—a virtual presence perhaps monitored by human beings.

I am giddy with the vision of facial recognition software running somewhere on the top floor.  Come on, we have seen these silly representation on so many television programs.  They are monitored by children who always seem to know how to patch across commercial and private networks to comprehensive databases.  In reality they are more hit and miss than with deadly accuracy.  I wave at the cameras and the minimum wage souls who are most likely staring at screens during an excruciatingly boring eight hour shift, as I step out.

Stepping into the hallways and out across the corridors I see a few additional cameras tucked anonymously in the recessed corners.  I am coming onto a series of suites that are a mix of businesses and living quarters.  I love the mix and the notion of straddling one hallway to get from home to work and then back again.  This is a convenient world after all.

Roxanne number two answers the door on the forth knock.  She is dressed in shorts and a t-shirt.  Both are made of materials that could be described as fine and thin fabric. I am only kind of surprised but quickly remind myself that this is her world, not mine.

"How was your flight over?" It is the beginning of a typical banter between residents of two continents. She is moving across the very large and ultra modern flat.

"Please make yourself at home. I am going to fetch some wine. White or red—what is your pleasure?" I cannot see the expression on her face because she keeps her back to me. I am thinking this may not be rude. I would really like some tea.

Soon enough we are sipping and we are reengaged. We share facial expressions and body language, as well as a common language. Once in awhile Roxanne switches over to the dialect of her chosen homeland and then back to common ground. It is only kind of amusing. I am certain she did the same thing in while living in Amsterdam.

"The ride over was not very interesting. That said my revisit to the streets of Munich brought back many happy memories. I walked over. Not much change in the inner city, but that is good I suppose." The cool and very crisp wine is delightful, but a tad sweet.

Roxanne is shifting her legs over the arms of the couch and I can clearly imagine that she is doing so with purpose. She does a good mimic of her original self. The first one was a habitual flirt. It kind of makes me sad because now I have to muster the strength to remind myself that this isn't the one who penetrated my life across so many meaningful occasions. The Roxanne in front of me is unflatteringly false; my appeal has to seem palatably real. I am lost in the paradox for longer than intended. I am staring at a large mirror fastened to the ceiling. Why is it above the living room?

"Are you here or somewhere else?" Her demeanor is friendly enough. This woman is drinking a fair amount of wine in the short span of time since my arrival. She has a noticeable stutter. Perhaps there was one bottle opened and consumed prior to my sitting here and staring up at the ceiling.

I muster a response. She is only slightly amused.

"So you think the Professor was generous do you. Well as a matter of fact he was but it came at a great personal cost, if you know what I mean." She gulped down the remainder of her glass and gestured for me to refill it.

I came too close and I had her hand on my stomach and she was tugging at my shirt. Yes, she was on another plain.

"I am not sure this is what I came to hear." Now I was kind of stuttering and I resumed my position in another chair. We played a staring game for awhile longer.

"Oh, there are always hidden costs. You came to me for financing for your little project. Granted I am interested to hear how those previous series of events have unfolded. But what made you think that I would want to fund it."

Roxanne had slipped out of one of the straps of her top. Now the evening had transcended into one popular cliché. I would have to let myself be seduced by this transparent act. I was supposed to be aroused by the one exposed nipple. I was not interested.

"Let me remind you of the relationship I had with his daughter. It was playful but it was real enough and it spanned quite a bit of time to allow it to grow meaningful. I am not looking for a fast tracked experience with you. I am aware that this might be a deal killer, but I am hoping that there is enough in our relationship for you to trust my instincts. This is simply not necessary."

Wow, she looked so hurt and bowed her head and slunk further down into the plush leather couch. The shirt strap was repositioned and then she sat straight up and crossed her long and slender legs. But this gesture was not the same—it was that different. We were back on a more reasoned track. I was sure of this and I tilted my glass in a response to the shift. It was all I intended to do and I place the glass onto the tabletop and indicated that I wanted no more spirits. It was time for me to either stay with the original game plan or make that descent in the high tech elevator that served this building so well.

My dignity was to be retained. Roxanne stood up and grabbed an equally thin dressing gown but the layered look did the trick. It flowed nicely around her body and acted as a barrier to entry. It was a nice trick. It caused me to move forward.

"Ok, I will provide the necessary funding." She stood before me and retrieved a business card from a crystal bowl on the table nearest the entrance. Her walk became more of a glide. It must have been a sobering moment for her as well.

I took the card but did not have to read it. Roxanne provided all of the direction I needed and I bid my goodbyes. I maintained the crisp piece of paper safely in my hand until I entered the elevator. The wine had caused no buzz. My focus was clear and I was alone for the ride down, sans the eyes in the sky. It was a long way down even though this was a super elevator; this efficiency could not be denied. It glided me to a whispered stop at the bottom and bid me a happy journey in several dialects as I stepped off. It was a nice touch.

Roxanne and I did not live in parallel worlds. Our worlds were separated by the traces to and from our individual pasts. Mine was linked by reality to family and friends—so solidly grounded—and hers was one pulled together on the fly and temporarily anchored to the next patron who passed her way. Some would think of her life as one of luck and resourcefulness. My view was one of apathy. I did not have an appreciation for what she was or what she had become. We did not survive on a common ground.

But at the same time I felt something else for her. I sensed the meaning of why she reached out and what effect the connections must have had on her life. To expose one like that was foreign to me, but that does not necessarily make it wrong. It was simply a necessity. How could I condemn that? I knew that I would not and I moved on across that busy intersection, went to bed alone, and spent the night thinking about how I would benefit from that which would imperil her to a life of continued loneliness.

In the morning I called Julia with the news and caught up on the activities on her end. Apparently she was just as successful but equally remorseful.

"Yuecan allowed me to take a copy of her programs. But she was emphatic that the data was left alone. Her argument was that it was not hers to give away. The good news is that we have another piece of the puzzle."

"I would say that you had success, but something in the sound of your voice tells me more." I was fishing.

"Oh, you do not know the half of it. She has retained someone to sell the estate. Her intent is to find a buyer for the equipment in their basement, scale down what is at ground level, and then move into a condo in town."

"Is there any word about Zhao?"

"She intends to leave his body in Hong Kong. Apparently there is an uncle that resides there and he is concluding the arrangements. Yuecan has expressed no intension to fly over. Do you get that?"

I did get it. Julia was most likely caught up in the transition of this older woman's life. Yuecan was alone—her mate passed on in a faraway place; that place which represent a point of no return in her own regard. She needed a buddy to get her through all of the hoops of her earlier life and that was her brother. This juncture in her life and she had reached out to the next closest person to her. That was the paradox explained by Julia over the phone.

"Look I do not feel that I can just walk away. I know we have a task to accomplish. I am still one hundred percent in. However, I have to run parallel tasks. There is no other way around it. Yuecan is alone in this big world and I do not want her to suffer in it all alone."

"I understand. Just how committed are you?"

I was after one piece of the puzzle at a time. It was all that I needed for now.

"So are we sufficiently funded?"

Julia asked this in a more chipper tone but she did avoid answering my question. Perhaps she did not know, yet.

I was pleased that she made the quicker transition during this particular conversation. I shared the details of my end, leaving out the more dubious parts. There was no need to burden Julia with the messy contingencies that I was now tethered to.

I headed out to the airport, and boarded a plane with mostly people like me: business or pleasure, the usual mix. This made it all the more palatable ride back home: across an ocean, a continent and a tarmac I was never alone. I could never fall asleep on a transcontinental journey but I could daydream.

There is no doubt that what Roxanne had said to me had me feeling a bit crowded. I had trouble splicing the end of the original to the beginning of the clone. Someone had picked up after the Professor gone; watching at a distance. There were scant details to go on at the moment because I kept drifting back to the original thing. I had insinuations and vagaries with little detail of the exacting crossroad. When exactly did the transformation take place? I can conjure up Roxanne's facial expressions and body positioning and here is little similarity in the version I left behind in Europe. The ongoing Roxanne says she has seen things in advance and extended advice that I should just keep on going. Going where—towards what?

I am the principle keeper of secrets about the past. Am I to understand that I am also controlling these goods for the future? What about the present? Who is keeping all of this straight now? Roxanne's intensions maybe are mixed but we were well funded on the other hand. Right now I didn't know. I just wanted to get some undisturbed sleep.

In the very early stages of my being a teenager I wanted to approach transition differently than my peers. Most of the teens I interacted with at the time were experimenting with their lives with artificially induced goals. Call this a cross section of being around adults teaching what at the time was normative behavior, and a line of reasoning called experimental by one's peers.

At the time it became so obvious that I did not fit into either end of the swing of the pendulum. I was off to the side and off center of the normative track, and my dealings with the experimental was more grounded in day to day living. There were several exception of course that transcended all of the pressure of the times; it got down to this: I wanted to be a man of knowledge.

I cannot say that I had any operative plan in my line of reasoning as a teen. I just wanted to understand as much as reasonably possible by my set of rules. I would keep to the pact that I had with my parents and be a good student and learn as much as I could in school. But I employed a different characteristic with respect to the manner of learning. I was intent to reach out far beyond what I considered the miniscule curriculums that were forced and offered to young people, and to consume what was available to age groups far and beyond my own.

Knowledge had to be above and beyond the matter of strenuous learning. Get good grades then and still is the mantra of early education. There had to be more to this most basic measurement matrices and I wanted knowledge and order that was practical. I sought out an order of necessary things—developed a hierarchical approach—as a way to think about all of the deviations I would become exposed to in pursuit of my goals. What I wanted, in short, was to perfect my own sense of critical thinking when I was awake and when I was asleep and dreaming of these things.

In short, I still daydream and night dream in critical terms. Of late I am dreaming about all of the conversations that I had in my own head. There was enough grounding in my leaving childhood and moving on to becoming an adult that I can attribute to these dreams. They were rarely dreams about physical objects that I wanted, or places that I wanted to go. Most of my dreams have been about conversations I have had or probably will have with significant figures in my daily life. I have also experienced a succession of things referred to as out of body journeys. Where most people describe this phenomenon as floating above oneself and pondering down, my experiences are typically listening in on my own conversations at a safe distance.

This woman seated next to me on the plane was stirring.

"Hi, are we landing?"

"Yes, we are just about there."

"Oh, I am so glad. I was having the strangest dreams."

I did not really know this person outside of the fact that I had been sitting next to her for eight hours. The plane's wheels had touched down and the roar of the engines braking is subsiding. She was still touching my arm.

"What do you dream about when you are flying?"

Her smile had been sincere enough but the flight attendant was making an announcement: something about our being deviated to another gate. This caused the deviation in our conversation. There was a stream of information coming from the overhead speakers with regard to the baggage carrousel for this flight and how to approach customs. I no longer had the opportunity answer the question. But I thought about it for quite awhile.

Fortuitous Event

# Chapter Eighteen

## *What I Dream when I Fly*

I RECALL THE PLEASURED DETAILS of the last time I was in Vesuvio's on Columbus Street in San Francisco. I can match the sounds inside my head with what's going on outside on the sidewalk, pausing for a moment in front of the famous drinking establishment across the adjoining alley called Kerouac Alley. Kerouac Alley was just a name in remembrance of a famous son that was adopted by the West Coast. The name of the alleyway was honorary in title only. As a child of San Francisco streets I remember crying out to my dad, above the screech of the brakes of the Muni as it made its turn on to Columbus and slowing for the steep decline at the top of the corner. I close my eyes with great pause and review the panoramic scenes of outside before walking back inside. I remembered why I had cried out.

The drinking place had a sparse clientele that day. That was not at all typical. I will return later on in my life and I get to know the place. But back then I made my way in and scan the over-decorated walls and ceiling of the first floor, covered from top to bottom with aging black and white photographs of famous people gathering in San Francisco during the height of the great Beat period. I am grateful as I pass through the double swinging doors of the bar's entrance, loving the fact that such a place existed during a favorite time in my young life. I recall each successive visit without over-scrutinizing the more lurid details of the drunks that sat at the bar for generations; knowledgeable that each one of these patrons that turns toward the front when I walk in will monitor my every step and the steps of each new entrant that enters after me. For some reason they thought it was perfectly reasonable for a child to wonder in off of the streets.

I returned their half amused stares with without secrecy. It is a telling means of conveying that I am not afraid of them; perhaps it is a local who has returned after a long break and see me who will be shock. He will pan to the right, and then back towards the center, seeing that old wooden stair case that leads to the quite serenity of the upper level. He will be looking deliberately through the regulars who have now lost interest in me and go back to their own introspections. Only he follows me upstairs.

After a ponderous moment on the next level I continue upstairs in bowed silence and savor the recollection of each ascending step that brings me just below eye level to every framed photograph that I passed by. Furthermore I am recalling where my dad must have been during the same instance in place and time. My hands find a firm holding on the railings and I take the time to read each knot and carved surface disturbance as though reading in Braille as I continue my slow ascent to the final stair summit; three-quarters aloft the atmosphere is less fresh, but not stale.

My breathing is deep. I inhale and then exhale; stubborn steps do not give way to my heightened and emotionally labored steps. Right now I can hear the people below, and I can smell the afternoon's stale air even after leaving that first level.

Now I am at the top of the stairs, turning right into to the long drinking chamber. The room is flooded via the many window panes that exist on the east side of the room. I is pleasantly surprised to find a few patrons sitting alone at a table on the second floor, huddling over half empty pints of stout; looking out; unlabored in their breathing and resembling another photograph from another moment in time. One is gazing through a wooden-framed window and out towards the large black silhouette painting of Jack Kerouac which dominates the side of a neighboring building across the alleyway named after the same famous author. I imagine that that Kerouac answers each and every stare. It is a comforting notion—not being alone. Perhaps one of these patrons is another silhouette occupying another obscure alleyway somewhere on the other side of San Francisco. I let my imagination run wild.

I sense that I occupied that same station of fate; another face of popular folklore; another portrait on numerous occasions; similarly lost in his own fixed stare. Everyone has a camera nowadays. I wish that I could be another author on that long list of famous faces passing through famous San Franciscan landmarks past in semi-permanent acrylic on stucco walls, snapped and transmitted digitally to the next virtual location. I take in one patron's stare in gratitude for the many pleasant years that passed became I shot him a genuine smile; pushing all of his own troubles out in his mind for a brief instant; begging him to take time to revisit his extended tales of a youthful lifetime lost in thought; time spent pondering San Francisco of another era gone by.

In the meantime I have a specific image in mind, already meaningful; whose framed intelligence reflected in a photograph secured that most precious gift of authenticity. My movement had captured the attention of another famous San Franciscan who certainly enjoyed that thoughtful ability of childlike observation sans the rigidness of bias which might deny such a moment in time to be committed to pages someone else's photo archives.

The owner of City Lights Book store approaches me and makes an introduction. The Book Store is neighbor to this bar. It is separated by an alley named after one of its most famous authors. I will earn his interest that day. Thoughtful artisans are taxed with the certainty and faithfulness of memory. Studying this patron of grand books hunched over his dark creamy beer lead me back to the source of the cool breeze that sweeps in through the open windows of Vesuvio's, onto and across the second floor. The breeze waifs in and it echoes the language of this coastal city; the chatter of this west coast region. I think that I know how it does this. Consequently I am able to think of it in terms an eloquently developed and streaming dialog not limited to sight, but also to include smell and touch and certainly taste. This was not an abstraction of my early life. It is my total recall, the way I want to remember it now.

If this breeze should make its way across the Pacific, it will prove that it is a testament to the devoted immigrants from the east coast region of China that make their way here and live in almost instant harmony with persons of local birthright. We are an instant melting pot because we share the same cool wind currents across one of the largest oceans; we feel its touch, smell the uncanny scent, and taste it like a lavish feast. Chinatown is only two blocks away. I knew that then and I definitely sense that now.

I am in the middle of reliving these streams of incited senses through the windows of one of the more recognized establishments on Columbus Street, leaning in closely to the wall and seeking out the details of a fine photograph on the wall, across the small wooden tabletop he leans on. The photograph is of two men sitting at the same table; perhaps a decade earlier; speaking louder to each other than the expected whisper given their close proximity to each other. Their conversation must have lasted over the remaining overcast afternoon. The two men are sitting with their backs against the room's western wall, under a black and white photo-montage depicting the first public reading of the poem Howl on the west coast. The photos are hung at eye level when seated and have dark yet faded framing and smoky glass. It is like looking into the cross-mirrored reflections at a barbershop. The owner of the Book Store is in the same picture frame.

The fabrication and placement of the photo series seems amateur yet entirely appropriate given the odd distribution on the second floor of this drinking establishment. There are many other photographs over the single entranceway and the eight, wooden-framed windows that dominate one wall to the side and to the front of the room. The smoky glass of the photographs is a result of both natural aging and film of decades of an establishment once dominated by cigarette and cigar smokers, and at the time something called Mary-Jane. I did not know her then, but I heard her name on some other occasion that currently slips my mind. The Beats knew her well.

The cross current conversation depicted by the photos inside the photos reminded me that I had narrowly missed being a beat artist by two stories and perhaps by one quarter generation. My time was spent part time in San Francisco and the other part south in suburbia, and was as colorful as the differing hand stamped and framed artwork on that wall in North Beach. I could equate in the smallest details, the artwork, the short stories and the poetry, the animated way in which they spoke, and even the clothing they wore, with the long habits of the locals who were still caught in the vortex of that era. It was strange, but in a way it was warming in this cold yet delightful City by the Bay: faded blue jeans and well worn sweatshirts or black t-shirts adorn all.

The furniture the patron sits in is old and dark wood, and was quite heavy, and of course it was the same across the rest of the second floor tables. On either side of the table the soloed patrons clunked down their pints of dark stout, looking out of the large framed window allowing them to oversee the activity of the locals which frequented this section of the city, and the tourists who still showed up in competing fascination. I wondered what would happen next. This man asks me to join him. But I am too busy looking out one of the windows at the far end and ignore his invitation.

A San Francisco Muni bus outside has just screeched its way around the corner and onto Columbus Street. Two Chinese women are standing at the bus stop just below the large windows and they are screaming at each other. To a local it is considered a normal conversation; one hundred precious trifles of cultural exchanges on a corner that borders Southern Italy with Eastern China and of course Hong Kong; flowered, thoughtful dialects brought into bloom by the eclectic nature of this truly fashionable San Francisco neighborhood. It was the only next imaginable world for me to be inspired by.

On each of its four corners are figures from small towns anywhere: shepherds in blue jeans and black tee shirts, marionettes with delicate bouquets of French bread, and Chinese with bundled take-out in their hands; a city surrounds them like a perfectly accurate platinum timepiece, inlaid with the dialects of one hundred points of emigration from around the globe, and simultaneously crossing into one very busy intersection. The cold and gray sky somehow sparkles brilliantly and the Bay off in the distance mirrors the sky. I found myself in the perfect location looking out and down; it was all framed between the Bay Bridge and the Golden Gate; two magnificent structures built as an exotic byproduct of the cultures that all at once built the Bay Area and simultaneously occupied it cold, orderly, and where all things were put into place as if anything else other than instant occupation were an option; of the gay and the lavishness of a happy homestead that was always a sweet place to come back to every time I wanted instant recall.

In the next moment several people are weeping that they can no longer reside here and the pain is sweeping when they leave. Many often do not come back. But they retain their photographs of the moment in time where they stood precisely at that time. A third man has just joined us upstairs and sits down at another table, and he is one of the dominant jazz players on the West coast. At least two of us recognize him—the patron and me. This is known enough to explain the amazing wardrobe he is wearing in the middle of this late afternoon. It immediately reflects his rank or station in the art world; this rich music haven; having pushed him forward in the avant-garde world of improvisational jazz, remains uncontested. He is after all the current revolution of jazz in San Francisco.

He was quickly acknowledged as he makes his way in to the top floor of the bar and sits across at his table as an equal. He sits alone and feels his company. He is as obliged to acknowledge us as we are to him. He is after all, one of us, and one of our predecessors. He does not seem to care that he is in the company of a child.

I stare back and have no idea what he has been through. It's like he dropped into this sparse crowd. I might have heard later that he got married, or that he returning from an equally important city, or from abroad. But now he is back here, and I indicate a youthful appreciation with less than innocent nod. I am here with Beat poets and Jazz greats. I never have hesitation when someone asks me who my earliest influences were. Soon there will be live music playing across the bar.

## We are the City's Polite Listeners

All three of us were bending forward on our respective table tops in earnest, with the attitude of polite listeners, and many talkers. We took turns providing the lurid details which were pressing us at the time to each other with the fraternal tenderness that was warranted of family members, occasionally noting our conceited discern, at the hand of anyone who landed in the middle of our makeshift neighborhood.

Our neighborhood in the day was not necessarily our neighborhood in the night. Society declares that we may be extended family at all times and under all circumstances. It does this to maintain order to distinguish us by age in rank. It was getting dark outside and I knew my dad would be wondering outside to this place, and places like it, throughout the early night looking for me.

I thought of this while leaning into the tabletop, watching the patron hunched over the last third of his dark stout and signaling the wait staff for another round—individual orders were made for the three of us—now that we were breathing slowly and deeply to suppress our joys and our sorrows, and now keenly watching another table being occupied by a Japanese tourist trio, wondering who I belonged to. They have arrived and are huddled in guarded conversation and looking at each other another kind of familiar support. Did I need rescue or was I a fixture at this place prone to surprises.

These newcomers are also dressed in jeans and black tee shirts with international appeal. We live a place where strangers from other spheres can adapt instantaneously to this West coast environment, and we can relate to the nuances of their huddled conversations respective of their chosen dialect, preserved on the spot, no contempt for each other and our own respective social union and dress codes. A quick glance at their faces will explain their particular situation as they begin to quaff beers that they have recently ordered. I will assume at this point that they are also talking in depth about jazz and the other arts. This environment demands this attention to code: recognize all of our artists.

We all heard the word jazz. It is the only word in their conversation that we have been able to recognize—so they are very engaged and smiling as they are caught peeking at us as well. They were speaking of jazz, in Japanese, while we were eavesdropping in English.

The jazz man gets up and greets another musician. He is setting up a horn and a microphone. In the corner stands a large double bass; I see the cigarette thoughtfully placed on one side of his round head. He thought about this object, fetching it and lighting it in front of all the others. He did not want to think about other persons at the other end of the second floor in hushed conversation and pointing in his direction. It is narrow minded to devote this much time thinking about the negatives of the intrusiveness of less than guarded conversation over an international crossroads, especially when it has spawned a new form of conversational etiquette—so sustained by a sense of obligation that one cannot go anywhere void of its incessant use of the words beatnik or jazz.

This reading was obvious in the faces of the Japanese group that evening in the bar. They were spending most of their time staring at each other blankly, and then quite expectedly, they turned energetically at the next incoming patron's conversation that each took in turn, and then in unison—passed as many times between the group—as they took turns talking past the entering faces, unwise and unguarded they yelled explicit comments into the night air.

I might have been aroused by their imaginative flair ups, expressions and accompanying body language. They had this animated and childish relationship with their each other. It was not dangerous at the distance that I maintained my vigilance, but at the same time I might have preferred a less rigorous and more conforming behavior in a place that ushered in a new era of poetry and mad literature into the ever changing jazz compositions of North Beach in San Francisco.

Are ringtones in the context of moderately crowded taverns the means of communicating one's favorite type of music, or are they the result of blander commerce? I looked at the table across from my adopted hosts in lost innocence. Was I a meaningful depiction for the next generation of tourists visiting San Francisco? Could they not even see the hoards of Chinese milling around down below intersecting with the Italians, Irish, Africans, and other similarly lost children of the future? Now I wanted to know who maintains the database of their ancestors who had to or were asked to flee the homeland and survive in this New World.

Everyone on the second floor has moved on to their third or fourth round of stout and the conversation became louder and much more animated; blended as well as the other conversations entering into the room. It was now English, Japanese, as well as hipster street talk; as if spoken in one blended run-on sentence it became harder to distinguish one from the other. The tender confidences at each table were no longer in whispers, or of a few short sentences exchanged as if we were alone for another moment in space and time. The room contained more ideas than the words themselves expressed in as many languages. I often shot a glance at another's table, without concealing this from other equally attentive stares—by which I conveyed to each other all of the emotions that are reaching pint after pint; like the poems of the melancholy silhouette that stares back at us through those windows, from across that alleyway.

Did everyone here know the life he or she roamed? The sight of those now borderless tables, the fragrance of strong beer, a turn in the pages of night life off Broadway and onto Columbus Street; bordering the Chinese district and the adjoining Italian district, arm in arm—so this was what is referred to as the shared poems of life.

Listening to the finishing of the next sentence ahead of the other became a source of enjoyment. This was the social circle of artisans: opening collective resources, stimulating collective minds, no darkness in ideas; not those they were ever made up of unique ideas, not tendered by cultural guardrails. These conversations turned on the point of differences which distinguished artists from the petty dispositions of being overly conformed to the rigors of some other type of life—that home bound body that had not come out tonight.

No one appeared sullen as the decibel level doubles again. We all have extinguished any possible differences—so we are therefore not distinct from each other. I however am in the comfort of the nest—a crow's nest. They protect me like one of their own.

I get up and head slowly across the crowded room toward the bathroom. Everyone seems to notice but not care. As I entered the bathroom I had heard the frenzy of the patrons that occupied the second floor disappear behind the heavy wooden door. I peed and came to reflect on the international personages of the bar through the silent musing of graffiti written above the urinal on the wall. I thought about the authors with their gleaming eyes and their expressive faces and varied languages as they wrote these uncontroversial pros on the walls of the bathroom. It was an experience, but sadly enough it breaks no new ground—haven read this on the bathroom walls of my school.

My hands were not the kind to be held in bondage, as exclaimed in one graffiti passage. I would offer no insightful retort even though someone thoughtfully leaves crayons behind. Life was not in compromise. If I had pen and a notebook then I might have jotted that down.

I was glad to have understood this distinction as I finished peeing. With the instinct of protecting a great prize I zipped up carefully, against the always pervading backdrop of this un-cloistered place and the few who passed inward as I was finishing. I quickly washed up and returned back out through the same set of doors, and back out to the assembled noise of the second floor. It would seem that I will no longer turn heads. I am a regular now.

As I walked back I passed two marines in uniform and was certain I could guess their next life's destination. They listened and pretended not to be surprised by my age. I instantly developed a liking to them and them to me.

My presence has permeated its way through the arts passionate strokes, chisels, lyrics and stanzas fly their flight to make the true nature and manner of conflict known across modern society. When artisans had executed some great work in a manner that their society declared to the point—that bulls eye—embrace each other in ecstasy and believe ourselves to be the most eloquent conveyors of right versus wrong. The news media used to ply this role in the theatre of life, but they have given up control in the name of entertainment and the bottom line.

These several Marines are just passing through and will no doubt recast tonight as one of their favorite rites of passage as I will do as well. We will all recant that night in unison—we are brothers.

I continued to walk slowly back to my reserved chair. This is such a strange tradition, not to be caught looking while hoping to be caught looking back. I make it back to my table, surviving the consequences of being caught looking back into my dad's eyes.

He is standing over me now. I cannot tell if he is pleased to see me here. Tonight is a festival. To the casual onlooker he and I were at the same table, but I knew that we were worlds apart. On evenings like this, I left him alone not out of cold timidity but rather out of fear that I might have to explain a momentary sense of uneven handedness. I didn't mean to run away, but rather to stay here now. I meant to give introductions but my patron was gone. The jazz men were nowhere in sight. I had been left in the company of strangers.

Did you see the Marines that just walked by? I had relied on my eyes and body posture to ask my dad to look at all of them while they drank beer and shifted their positions to take it all in.

Called to duty, I suppose, my dad spoke with his eyes alone. He will continue to serve as a carrying parent, but now how willingly. I was in his line of fire alone. He assumed the other two men I had been seated with, given his judgment of their approximate years of age, were completely out of line.  He reminds me that his own father came to him and escorted him outside another bar with equal exuberance.  Under the supervision of a proud and knowing parent I did surrender and acknowledged a pledge that he had the right to remove me from my birthright.  It too was a rite of passage between fathers and sons.

Somehow I knew that my dad would show restraint. These other men finished their beers approximately at the same time and made indications that they would soon be off, inclined toward a deeper set of circumstances and sentiments.  Perhaps they had children of their own  The interior of the second floor of Vesuvio's on Columbus Street in San Francisco was thrown into a different light as we passed others silently as we passed through the door and back onto the busy street.

What were those sounds outside on the sidewalk that I heard while pausing in front of the famous drinking establishment?  Was it a siren crying out excitedly or perhaps the screech of the brakes of a car full of young partiers making way onto Columbus, and slowing for the steep decline adjacent to the crowded corner?  I shut my eyes so that I can hear, smell and taste the panoramic views of the outside before walking toward Broadway and back to our car.  My dad and I vanish into the night.  There was this cumulative evidence that we were part of it—enough to go around.

## Howling Memories

What is it about those impossibly important things from our childhoods that we think were left behind?  I wonder now in my fifth decade what was so important about being young in the first place. Have I really changed all that much; was change the real goal after all? I am old as today is young.

I needed a break from my daily routine which somehow had slipped into part-time detective attempting to unravel the tale of Chinese immigrants over the past century. This is not what I had in mind when I say I wanted to reinvent myself. Notwithstanding all of the real noteworthy evolution that had stratified my lifeline, I began to look for those hints of what I was and what I had become. It was not so impossible a task when one focuses on the smaller, key notes.

The first key note of the world would have so grand an impact on my life; experience at the guiding hand of my dad. There were so many times he had guided me through the unique neighborhoods of San Francisco; walking on with keener interest as we turned the next corner to witness something else happening that would be bigger than the last. A next corner is rounded with a smaller, impressionable hand in the grasp of this bigger than life man in the center of North Beach. We had started out on Market Street and then walked on. It was an intermediate neighborhood for our walk on through to Fisherman's Warf—the destination. Did we even get there that day? I remember so.

This walk took place in the start of the sixties as we rounded into a steady stream of cafes, bookstores, music shops and open front eateries crowded with the differentiating look of those who flocked to the next big reading by one of the Beats of what we now call 'that era'. What a rousing surprise for my open mind and the older man who was trying to open his own as a means of bridging an already expanding generational gap.

I was as young as I felt sitting in the front of those crowds of mostly young adults and listening to the series of poets screaming at us. This was as far a departure from both school and church as I thought I would ever experience in my (oh) so younger years. But it was an important event even for my dad. We had come to bear witness to that era already in transition.

There was a wild eyed guy with long stringy hair and an even wilder face full of hair committing another free reading of his book length poem called Howl. I sit as wide eyed as the screamer taunted the crowd and they in turn chant back key words as though they were echoed across the Grand Canyon. This is now referred to as epic. This was such a mad place but in the end everyone just looks so satisfied. I stand mystified and searched the much taller crowd for my dad. There he is; I do see him. I want to recant what I had just heard; that was what I had first encountered. He was standing in an opposite corner and was engaged in a conversation with a police officer. When I broke through the crowd I thought about what I had listened to—a first line of conversation—it sounded so foreign to what they were teaching us in school. But I liked what I had heard. And when I reached my dad he was saying goodbye to the policeman as though they were long time friends. The policeman bent over and shook my hand and said it was very nice to meet me. He and another man in blue then arrested some fellow in the crowd (but not one of the poets). This was the start of a very mixed day.

We continued our walk toward Fisherman's Warf. It was there that we settled in and ate cracked crab, a loaf of sourdough bread; dad with a beer and I sipped iced tea and we talked mostly about what I had just witnessed.

Five decades later I am in the basement of an independent bookstore, taking a break from my research and planning with regard to that large database and I am listening in to the conversation of a small group of people who appear to be lifelong friends.

There was a pause in the conversation. They continue within earshot. One asks the group: When were the Beats? I look down at my faded blue jeans and sneak a peek at the old sweatshirt I am wearing in the reflection of a store window. My hair is slightly longer than the others around me and my head of hair is still mostly full. It dawns on me now that I can answer the question about the era of the Beats today, because I was a witness during that era on the San Francisco Bay. I know who they were, I whisper toward the small group who wanted to know. But then they never turned around and acknowledged my answer.

But they are right to walk away. I think that I had done something so extravagant—a sort of bragging right. Not so, at least not so much as a small child that is led across the expanse of the Pacific Ocean, hand and hand with a brother that had little choice in doing so.

# Chapter Nineteen

## *The Need to Escape*

JULIA CALLS ME TODAY and knocks me right out of a self induced funk. No, nothing happened and that is the whole point. I could not even begin to explain what having this project transition so fast did to my sense of wellbeing. The funding appeared in a special account with little strings attached. The modern and palatial estate was only on the market for twenty days before a suitable offer was made. I mistakenly thought that we had more time.

"Look, I just dropped Yuecan off at her new place. She really seems happy to have this part of her life behind her. I cannot press her on a more direct approach to the data. She might start to get suspicious."

My heart rate had increased slightly as our conversation started to get more animated. Her voice was just shy of a shrill and I thought for a moment that she wanted to back out gracefully. I did not want to go at this alone and I feel that I am starting to like this woman in another way.

"I've had time tables move up before, Julia. This is not so insurmountable a task. It does mean that we have to move fast and nature is on our side."

I began to lay out what I had already laid out as a feasible plan. The tide table would play a role. They always do this far north in the Sound in mid winter. I probably mentioned the fact that the winter water conditions in this region were ideal for diving. But she was still hesitant. Her only push back was a dread of the impending cold plunge.

"This is coming from a woman who does a group splash and swim in Lake Padden each winter. Come on, you do it in swim suits. We will be in complete wet suits on the other hand. Is this your biggest worry?"

I looked at the clock on the wall. I was thinking about a test run so that she could be convinced that my words were not some cleaver joke. I made the suggestion.

"I thought you were picking someone up at the airport." Her protests continued but were weakening all the same. I could hear this in her voice.

By the time we hit Cove Road the sun was already just above the horizon and a beautiful kind of winter glow settled behind Lummi and Orcas Islands. Their collective mass looked like one continuing silhouette of a dancer stretched to the maximum and holding this pose. The air was quite still and the surface of the water gleamed in a close to a mirrored finish at this end of a slack tide. The only noise was the crunch of the belly of my hollow kayak as I pushed it over the last several feet of shoreline gravel and into the water. It slips through the floating kelp without much effort and the tall eel grasses are undulating under my booted feet. We are both entering this place dressed in at least seven millimeters of close to zero pore material. But the cold seeps in as expected.

"Oh fuck, it is quite cold. You lied to me." Julia shouts this but is laughing all the same. She steps forward and wastes no time straddling the kayak and swinging in.

I am taking my time and push both of them out into deeper water. It has already passed both knees and I feel the slight pressure around my legs as I mount as well—pulling me on board with a steadiness that is paramount—I do not capsize the craft until we reach our destination.

Paddling as the sun sets is my favorite sport. There is this sense of the surreal and that something surprising lurks around the next bend that I think that I paddle steadfastness that is lacking during the day. I can already see the moon lifting up above the mountains behind us as we begin our turn and make way parallel to the coast. Mount Baker is almost a complete silhouette if it were not for the glistening snow covered glaciers that make it a beacon of light in the night sky. One cannot get lost off of this shore with the easily distinguishable shapes of the San Juan Islands to the west and Baker to the east. Soon I will be able to make out the slight glow made by artificial lights on Vancouver Island, the furthest monument out toward the ocean.

"Look at those snow caps on the Olympic Peninsula."

Her steadied point glides my eyes in the dark to the south west of our position. It seems strange that we are paddling in this large body of sea water, yet we are still one hundred miles away from the Pacific Coast. The distance seems impossible riding this low in the water, dipping far below the real horizon.

"If you could be anywhere else on the earth right now, where would it be?"

Julia seems to have settled in. Her strokes are matching mine. We have a rhythm as the flat and curved paddle blades cut through the water.

"I suppose it would be hiking at night in the desert. I am quite sure it would be just as cold." I regret the last part of my answer.

"Oh, so now you admit that it is bloody cold." She twists her body around because she wants to see my face.

"Yes, I admit the air is cold, but when we get into the water you will be amazed how well you warm up."

"Liar," she cuts herself short but she is laughing. Our synchronous paddling resumes.

It is some time later that we pull into a familiar looking cove. The landscape up here is mostly wind and water carved and the faces of the cliffs are distinguishable yet are constantly changing. If you witness a face carved in one year, it will probably have morphed into something else following the next four seasons. Tonight it is relatively calm. When it gets rough the wind whipped waves and strong currents and tides strip this coastline of a layer of sandstone each year. And the color gradations caused by this successively rough erosion is as magnificent as any around the globe.

"In reality though, I do not want to be any place else."

The conversation has been picked up again. We have our fill of beauty and cherished it for a while in complete silence and near darkness. We are in the cove, surrounded by tall cliffs, and our lifeline of illumination is not due over head for at least another hour.

"Would you like to try entering in complete darkness?"

I want to go in but I do want her to enter first. There is little else I can suggest given her reluctance to answer me directly.

"If this is just a test run, why did you bring all of that equipment?" She answers stubbornly. She wants this to be all about me.

"Well I thought we could get a little bit of work done. It's just a pigtail extension. No big deal." I had raised the long length just to emphasize the point.

There is another long pause. Julia is slowly turning in the kayak and extends both of her legs over the side while I steady the thirty eight inch wide vessel. There is a look of feigned shock on her face.

"Oh man it is cold at first. Now my legs are kind of used to it. I'm going in. Make ready with the lanterns, captain."

Julia has slipped into the waters. She dips under and then splashes to the surface again. The snorkel is cleared and she pushes it out of her mouth.

"Ok, you were right, again. This is not as bad as I thought it would be. Are you coming in?"

There were some last minute adjustments to be made ready before I splashed over the side. As I entered the water I un-looped the long leash, swam toward the cliffs and then lashed it to an outcropping of tall and slender boulders. The other end is attached to the kayak of course. With a second line I pay out a moderate load until it reaches the bottom. This line is attached to the kayak as well. Between the two anchoring we should find my boat still on the surface and tucked away inside of this cove when we resurface. At least that is the plan.

After a final equipment check I signal Julia that it is time to descend to the bottom. We are in around twelve to fifteen feet of water now, but we will slope another five to seven feet below until we reach the face of the rock and the conduit covered coax extending out into the sea. Visibility right now is in inches.

I swam with a mighty burst of energy and beat Julia down to the floor of the sea. The bottom is the scene of an ongoing natural history of erosion and there is a thick layer of gritty sandstone blanketing as far as I can see. I can make out the larger rocks poking out from the sand and they are an interesting contrast to the grain brown and are several start shades of purple. The areas that are not worn bare from the undulating surf show signs of algae and vegetative life for which a photosynthesis process keeps these undersea gardens flourishing. As opposed to areas in the South Sound which are oxygen depleted, the North Sound has an opposite scenario. Everything here is in abundance and is attached, crawling, skittering, swimming or just floating as do the jellyfish that are grazing on most of which is carried by the several underwater currents.

Most divers find the North Sound most attractive because of the more common critters which are features in this region. I am encouraged by the significant crab populations and see so many fish species that I have chosen to lose count. Although it is not our main goal here today, I would love to have some extra time to search for the Pacific octopus that are cave dwelling in the area. The carved sandstone is a perfect natural habitat. Although I would not see one on this dive I marveled at the very large sculpin that dart away if I get too close. Julia and I are using re-breathers so our output is not as noticeable by the more than abundant locals.

While Julia plays at a safe distance with a small harbor seal I attach a coax pigtail to the junction of a major trunk. The task is fairly easy on dry land but proved to be a tad more difficult at twenty-two feet down. I have made a bit of a mess of the job when I stir up the bottom and visibility drops from feet to inches in a record amount of time. The original cable layers need to provide good points of service is making the site almost far too easy to attach and link into without causing a signal short. There, it is attached and my meter never registers in the red. I am certain that I did not spike the line with the vampire tap. I had a good instructor—so I was an excellent student in return.

The problem with multitasking under the sea is that some order of task is bound to slip beyond notice. I have lost track of Julia when I am feeding the last of the tool back into the bag and back up to the kayak on the surface. As I ascended I was sure that she was in my direct line of sight. However, as I began my descent I could only see the tip of one of her flippers and it was flailing wildly.

Rushing to the scene is slower than normal. I am fighting a cross current. When I do reach her location I can see that she is breathing too rapidly. When I am on the scene I can see that one of her hands is in the mouth of an adult wolf eel. Their population in these waters is most noteworthy in terms of spread. The abundance of fish species I mentioned earlier sustains the population and they do get to big in these waters. They love to dwell in the sandstone caves that cover the bottom of the Sound and its multitude of reefs.

There is one truism which carries forth the majority of cases. If you stick your hand into a cave under here something will bite back. This location was no exception to this usually strictly adhered to rule. Julia was an experienced diver and snorkeler so I did not understand how she would have gotten herself into such a foolish predicament. I know I should be more sympathetic but this was killing valuable time in the water. I would assist her rather than look for an elusive species as per plan.

The wolf eel has a dangerously large head and a big mouth full of teeth which all but guarantee that it holds onto its prey. This one was three-quarters tucked away in its underwater den and there was no pulling it out. Getting her hand out of the jaws of this monster was even less likely. She was pulling more frantically and hyperventilating as a result. Panic has set in. Her free arm is braced into another grouping of rocks and both legs are kicking so hard that I am hit several times as I survey the scene.

Julia is gulping in and exhausting an excessive amount of oxygen. Her face is darker and bloating. There is only one measure I can deploy and ensure that I can get her breathing back under control before we even think of returning to the surface. Our biggest problem right now is no longer the eel but it is the danger of an underwater blackout. Her body is contorted. I must react fast.

With one continuous movement I unsheathed one of my dive knifes and lashed out across the back of the eel's head. I had cut only half way through on the second strike, and then severed the head on the third round. It finally let go of Julia's hand.

The head floated a few feet away due mostly to my final stroke and to a lesser degree the current. It stared back at us with two bugged eyes and an open gaping mouth. The rescue of Julia was only half over. I had to calm this woman down enough to get her to reflect on her surroundings. She calmed: a more normalized breathing routine, cognizance of my presence and her surroundings and of lesser peril. She let go of my arms and pushed a few feet away. A moment after floating almost in place she gave me the ok sign. I looked at my gages and then hers. It was time to surface.

When we were floating and taking in fresh air I had at least one hand on her at all times. She apologized too many times. Monitoring her breathing just below and then on the surface I was more certain that she would not experience anything close to a shallow water blackout. The cardinal lesions of the underwater world are learned over and over sometimes. She would not drown today, but she was certainly more aware of the consequences of her actions and the rookie mistakes we all make over time.

"Thank you so much. I knew the instant I extended my hand into the cave that it was a huge mistake. Fuck me; I can't believe I came so close."

"What were you after?" My breathing was good as it needed to be at the end of a rescue.

"Oh, you did not see what I was following? I came upon a small Pacific octopus—a juvenile—and spooked it under a ledge. I reached in because I thought it might cling onto my glove. Then that damn eel lashed out and bit down hard."

"Climb up onto that bolder. I want to inspect your hand."

Julia removed her glove and I could see the bite marks and punctures. Although she was wearing the most appropriate hand coverings for cold water diving, nothing would have protected her from the wolf's mighty bite. Her hand was bleeding.

"Put your glove back on. The good news is that the wounds are bleeding freely. I have isopropyl alcohol back in the truck. We can clean you up there."

I assisted Julia back into the kayak and helped her remove the extra gear, before I removed my own. Probably the greatest deterrence to moving around on top of this kayak is the weight belts we both wore. Once we shed these we were immediately comfortable and began to review what was accomplished. There was a modicum of success all around. It was a good dive sans the crushing of her right hand.

The second phase of the night sky was over us and the moon illuminated our position to anyone looking toward the mainland. The good news is that we would not be in stark contrast against the dark earth of the high cliff behind our current position. When I looked straight up all I could make out are expected—still unusual—stucco walls of the modern dwelling that housed the histories of numerous generations from across the vast ocean to the west. The view was somewhat amplified by the arc that the three-quarter moon was making across the sky, bleaching out the clusters of stairs straight above. I attempted to fixate our position by celestial means but was frustrated by the moon's glow. And now I was eyeing the food that Julia was pulling out of her bag with one hand because the other one would be throbbing painfully so.

There was a hint of discomfort in her facial expression and I knew well enough to leave this alone. The woman insisted in staying for a while longer, at least until we had eaten something before the paddle back. The spread included a block of cheese, strips of toasted nori, and a half loaf of rosemary baked bread. The chief components of the meal are doled out and we eat mostly in silence until I first hear the steadied drone of an outboard motor. It seems to be coming from the north and is operating at a wide arc away from our current position, kind of hidden against the tall cliffs of sandstone. We are not alarmed but we do shoot each other telling looks.

"You know, they seem to be operating without running lights." I say this casually enough between bits of bread and strips of dried seaweed. The night filled picnic is filling and quite good and I swallow mine down with chilled water before passing the bottle to my paddling mate.

"There is nothing on the bow or stern. I think this is very odd. I wonder if they are heading over to Lummi." Julia asks for my bag and fishes out the night scope.

On most moon lit nights in the area there is an abundance of waterside activity in warmer weather. However, I am reminded that this is a cold and very crisp winter night and the activity that has dropped south of our position. But then the come about.

"Julia, I think that we should start back to the cove. It looks as though we may intersect their path, or vice versa."

I am the first one to put into action and my initial strides with my double bladed paddle lurch us forward while Julia repacks all of our gear. At the very least if that other craft throws up a sufficient enough wake we will now be clear of the cliffs and submerged boulders. And if my calculations are correct it will come very close to our last position. There is a moment when I believe that I did in fact put an electronic ping onto the coax. I hope that I am wrong but this damn craft has changed its heading again and it is almost above where we had been diving fifteen minutes ago. Our dual paddling moves us silently and swiftly in a southern heading and fortunately a cloud has drifted in front of the moon, making visibility is a whole lot harder. Soon we are a blending of shadows over the sea. Our kayak barely makes a splash against the small incoming series of waves and we are easily riding over their insignificant crests.

The other craft has come to almost a full stop. They are no doubt just above our last location. All of a sudden two flood lamps wash over the sea and the upright walls of the sandstone cliffs. They are searching for something—most likely us. Using hand signals I tell Julia to steer us into an outcropping of boulders and we barely squeeze the thirty-eight inch beam of the vessel between the last two boulders. One moment later the floods illuminate where we have entered and disappeared beyond. It is chillingly close but we are well into the dark recesses of the rocky masses. We grow cold waiting it out in complete silence.

"Julia reaches out and whispers, "Can they see down to the pigtail?"

I am in pause. My heartbeat is racing faster and I am guarding my breathing until it is closer to normal.

"No, visibility is pretty bad tonight—at least below, that is."

This comes out barely in a whisper and causes her to lean in all the more closer. I can taste her breath and I can sense the heat of her body she is so close. In one moment there is another change. It is something I was not expecting. Her lips touch mine and there is no attempt to pulling away by either party. We are softly and quietly kissing.

My heart rate picks up where it left off. I know there are people out there lurking in the night and looking for something on the surface. But at the same time I am feeling like there is no immediate need to escape. Right now I am hovering in the dark recesses of another small cove and the smell of floating kelp beds and the sea air fill my nostrils and the lapping of the shallow waves is barely audible against the side of this hollow body kayak. The person who sits across from me looks straight ahead and the one thought I have is one of anxiety of rejection. I do not want one series of kissing to reshape this relationship in a negative way. Do I have regret? I am heading that way.

Fortuitous Event

# Chapter Twenty

## *A Critique of Surveillance*

SITTING IN MY HOME I was trying to put together a framework for what was happening. It would need an excellent choice for organizing what and who I wanted out of this series of events that just kept on cascading. I was also hopping that it would allow me to take one giant step backward so that I could visualize the entire picture forward, notwithstanding all of the emotional baggage that was layered through the whole thing.

First things first: I was finishing up the preparation of a pulled pork and Pico de Gallo mix and spreading it out as multiple layers on top of two thick slices of Tuscan bread. It would be toasted appropriately. The spread included a lather of spicy and tangy mustard, of course. The main course was to be washed down with an ample supply of blended chocolate milk and ripe bananas—a sort of shake to wake up my body and my spirit.

That thing—so what was that whole thing: What makes independent judgment possible? I needed fuel to give me the energy to garner an impossibly cleaner approach because this thing has been sliced and diced beyond recognition.

I had a need for purifying this thing and I knew that I was really close but I did need to take that one step back without casting myself off of a self induced cliff so to speak. Almost everything becomes organized in this manner sooner or later. It is like I have a giant conversation going on in my head: barreling down one straight and narrow path I can see some of the competitive advantages coming in at several angles—all at once—all of a sudden. There was a premise in there somewhere and I was working up an appetite to work it all out into the open. Perhaps there were several.

The first premise of this framework I wanted to clarify would include the notion that the use of data farms in worldwide commerce is increasing substantially. This was a given. The downfall of the more traditional means meant that for every attribute described, ten million permutations still resulted at a minimum. Data farming, especially the social kind was a gold mine so long as one had the patience to weed it all out using very specific Boolean Logic Descriptors. Non math majors need not apply. The follow up premise was that simplicity is still kink: who knew what then; understanding where to plug this in now. This premise is quite appealing obviously.

China's growth in output was viewable from many angles. To say that there seems to have been no spontaneous understanding then as now would be a falsehood. We all are witness to the monster growing additional legs, arms and heads in vivid detail, and we all know that China's greatest export continues to be people.

That was a pretty simple framework and I was certain that the picture I wanted to paint was more of a desire than a thing. There was this desire to find some profitable commodity that could be proposed to the international marketplace and thus promote the success and prosperity of the earliest Chinese settlers in the United States and most importantly their ever successive links (lineages). I was driven not so much to who controlled the data. It was clear that there were as many interested parties as there were taps into the undersea web of cables, just in this region. The motives which drove Zhao and Yuecan that begot this abundance of data were so well organized; like that of a patient gardener: the ideal is to simply grow and nurture the data, plant only that which would yield such a tremendous influence on the history of future commerce around and across the United States and its business counterparts.

See it was that simple. It just needed to be framed—a factor that must not be overlooked—one of the basic aims of when to focus your eyes inside of the framework once assembled. The basic aim if the approach works was to project the development of resources which would at the same time create a colossal demand for such a staple, feverishly growing the demand for the goods and services that would feed on this thing from everywhere else infinitum. There would be no foreseeable drain of the one high demand resource from inside China's shores, so long as outside of China could produce an inexhaustible supply of rare minerals in which to use.

But in the history of the running up of things up in business and commerce we would be looking for the likes of the embodiment of ITT, ATT and now Google. I was a single entity with access to a thing that was already no doubt going to go global. I had access to this thing from the high seas but I was certainly no multinational pirate. I simply had a tap, and so did the multitude of others. The question was who would understand its usefulness first.

Julia and I did not make the mistake of adding a tap to an already existing network. We knew what we were doing and the ripple it would cause. My background had prepared me well given the electronic spike our tap would place on that existing length of coax and it was always part of the plan. What we did not count on however was the (oh so) quick response.

That single boat had motored into our space of operation within an hour of our placing our tap. That meant that it was live from several directions at one to be able to triangulate our position. Yuecan had already moved into her condo and although Julia did have access to the house to finish up her own research, no one else was working on the inside.

While Julia explored the data mapping software she was also further enabled to look at the other recesses of the basement level. What she had brought to my attention earlier as several additional empty chambers, they turned out to be anything but. At least two of these rooms contained hoarded materials of past places explored but then rejected as possible homesteads. The neat and no longer growing pile produced some very exciting insights into the lives of this brother and sister, and their earlier attempts at settling down roots in a new land.

Like all explorers of the past we take strides and peaking under the layers of debris of discarded items thinking they will be insightful in themselves. But as it turns out the refuge is not in its constituent parts alone; it was the collective histories of what someone regarded as worthy enough to carry forward, yet left alone. And that provided the better storyline.

In one particular battered and disregarded box Julia found some astonishing pictures and a diary. The text of the hand written book would require translating if that were to be the desired end. In the interim the photographic montage was enough to carry all of the bitter transitions with it to a more understandable climax.

Yuecan is in one photograph that is noteworthy. She is sitting cross legged and turning almost toward the camera. However, looking at the details in a more astute manner reveals something quite different from the more casual first or even second glance. Yuecan is not seeing the camera at all. She is left looking at some faraway place and this moment of longing is witness by the study of her face and her body position, and more likely by accident by the photographer.

"Was she looking at a new landscape?" Julia reveals this with great anguish as a recent meal. We had stopped eating for a while because there was something that needed to be watched before said.

The direction of the gaze and the positioning of the body gave this one stilled shot a new beginning. This is a more honest critique of surveillance.

"It is not possible to live inside of that judgment that is expressed by the face in the photo. But can we still comprehend the desire it expresses." I was reaching— so perhaps too much for a glutton for more. But the image is that haunting.

Yuecan's mouth is closed and her very thin lips are pursed although I cannot say for sure this it was in anger. Her eyes are wide open and its intensive stare reflects not that which one was supposed to have given up. Her stare conveys what was brought forward. I wondered if Zhao was indeed the artist behind the can did he understand what he had just captured in Yuecan's tortured soul.

"Why do you think that her head was shaven?" Julia has asked the most pertinent question. "I have seen photos of women with cancer exhibiting the same intensity in their stares, but this is different. As far as I know Yuecan is perfectly healthy."

"My first impression was that it shows a hint of Yuecan's forced journey. Perhaps she was in between places to live and she was fatigued at the time. I don't know for sure, but that is my best guess. Why don't you ask her?

It was not to be an immediate challenge but I had hoped that by planting this thought Julia might be moved enough to ask her to translate some of the image and the book that went along with it. The photo had a hand written date on the back that corresponded with a calendar translation of 1962.

"I looked through the pages of the diary and attempted to match the dates. There is a mention of Mendocino, California—written out in English. You know it is interesting that she writes out English words to identify a place, but all of the details leading up and away from the place and time are in Chinese characters."

"I have seen that before."

272

"You have, when?"   Julia is handing me another photograph.

"Do you remember the old man I interviewed in Half Moon Bay?  Well his daughter once showed me a stack of hand painted scenes of China's wildlife.  Each one painted with very fine details, and on the back was all that was known about the species including habitat, what it eats, how it mates and so on.  The details were all in Chinese script except one or two words that were in English Characters."

"That seems strange.  Why would he do that?"   Julia was sorting through another half dozen photographs, many of which we in black and white.

"It is in the power of observation.  It is what he wanted to teach me.  His daughter pointed out that the English texts were added in after he had met me.  The ink, strokes and hues were all but perfectly matched to the original scribes.  She laughed when she handed the stacks to me because he had made her promise not to reveal his secret."

"He wanted you to learn, I suppose."

"He did indeed.  I was a very astute pupil."  This made us both laugh and I was starting to let my mind wander when Julia handed me the next photograph.

It was of Zhao and he was sitting in a very tranquil pose looking out of an opened and large bay window at a wonderful garden.  It could have been in mid spring.  Zhao's face is mostly away from the camera so you cannot see his expression except for the furrowed lines around the outside edges of his eyes and across his temples. Interestingly enough his head is completely shaven as well. I look at the back of this photograph and translate the character set representing 1962.

"You know, I would be interested in having the diary translated by a friend of mine." I had reached for the book again but Julia snatches it from my grasp. She gives me a piercing look that did not require translating.

"I am shocked that you might do it. But then again she did leave all else behind with expressed purpose."

Julia is flipping through its pages and she stop and dwells on the importance of the content before flipping it to me. When I catch it I am not sure what I am supposed to do. I am touched my the careful calligraphy inscribed pages that just about spring to life with their exquisite strokes and carefully pointed or blocked ends. It is all done in black ink, but not from the same pen. Every once in a while the carefully written lines appear to be brush strokes.

"Look, how is it we are able to do data dumps of their ongoing genealogy study, yet we hesitate on this one book. It seems to me that it is all a sort of diary, just differing media."

I was not being smug in my assessment. If Yuecan did leave this part of her history behind it was intended to be found—the first premise. If found it was meant to be told—so the second was lining up. It was convincing enough for me, and it really did help when Julia shrugged her shoulders and nodded semi approval.

"Your logic is sound enough. I would not protest. But if you do not mind I will hint the same at our next meeting.

She and I are meeting at her place for tea later on in the week. I will not be blatant about the approach, but I will probe the 'what if's' if you know what I mean."

So this is the challenge we face when we critique the means of surveillance. These stacks of photos and hints of words that describe someone not so hidden past are honor bound by what? Should history not be told when revealed? Is it the right of the human species alone to leave their marks and not have them scrutinized by another generation? I did have mixed feeling. But then again, I love to piece together puzzles.

Two days later I received a phone call from my counterpart; we had a chance of opening up a new chapter on the life of this family duo. With all of the attention we gave to these photos we had not learned anything about the audience as subject unless in retrospect. Yuecan had used her tea with Julia to unveil the horrible truth about the expressions behind the face that pondered a life that can be so unforgiving. She had used this invitation as a means of another kind of discovery—the taking of her own life.

Yuecan was gone. How she did so did not match the void of life of my favorite old man in Half Moon Bay, but it echoed a statement made by my old man one half century ago. If you really think that you have gotten lost just seek out the next interesting face in the crowd. They will be able to tell you where you have arrived.

I will be look for that familiar face in Yuecan's journal. It is lying open on my couch, opened past the first pages that are neither yellowed nor crisp with age.

It was then that another vision of a prior quest came into my mind. Scanning the pages of another's life often has the most common of effects—that is to prompt you to scan through your own. It was not long ago that I wondered about Julia's own relationship with her husband, and the ensuing relationship with her friend on the island. It was a weird kind of connection to make in most instances. But what was it that she shared about this woman earlier? Ah, yes it is coming back to me now. Her house host was an Investigative Genealogist.

Funny how those pertinent little details slip the mind. This puzzle was growing interesting by the turn of the page. Yes, it was a hopeless transposition, but I made it all the same. This rediscovery of something already found was just getting interesting.

Michael O'Connor

# Composition of Change

Fortuitous Event

# Chapter Twenty-one

## *Across a Natural Bridge*

I SOMETIMES CLING to this repeated path so tightly that I know every fallen leaf and every exposed root before I place my next foot forward. The natural trail has ended just up ahead of me and I know that the only way over this creek will be a downed tree. The tree has been here for a very long time. All around me I can hear the echo of the swift waters rush forward because the last several days of rain have emptied into the hills and short valleys and have trickled into the earth crevasses now seeps into the only conduit that bisects this place. My movements are being studied by every creature within the sound of my footsteps or within direct line of sight. This is the challenge we face when we are critiqued—so the most intimate means of surveillance is a natural one.

These stacks of photos and hints of words that are in my lap describe someone's not so hidden past. Am I honor bound by what I read, I handled them so freely. I re-ask myself when history should be revealed in its entirety— or should it be revealed at all? Is it the right of the human species to leave their marks in a society and not have them scrutinized by another generation, let alone by me? I might just be so wrong; exploring these private murmurings not for enjoyment as much as for gaining a necessary perspective as to what to do next. I have opened this private journal and the words lay open and are thus translated and summarized below.

## Yuecan's Fragmented Journey

I can see my brother far off in the distance and he is coming back down off of the mountain and he is hunched over with the weight of both of us. This place where I am standing seems so empty to me; it is like looking out of a window and seeing nothing. I want to go up this hill and greet my brother but I cannot because he has warned me to stay inside but it is cold in here and I want to feel the warmth of the sun on my face. It is a golden ball in the sky; it is brighter than I can remember than in my past and I see that there are no shadows on the ground under its intensity. I am frightened because I used to feel that the shadows on the ground reached out to me. They were soft and perhaps colder but they embraced the thoughts that were in my head and I can remember when they made me feel glad that I had something to share my day with; these things that danced slowly across every living hour in my village.

There are no shadows in this hot place but I do not think that I should be unhappy. If I were not here with my brother now I could not do everything I would be permitted to do. I will pretend that I can do everything the same as back in my village, but it will be different now because I will not have to ask anyone's permission.

I want to sit down in this chair and I do not care that it is too big. I will call this my long chair from hereafter and I will learn to rely on it when I am tired from looking for the shadows. I must rest here inside until my brother has returned with news of what he can see from the top of the mountain. He will see if there is any water and if any water can be made to flow down to this place so that we may start our farm together. Look at him now: so hunched over he cannot bare himself to not stop looking at every bush or tree to inspect its leaves and branches. I will hear about his discoveries in so much detail when he returns to this place that we are now supposed to call our house. The walls of this place will protect us from the hot sun outside and I am quite certain that the small table in the corner will be large enough for me to make our food and then write in the cool and late of the day. But right now it is so hot even inside of this place; I am certain that I may get used to it if I try.

I can reach my hands outside of the window and I can feel that the air is so dry here. There are no forests to hide under except for the tall pines that are so far away that I cannot even smell the sap that they ooze sown their branches and drip to the ground covering everything with a sticky clear paste. My brother has brought me a small pine the other day harvested from the top of another hill. It is in a barrel on the other side of the house and he promises to put it into the ground some day this week so that we can watch it grow and eventually provide some shade for this house. I will welcome it resulting shade and I will sit under its branches and enjoy its long shadows someday.

This house has only one room. It is quite adequate for two people who are used to living in a place so much smaller than this one. I was horrified when I was first entering in through the door because I was not used to the sights and smells of a house that stood so empty for so long. I cannot force myself to write down what this place made me feel like as the first month passed so slowly; it was not a household yet in my heart. But now every wall has passed through our hands and has been cleaned and made to look presentable. I think about my mother and all of the time she must have spent doing the same thing and never complaining. She had been asked to move into another place and never see or hear from her mother and father again. But she made that place her home and I will do the same here. That is what she passed on to me even though I ended up have so different a life than her own. But what she did pass on to me: understands what we must do to bring honor to our lives, and that we must live within the limits of modesty. She never understands why I must have needed to go beyond that; womanliness also meant that I could pursue something beyond what was simply offered. I had wanted what I could demand, not what someone else would limit me to have. When I made it into the university it brought tears to her eyes. But then it brought tears to my own because I relished what would come with the crush of ushering a new chapter of my life. It was in my hands and I could feel its weight. I wanted it; with each stroke of this pen I cherish it now.

We now have water flowing to this place. My brother and I have dug until our fingers bleed and the first trickles of the cool wet were blushed with our sweat and salty tears. I do not have time for sadness and longing for my old home now that the months have passed by. I know that I am feeling something new in my heart and I think it is because everything is not so different. I can take in great breaths and let it out; now it feels no different—so this must be done in my daily tasks because it is what we are surviving on. I sense my brother and I have been handed a key to a new kingdom. We will not wait for someone else to provide for our means to live day after day because we have been shown that we can do these tasks ourselves. This is not an empty valley. There are many other families who have made their way here and they keep to themselves and are quite busy. I come to my brother's side when someone visits us even when I recognize their faces. And although we do not have a lot to share we will always offer something so that they do not go away empty handed. Our parents had always done the same.

The one great consolation of our living in this place is watching it grow into something else. The once barren planes and soft and lofty hills are showing signs of a new life. They are covered with things that did not used to grow here or even over the next hill. This valley has become so fertile that we believe that any seed we put into the ground will grow an abundant crop that will swell at least twice each year. I no longer feel that it is hot and my nostrils are full of the sweet and pungent smells of food that I never dreams of harvesting or eating. But that is what we have come to expect as we watch our shelves fill with an abundance of goods that we no longer have to guess what we might have left behind. There are tens of new foods that we eat and cloths that we ware that are no longer foreign to us. This is the one great consolation of being here now is that the swelling of our daily hearts are filled with what we recognize. I have made this procession on my own and my brother has done so likewise.

We share one bed in this one room house. There is a silk cover across the two windows that let the ample sun in each day and there is richness in the folds of the bed coverings. Although many of our things were painted in red lacquer in the past they are now washed in mush thinner paint and in colors that represent what we see outdoors: yellows and browns, with hints of purple and green, an a front door that was painted blue because we are able to survive due to the water that flows to this valley at last.

I have a table that I can set with cups and platters that have new value to me. There are household utensils that we labored with initially but now have under our command. I am still enjoying the same abundance of vegetables that I had in the past be these are the tastes of our present and of our future. Even the baskets that we use to transport them into the many small towns that have come alive each new season are different. The smells of the weaves carry forward the smells of the earth that I let flow through my fingers, and let stain my clothing; I say with all my heart this is my home and I do not have to look back over the last ridge to remember what my past was. Every new day is a next volume of the collective history of my brother and me and the thousands of others who came from just as far away places. Enter our new home and we are secretly chanting the familiar songs we learned when we were both children. I find this welcoming and I do not dwell on what has to remain my past.

My chanting is of the future and I do so sitting in a new chair that I have assembled myself from the branches I gathered, shaved and smoothed away all glaring blemishes to support me now. My breath is no longer any different than my closest neighbor who sits with me from time-to-time and offers her own details of an ongoing dream. Her hands shook mine when we first met and we exchanged our greeting in the language of this new land. She stood so bravely before me with her hair twined with flowers picked along the way and her thin and lacey fingers hold another bundle away from her body and toward mine. We are no longer frightened because we are both of these valleys and we share the food I have prepared without all of the bitterness and we discuss the next of the moons to come because it is at the end of another growing cycle. Both of our harvests were good.

I have made it clear to my brother that we do not have to obtain from living a richly full live. When he reminds me of all our ancestors predictions of an uncertain future I do not fall back or land on my knees and feel pain or sorrow that I have chosen to leave most of it behind. I still do honor our ancestors. But I can no longer remember their callings and when I raise my eyes and spread my arms I tell my brother to look all around him and tell me about what those fears will dispel. What should I remember about the honorable land of my past when I think about how beautiful our future will be if we choose to embrace it? At that moment I scan the tall pine tree that has grown so large in so short a period and how its thick branches cool this part of our house throughout even the hottest days. I remind him of how just last winter he had expressed his love of the sound of the rough bark of those branches as they danced across our roof in the wind and the rain clearing a path as they swept away debris under their laddered weight and provided a path for the raccoons which made that tree home. We have witnessed several generations of offspring that scamper across those laddered branches to explore and eat in abundance because we have tilled this land and made it our own.

At that moment I see that his eyes are wet and they are so beautiful and they are almond shape, just like the fruit of our groves outside. I wish to scream at him because I do not want to think of any other place as our home. I think to myself that I am so happy here, and that if he remains so strong he will see that nothing at all was lost or needs to be rebound. The next days are in sight and we can reach into them and pull out of it anything we desire except of our pasts.

The clouds above are like pearls when the sunlight pushes through them. I know that he sometimes prays to our ancestors when he looks up. I place a great deal of gratitude that he remembers what I cannot allow for myself. My own mother passed along a key in my mind that opened the door of my own choosing. She had a past place in her heart but did not mourn because her days were filled with duties that arise each morning early enough to push out all of those dreams that would otherwise haze what we have come to accept. It is a new cup of tea that we heat up and then sip out on our front porch in a place that we built with our own labors. This place now has water because we choose to bring it to our steps. It is our wishes and desires that created these present and future days where we can finally rest and take it all in. Each morning that I rise I must take into consideration that I am the lands consult and its steward. The vegetables that we eat and take to the markets and the prices that we ask and that are paid must be regarded carefully. It is not the past that we can bargain with but it is the present and the future and our next breath.

I tell my brother that I feel so much pride each morning when I open the door of this household. I am the key holder and I do not want this to be a rare experience. I want someone to share it with; someone who sees it the same way I do when it is heavy on my mind. Then I want to step out together past our garden terrace and out into our fields and arrange the harvest for the day, works against the terraced hills, rest sometimes and look out at the tops of the mountains and the skies beyond, which this land clings to. When I step through the front door I always look out over the length of the valley because I can watch the morning march across it and up to our doorstep. I wait for it to return each morning; because I say goodbye to it each night. I know that it will return if I just bring myself to step out of that door to embrace the brightness and the beautiful rows of orchards that it casts its light across until it blinds me because it has become so vast. It is my current happiness that I am clinging to and the only memories I have are of the previous days where I can still hear the rustle of the branches against the roof above me, so this happiness can be carried forward on the hillside down into town where I am greeted because I am recognized for all that I have done. Each face in every doorway shows me an expression of recognition as I pass by. And for as long as I am recognized I will love this place as my only home.

My brother, the hours have passed and you no longer look as though you are my twin. We are blossoms from the same tree but we each have a story to tell. This morning's duties are what distinguish us and I am a woman and I have to take care of this household as well. I stood alongside of you when we terraced those hills and I am reminded that I am still your sister as the long hours pass and finally we do see the shadows cross the length of the valley before us. I am as different the blue smoke curls from the chimneys in front and away from us as we review the labors of our day and watch the sun getting lower. I think of myself in the way that all women do when they are made comfortable.

There is a sense of inner peace, and this peace is wonderful but sometimes disquieting all the same. When I take the time to mend or embroider on the front porch, looking at the valley below I think about the other women and what they accomplished across the very same day: planting seeds and harvesting, looking up and across rooftops and following the antics of small animals that make our buildings their home. There are times when I watch them cross open territory against the dangers of being lost or hunted, and drag the rich mud and twigs back up and across the rooftop to make that nest for their own. When they build I can hear their chatters and thrilled whistles and I am witness to the insects they hold in their mouths or the almonds they rob from our trees. It is an ongoing procession and it can be followed while I sit in this chair or stand on this porch leaning against the balcony and looking straight up and waiting for the next sound I will hear.

Yesterday I saw that procession and it brings a clear remembrance that began the lifespan of this brother and sister. It is clear that this has been done in the many millions. But this does not bring me any satisfaction if I cannot experience the burden and the worn out feeling and not knowing whether I could survive the same as our mother did or the sense of her good fortune.

Yesterday I saw a friend riding by on a buckboard being pulled by two strong horses, being led by a man on another horse and I counted another child among their brood. She was carrying this bundle like a banner with all of her rank and virtues into the community to be witnessed and be counted. I sense that she felt beautiful on that wagon being pulled up a hillside in autumn with the wave of the grasses so golden and so strong against the breezes of the afternoon and the leaves that were already falling and drifting across that ground. That child was somehow sleeping against the racket of the day and the bouncing of that buckboard and in the face that more wind will come before they can reach the middle of town. And when I suddenly looked away and up to the sky I could see pairs of geese flying across the valley making ready for their brief stay.

My thoughts are not carried with tears and I am not saddened by the next bank of clouds that cover the outline of the moon. The geese are on their way and I feel their happiness and the endless days of flight they have before them before they can land in a large pond just on the other side of this hill. This sighting will become endless. But it makes me wonder—so what about me some day.

I have so much more I want to share with you, brother. I had so much more I wanted to say the other day. I was not unhappy and little else changes my mind that I have everything I could ever hope for: joy not sorrow: what else could I write down in words in my journal. Why else would I write at all? I must someday tell you, brother, that you might have a similar kind of day and long for some other woman to fill your hours with such unappreciated talk. I cannot let these thoughts govern my life and what I want to do next. We have this arrangement and I do not want to damage it so much that the repair cannot be done without separation. There are many other things that can draw upon my jealousies—so I pray that I will be able to maintain discretion because I do not want to disturb the harmony of our home.  My loneliness carries with it a greater beauty; I rely on my education to work it all out.  Why else would I take the time to write all of these words?

We have an arrangement, my brother and I:  it is one of great beauty I can see, a perfect song that I can hear, and an aroma that I can fill my head with until all the other things I am disturbed with fall away.  We have an arrangement to share something that grows within and that eventually I will grow without.

I will sneak back out to the porch and I will view our land and sit in my favorite chair and do embroidery.  It will open up my heart to the next pattern in cloth and I will not talk too much of that other thing that was known by our mother.  This is not some great famine or a disaster that need be endured.  It is simply desire and one more thing that I will need to control with my next breath—a head full of so much wisdom cannot use this as an anchor.  Here I am.  I am a farmer, and a merchant and I have been richly rewarded because I am wearing trousers and not the pretty dress of a girl controlled by her own laughter; stuck with a blossom that would be too helpless to survive on its own; her hair is so coiled that it pulls painfully against her skin.  I would only want to shave my head if it made me at all helpless.  I could never question why my mother did what she had to, when I can draw upon my own day.  It is my voice that I want to listen for in the middle of each night, and it would be a heavy price to pay if I could only have the dreams of someone other than myself.

We are in the middle of another winter, I am not afraid.  There is a cold blanket across our valley and ice veins hanging from our rows of trees.  We have gone to a great deal of trouble wrapping thick material around each base but when I feel the numbness in each of my fingers I am rewarded. This place has silver and gold. There are so many riches in this valley and I am proud that we can reap reward from the canals filled with cold water that continue to flow but not over its edges. There are parts of this land that we want to stay dry outside of the rain storms that are now coming in succession. The water wicks easily into the ground. This place is not flooded this year end. I vow in my heart that I would have given it all up if the water overflowed and ruined the promise of another bountiful spring. My heart is at a comfortable pace again. The water gates we all put up are working and my face it not wet with the bitterness of too abundant rains. I vow again that I will stay.

The summer time is upon us and each morning starts with the song of the numerous flocks of birds. They are already hunting for insects that hurt us rather than help us in this valley. The early morning gray-blues are now replaced with great sheens of golden light cast across row after row of almond trees. The branches are laden with fruit and I am outside on the porch wearing a new dress hat is spun with a golden yellow. My brother has given me this as a gift. If I have one flaw in my character it is due to my stubbornness. I did not want to be a brightly colored lady carrying a matching parasol and a glimpse of my shadow on the ground fills me with a sense of agony. I want to sink to my knees and pull an armload of earth into my lap to show what real beauty is to me. But no one wants to hear my pleas to be left to dress alone. This time others gather and offer all sorts of unwelcome compliments about how glad I should be for the yellow and the gold spun bolt of cloth that has been used so unwisely. I am not in this garment for long.

My brother and I have been very successful in this valley and we have added three other rooms to this house and have expanded the porch around the new sections. I am certain that my brother wishes that I had a room full of garments faithfully following all of the changes in women's apparel over time, if they could reach out to me. A far as I am concerned I am most comfortable when I am dressed in the work outfits of the day. But this is where my brother and I really do differ. He does not call his clothes outfits. He has little to say about his own mode of dressing. They simply are, and when they wear out they are replaced. I too like this manner of simplification. But there are other things that are just as noteworthy as to our differences with the outside world. There is a small cry that I must take note: all sounds are pushed from my mind and my spirit and I grow accustom to the silence: I do not remember why that cry seemed so important.

Ours is no longer a little encampment. Our neighbors have grown as well. Our most immediate garden has blossoms that match if not surpass any other garden throughout this entire valley, but we do not cover our floors with rugs that mimic the outside primary colors or patterns nor do we hang plaques with the sayings of Confucius. When visitors come into our house for tea or for a shared holiday meal they are witness to simplicity, bare wooden floors and a host of decorations that are both plain and reflective of this country that we had adopted as our own. I am honored when I see the looks on those faces which suggest that we live no differently than they do. I am satisfied with the non distinctive living we have carved out for ourselves among the masses around us. This valley is now quite populated with towns and city centers reflecting the new age.

Our front door now has a screen hanging in front of it. It keeps insects and the many pets we have out, unless explicitly invited in. There is one cat in question that is never refused. She is like me: never bearing offspring and hardly complaining. Because we are prosperous we have workers who toil on our behalf for wages that are maintained and do not exceed what our neighbors are willing to pay. We have ton meetings and merchant gatherings to appeal to the status quo. Although our inventions are individual they reap a common reward because we all make sure we adopt them in the same way. This is now a community. It is our home and I cannot remember the last time I thought anything about where I came from outside of short and passing conversations in my now second language. The necessary transitions have been met head on by me, and perhaps less so by my brother. He is still in attendance in secret meeting of Chinese. I ask him, why bother al all. They are as American as we, perhaps even more because some of them ended up here in advance of my brother and me.

In a time honored tradition goods from our harvests exceed market capacity to carry and they are offered to those who own less or are simply less fortunate. Sometimes my brother and I argue this point because I have come to believe those who adapt survive, and those who hold on to the past are crushed by its accumulative weight. A courtyard of another family we provide charities to bears great resemblance to our country of old. From time-to-time we take our tea at a small inn that they have opened overlooking a very wonderful stream. They hang knickknacks from their original village and sig song of the past. Most of their customers find their way off of this compound when they do and they are left all the more baffled that few want to listen to this mimicry of their past lives. The emptying of their place is swift and nothing can change them from these ways—so they are holding on to the past steadfast—living and doing little else more.

Insects continue falling against the screen. Our porch is just at the right angle to see the best sunsets throughout the year. I do not think about evil spirits flying over us or falling against our screen. I gravely remind my brother that the special items he is leaving out at night will do nothing in advance of good luck or misfortune. It is evident when I take them down that he kind of gets this and he protests less each time. This is an organized household and it will contain little else. Some precautions are taken where necessary and I seriously consider the roof and it's all too abundant population each coming spring. Nesting animals also hang on to their pasts and if they do not seek out new place to grow they will grow sick with the even smaller pests who do the same. I will follow nature: rejuvenate, move on and be prosperous. If you do not take precautions and over task your environment it will lay claim to you soon enough.

All lines in my life point forward, and only a hint retraces to the steps of my past. I am mindful of the origins of all of our beginnings and not retracing the bad for the good. I am happy that I am thin. My mother was large because it was an expectation. My brother wanted to install a large and round bottomed cooking pot into our kitchen because he wanted to rejoin with the tastes of our past. To me it just represented burnt oils and rancid aftertaste. My shallow and flat pots and pans are cleaned thoroughly by my kitchen staff and our cuisine is as modern to the tastes emanating from the kitchens in town. Yes, some of these kitchens are Chinese. The ones we frequent are blended cuisines. I like this world of blending. I do not want to stick out.

My brother would do so—he is often sullen if we do not speak of the past. He yearns for the ways of a country that cast him out and so many others like him. I cannot forgive this wisdom and I will stay with my new place in life for as long as I stand. It is not my longstanding tradition to die where I was born. All this talk about going back; those days moved too slowly away. The one time I do want to quote Confucius is that birth is not the beginning nor is death the end. This is just a journey—talking, always talking about the past as though the present is never good enough. I beg his pardon when I get so angry with his insistence on going back for a visit. I will not so—my soul and what is on my mind is here, with respect to my honorable parents.

The worst things that can be inflicted on women are the traditions of gender including discontent with their physical beauty and the silliness that they cannot make it on their own. This country is moving so fast that I can now hold my head up higher and say that I am a business owner. That does not sound familiar in the China of my past. There we were educated and placed into the work field and told to stay—when to leave. I take my ownership of this plot of land very seriously.

Yes we own it together but I am very quick to say 'we' when I hear others say him. I know about us because I have seen the words written on the piece of paper that notes our joint claim on this land. I have confidence that nothing is lurking in the shadows when I witness my hand written signature on that deed of land, and all that goes with it. So I am not quite as worried as other women around me who wonder out loud whose sons will continue this legacy. That does not sound familiar, I tell them. I see the resulting smiles, as though they have a secret of the ways of life. Another decade has passed and there are no signs that either of us will court and marry. We are seen in the community as an older couple—so most no longer remember—our youth has spent away. What else should we remember about when we were much younger—so many memories fade.

Most do not even recognize the fact that we are just brother and sister. I have acquired so much knowledge and resultant wisdom on these matters. Be me or do not be at all. I live my life in my allotted time and I gain daily strength in my body and my mine because I have willed this so. I live with this knowledge and wisdom because I am not afraid to do so. If I love the truth at all I will think of my life not barren, and I will not allow myself to be reprimanded for doing so because only I can choose who will be inside my courtyard. My duties as a woman are the same as my duties as a landowner. I have responsibility for the quality of the earth, the purity of the water, the harvest of an abundant and repeated crop, and the manner in which I seat myself each morning to let the sun hit my face and remind me why I come outside at all. Vanity holds the mirror but self awareness holds the quality of the reflection. When my face is covered with the sun's rays or the honey smears with sweet perfume, and my cheeks are naturally rouged from being outdoors weeding and digging the ground and dripping with perspiration, it is then that I feel I like being me. If I am adorned with pearls of sweat or the wisdom that comes through the day's torturous work, and if my hair carries with it the occasional twig from the winds, then I feel that I am fashioned properly as a queen. When all things in my life are in place, and I rise each and every morning with a song, all this carries the glory and the beauty of being a woman.

I do take these duties so seriously. I do not have many needs: for a husband in the second half of my life I am not so sure this is even warranted. I am sometimes alarmed when I catch myself looking at my brother as someone else. Have I made myself too seemingly for his eyes? I chose to be alone during my day. What about him?

It is summer again and I am still inexpressibly happy. This is my destiny. I can sense my brother does not share the same kind of happiness. He had started in on this very strange business of gathering names and places of other in the community but only that of the Chinese population. I think that this is rather vain. What is it about us that seem so important? The others: English, French, German, Native, Italian, Irish, Mexican Russian and so on: we are all abundantly represented here in this enormous valley. Our shared laughter and labors fulfills our destinies. None of us are so desolate, inexpressibly isolated. We are called the melting pot after all. I like this phrase. I want it all around me. I must respect my brother's obsession with people of a single race, but I cannot succumb to it nor can I subscribe to it now. I see that this task brings him joy so I am happy as well. He wanders around with his daily logs of who was where and when. The logs have grown to books and they have become a library. This is no longer a hobby to take to task, I am afraid. I am afraid because it is consuming him and he rarely ventures outside unless it is to talk to someone else that must be Chinese.

Last night I hear my brother wander outdoors and soon he is laughing with someone else. The rains have come again and the days are much shorter. All of our workers have gone back home and the fields and the orchards stand empty. Yes they are prepared, because it was by my actions that crews were hired and dispensed to take into account this whole affair. My brother is outside now and he is talking reverently in a Chinese dialect that even I cannot fathom. I do not know if he is in trouble of if the danger lay with his unknown associate. The two men never do come in out of the rain and instead argue audibly louder until it is a yell. I stay inside but sense great trouble; not the task but because he has held me here against my will. I will likely interfere with him when he is finished and come in to dry off. My hopes that he had some affectionate rendezvous with a beautiful woman were dashed long ago. I can make out that they are talking about gathering data against someone else's will.

We are more likely to fight these days and nights. His vast library is more the act of foolishness in my eyes because they are filled with the stories of others, not our own. I can no longer say that I am in command of the entrance to this courtyard we built together. He has opened the gate to anyone who proves that he or she originates from China. I can no longer relate to or react to these constantly changing faces. It is as though he is pulling us both into some cult. The outside world is now more bounded by these walls that our own life together. I want it all out and I ask for no more to be allowed free entry.

I am is devoted and loving sister. I can tolerate this no more.

I have been living alone for some time because my brother has elected to go off with a group of local Chinese and form a living group. All of the women in this group shave their heads because the men-folk have been doing so for a long time. They elect to look as though they are monks of some religious order when in fact that all they have in common is a desire to gather information about each other's lives. This is an almost unheard of event for the valley. Many of the same friends that visited or greeted me day by day have gotten smaller in number and so have the party of merchants which gather at the end of each week to review business. At one point our courtyard had been a gathering place for this living group that is until I put my foot down. I did so literally at the base of the large winging gate in greeting them with a polite good morning but would you please conduct your business elsewhere. I became rather good at this achievement even though my brother does not want to hear this.

We both know what we want out of life and that to retain good order there must finally be a separation of this brother and sister effort. At first there was a long procession of nodding heads whispering that the famous orchard couple had finally broken up. It was a very long August and I became the humbled but forgiving wife of this man and what people were now calling a cult. Imagine the effect of hearing that one word, then becoming his humbled wife. I was outraged and then silent once again because I knew he was my brother and was simply following one of his many strange instincts to follow all too closely in the steps of our ancestors past. He thought that we should be the bearers of proud family names and clans from specific areas around China. I thought that was a very foolish gamble in a town and territory that scrutinized all outsiders, even those who lived here.

That was all about to change. Even though I keep my visits to the town center to a minimum, I have donated monies to erect a fountain and plaza at the center of this place. It was voted on in design by a very narrow margin and it was more Mexican styled than Chinese and this outraged my brother and his cult. And be a very large margin the cult has voted me permanently as a persona non grata. What a phrase—so astonishing. And to go with this banishment the city centered monument has received another name on its plaque so as not to stir up any further resentment with the merchants and traders within the town square. This vote is unanimous.

So I rarely go now to the center of town, and I am left to conduct my business in offices and halls at the outskirts of the business center. On the bigger market days I do sometimes venture in but keep a scarf wrapped around my full head of hair so that I do not alarm anyone. It is rare that anyone offers me a basket of fish, vegetables or any sort of grouping of flowers lined pots in any way. I am recognized at time but I have never been so lonely. My brother's torturous behaviors have scared me so well that I have trouble locating even a single set of friendly eyes gazing my way; women with new dresses, men carrying bundles, children with small baskets step out of the way because time has moved on and few people recognize my scarf covered face in the crowded marketplace. And when I go to visit my brother on their expansive compound, their constituents swing around and chant their silly little songs and seldom is there a recognizable slant of a shoulder or blink of an eye that I am any more knowable by this crowd and they speak in a tongue that I no longer care to understand. I consider this to be the resting place of the dead because it makes no sense to me that they just ignore the fact that they ever left China.

There is prolonged sadness in my heart and I can barely bring myself to talk to anyone other than my ranch hands and crews. I have had signs hung up around my property that were painted yellow against black background that this is private property. Too many stranger come to this place looking for my brother and his band. My friends would only fit into my smallest room. I hear that my brother has transferred a significant amount of our once shared funds out of accounts and into another. It is for his cult and his projects. I have let my house keepers go to use what is left so sparingly. I have begun to sell off some of the orchards and non used lands to groups who I thought were independent, but then only to find out that they are connected to his principle ownership in the interim. Nothing I can say will sweep this away. He is certain that he is well within his rights and even a single court review has stated the same.

All of the silks that I had purchased, all of the furniture we had built by our design, and all of the things that we bargained for together are now being priced apart and offered up for sale. Either I do this safely, or he will do so in the dead of the night. The luxury of being one of the earliest settlers in this valley had been switched to unhappy tired, and hunger for days of old before any of this happened. I am trying to think of happier times and I am listening to the hissing of the tea kettle on top of a new stove. I am smiling because I am starting to play the game as well, and I am winning for the time being. That inner courtyard that I was entrusted with is deathly quiet and walled in and I feel that it can only protect me for a while longer. Life around me is hurried and I am distressed by all of the change I will not have caused and the shrinking wonder of my new world.

Another year has gone by and now I am carrying another burden that has caused me an equal mix of sorrow and glee under my own terms. I have received a young woman into my house and she is the offspring of a woman from my original province, married to a first cousin I had long forgotten about. The woman had this child in Hong Kong and it is the first time the two have been separated. The girl was sent to find a way of making a living in the United States: constant and steady stream of exiles from the homeland, enraged by internal strife of a Cultural Revolution gone all wrong by a set of ideals that were never adhered to anyway. Hong Kong was a first stop along a very long highway into the United States. I barely even remember her mother but I have the letter of reintroduction in hand and a very scared girl standing at my door with the local Police. Will I be taking her in, they ask. And of course I do when they left her at my homestead and the moon is bright above in its second day of full phase. I am taking in this girl in distress. She cannot go back home. I am her only family that is not shamed by what she has done. I am inexpressibly hopeful that we will be able to get along.

It is not too long before I find the trouble of knowing that I am not to be her mother cannot be undone. She has her own pride and she does not want to be left out of the principle promise of what is being offered to young people her age at the center of our town. Since I am too weary to make the daily tracks across the valley I do give in and put up our house and land for sale and leave, subject that my brother does not find this out too soon. I have my own honor and pride that I can accomplish this unusual contract execution with only one required signature. If I get caught I already know that this merits condemnation. But the first thing I want to accomplish is helping this young woman to understand that she too will have to learn how to go her own way. The pace is hard and I lay awake throughout many nights while she waits wide eyed in the next room in our two bedrooms—my new home. I think through this move very wisely and my brother is out of the area for some nationwide conference involving other like souls in the business of tracking the movements of Chinese immigrating into this country. I must think for myself and I leave him alone to go on with his business and his shaven heads cult. I want to be absolutely frank about this—they are all probably insane.

In one conversation with my brother he informs me that I must be eating a very bitter bowl of cold rice; one grain turns the rest sour. This remembrance makes me cry and laugh out loud because when I committed the thought to my journal I was in the same room with the girl and I had to explain my behavior and the odd reference. I remember her looking at me with great astonishment: Yuecan, I have never witnessed your eating rice at all. You are a very skillful cook with fish and vegetables and the grains which grow in this valley, but rice has never been one of them.

I remember that one piece of grain: the taste it left in my mouth, the sensation of its shape in my mouth, and the stubborn bitterness that remained after I had spit it out. And then I forgot it all the same. There is no safer place for my mind to rejoin than the last time I could remember laughing so hard and for so long.

There was one other time when we shared a laugh so ruckus that we were nearly asked to vacate our places at a restaurant. One woman had asked me where my husband had gone off to. When I clarified the mistaken identity and exclaimed that he was my brother the other woman gasped. It was here I had to share the very odd relationship that I had maintained with my brother throughout all of those years. The girl thought this was very clever.

I must not, I promise that I will not, bring forward sorrows of the loss of another. Both of our parents are dead now. This girl and I cling on to each other like sisters. I always wanted a sister with a deep heart and sound mind who would cherish me and love me always I cannot wait to share this with anyone who will listen. My circle of friends is growing again. Time and distance away from my brother's other business has sealed my fate. I am freed from it everlasting. The girl and I are treated as equals by this new circle of friends.

I cannot wait to update this journal and I have traveled a great distance to do so. I am just back from a journey up north to a place they call the Pacific Northwest. In my mind this is a place where the climate is moderate enough all year round and I did not have to suffer through another long and hot summer in this valley where temperatures average between ninety and one hundred degrees. The trouble is that the distance is so grave that I cannot attempt this on my own. So I brought the girl who has by now developed into a fine young woman. In my mind she is everything I had wished to be but was too afraid to be alone. She is without fear traveling and her answers about the possibilities of moving along with me are so piercing that it is as though they stab me with a sharp edge in a narrow time. But she cannot be blamed for wanting to be so fearless, because she had a generation before her to pave the way. I am not making this up and she has told me as much over the last several seasons that I believe it myself.

My brother's distance is equally far away and he has moved his contingency to a place further north where he believes that people will leave them alone. I am told that they number in the hundreds now, not just at his immediate location, but spotting along the ridge of the Northern Cascades. When he visits us I feel like I am protecting the girl from an oppressive father—someone that she will never know. I am the only one who reminds her of his strong will and desire to increase those who do his bidding. She is not afraid, she says, because he is only gathering information of a first order magnitude. Even I realize just how much information he has on families which stretch back for several generations. Some of his other members have told me so. This is beyond gossip and courtyard dialog and it is all I can do is occupy a place in his life that hopefully did not warrant so close scrutiny. But there are only several walls between us and I am sure that I am but a shallow knoll in the mountain of data he has amassed on the behalf of some benefactor back home in mainland China. This I believe is much more than mere gossip.

As time moves forward I dress the part and I am also being groomed by the girl; she is now so much more than a sister. I am in love with her youth and her cheery outlook on life in general. I never hear one complaint from this young woman yet I use each opportunity to fill her head with my discomforts and desires for a more meaningful relationship with someone outside of our immediate family.  Our quarters are in such a fine state as she assists me with each and every detail of our home in the middle of town.  I am no longer wearing a scarf because I believe that it date me in a not so beneficial way.  I do not want to appear older and constantly in what some people refer to as old people garb. At time I must make her life more difficult because I am so guarded about mine.  Have I made this young woman's life quite impossible?

It seems like the smallest details read out the most promising news these days.  I am so distant from the calamities of the day to day grind of inner city dwelling, and more inclined to align my time to more natural causes.  I find it necessary to explain all of my actions but she barely scratches the surface of her own needs. She is holding a very quiet front with me, but I assume that she is more open with her many friends at school. When I ask her if she misses home she states: I am home—what is there to miss.  I warn her that she might be allowing too much time before revisiting her home province and whatever ties she may still foment.  She holds her tongue with great deliberation until she can hold back no more.  As it turns out I have been careless in my assessments.  Things are better here than they were ever at home.  How could I ever suggest that she leave here?  I call her into my new courtyard; one shared with a multitude with others for the last time. You must go I implore her.  She laughs in reply and it makes me cry.

What must I ask her to do something I never plan to do myself?  What indeed is the point?  I will never go; will she leave this place of immediate salvation.  This young woman and I are slowly becoming as inseparable less than one rooftop.  She in turn asks me embarrassing questions about my brother. Were we ever at a place that would soften for lovers? How is it that we shared only one bed in the beginning and that we were able to play down the curse of close proximity, even behind closed doors? It was a question that I would never get to ask my mother—about the actions of so many men that history claims—not of his virtue but rather of mine. Sometimes I am indignant when she asks these probing questions. Little does she know that I have explored the obvious answers inside of my head too many times? My answers are well rehearsed.

We do share questions and answers about our shared family tree. This is a verbal contraction. I trust that she will forgive what she hears. My brother on the other hand dictates these answers into a shared storage that can be accessed by anyone within his circle. It would be too much for me to bear. Evidently they record everything. I cannot say that all of the actionable events are worthy of record and playback. What kind of a family does this portent to be and what will they be willing to betray? I am not impressed with this project that has produced so strong a will in my brother. When we are together I cannot forgive, and when we are parted I will not forget the moments and sounds that we caused together. This is in my past and no one other. To think that our future ancestors might become so unruly if they knew what we had known back then—at the end of three days or three hours it is a place I wish to escape the fate of being a woman—the servant of this man. I will go to my grave with only the disgrace and shame I am able to comprehend. Mother, oh honorable mother you did not prepare me so well in that far off place you called country. If it is self restraint that I did not virtuously practice it can be all that was expected for the times. I was overcome in my shared chamber. I will go to my grave without ever sharing those details over tea.

My new sister implores me to forgive and forget as she alone knows better because she had brother as well, and close cousins down the hillside from her village and a monastery just as famously. It was a place that she was brought to pray, and pray she did to escape by the sound of the next bell. She tells me that she has her own little gong that goes off in her head until peace and tranquility is restored. And when sleep comes to her eyelids I can witness the squeamish dreams that send her limbs flying so frequently until I lay by her side and cover her with my arms and my legs. In the morning we talk and we sing and we watch a new day being born. Outside there is a chorus of insects and I attempt to explain things that I never knew or will know to understand myself. If a fine piece of art is carved into a wall, does it remain a wall? I am not so wise that I can answer this question, but I am sure that mothers have had to throughout time. The next time I am with her things are not stormy and this makes me happy about the often forgotten times in my life. One cannot allow these periods to weigh heavily on ones shoulders forever. To forgive one (self) is to move forward. I know all about this labor done for the sake of happiness, I find it more helpful if I do not allow it to penetrate my dreams. I will morn for no one.

My brother's cult has grown to a level that one could only call it absurd. He has invited me to attend a summer festival at the 'Temple' and I have decided to go with the girl in hand. There is no need to do this alone, since I still do trust my brother and he knows better to leave us be to explore this place and this thing.

We are told where to meet at the train station at the end of the line.  The train ride itself was so exciting and the windows in our car were large and well maintained.

There was nothing to obscure our attention to the details of the mountains, plains and vast meadows that we passed through along the way.  I have started calling the girl Li-Li, imitating a sound my mother used to make when she called me when I was quite young.  I have told the girl that this will be one of those great pleasure adventures that she reads about in all of those magazines she has in her room.  It will be just her and I for quite a number of hours in the train car and we take turns telling elaborated tales we made us while looking out of all those windows.  Each window led to a new tale.

Here we are at the close of our first day at the Temple: created by my brother and his business partners, as well as nature.  It is explained to us as a place of business for pleasure and for meeting other Chinese.  It is late August and it is very hot.  The girl and I have made friends already and we have planned several outings for the next several days.  For the most part we are left to our own because it becomes clear that we are being guided away from all of the business oriented events on the other side of this expansive compound.  This is also a time of traditional feasting.  We are enjoying so much regional cooking that it is as though none of us ever left China.

I am sitting alone right now gathering my thoughts near a long canal which divides this property.  The girl is swimming with her new friends.   Later on in the day I am left alone to observed the changing light of the day from the height and clear view of a floral terrace.  It was different from and view I had witnessed from my own valley. The water in the canal passes slowly below and I swear I can still hear shrills of the children as the splash at some other location. On an opposite bank of the canal a large water wheel slowly turns and I feel that I could spend my last days watching the water passing from one flat and angled paddle to the next. It is a wonderful distraction.

The people in attendance here are very friendly and are so old fashioned with their deep and reverent bows. I have gotten used to the more westernized wave and hand shake that I do this out of habit while I am here and I am greeted with strange stares instead. In areas where the women are gathering I see no men. It is true that some of the older perceptions of doing business have clouded the judgments of these women. During introductions I became clear that I may be the only woman in this crowd who has owned her own business. I find this shortcoming most baffling and later I ask the girl if any of her friends discussed this plight. Li-Li answers sadly that she cannot help me. She was so busy playing that she had forgotten what I had asked her to do discretely.

I look down on those banks and I can see people lining up to do their morning exercises. It is practiced here, but I could assure them they would be forbidden from such activity if they were back in China. I will not bring this topic up because I am sure they would be embarrassed. I do however enjoy watching some of the elders straining on their woven mats to keep up with the younger people on the banks of that canal. When I look down again I can clearly see that my brother is beginning to address this crowd—this village within.

All of the buildings on this property are painted in a soft blue-gray and they have earthen colored roof tiles and open gardens. There are small groves of bamboo growing in between each row of buildings. Li-Li and I are taking a long walk after a sumptuous lunch and we make our way past these guest houses and watch children playing in the gardens and adults leaning on the balconies above and many of them are smoking cigarettes. There is not a spot on the compound where you can get away from all of the gossip of the mainland.

These people seem so obsessed by China and spend little time talking about home—the here and now. When I do participate in conversations I try to gain access to their insights on contemporary issues more close to home but I only receive polite laughter in return. No, they all want to talk about China and many want to talk about Hong Kong. They do seem happy so I am not too alarmed. We all take a group walk along the canal before dinner the following day a flotilla of little boats have been launched by the children and for our amusement. I found it strange that they all had the small, medium and large shapes of what we refer to as 'junks'. I watch them float slowly by and I am taken back in time to my childhood and the vast fishing fleets along the large rivers near our university. All of those boats went by so slowly as well and I am strangely homesick. Perhaps this is the whole point.

It turns out that the compound is the whole point of all of these activities. At long last we adults are waiting in a large room at the center of the Temple. There are long graveled paths which lead up to this central house and this is where my brother resides on this compound. Here he is master.

Li-Li has gone off with her friends. It is time for the adults to come together for the principle talk, to be given by a great orator—my brother. The remaining adults are streaming in and looking for the most ideal vantage point. Some of them are disappointed and are push back to the back of the large hall outside of the main room. My brother is already up and centered on the stage and he is being fitted with a microphone to elevate his advantaged position in from of all of these people.

We are all Chinese; no deterrents from the outside world getting in the way of this upcoming and grand speech. It seems that all of China is squeezed into this room and I suppose that we do not represent the poor or the disadvantaged. Everyone in attendance is dressed so fine yet intelligently casual. We are ascendants of privileged, historical hierarchies and it is our money not just our spirit that is of interest today. I almost wish that I were appearing in this place with a woman beggar; I suppose some do live well beyond their means and are in fact quite poor. But each day is a new day and we all dress in accordance with expectation set when we entered the Temple, placed out incense sticks into sand in front of a marvelous array of photographs and inscribed sayings, and we make our homage to the great people that stand elevated above us and make us feel special as well as humble at the same time.

I suppose I should have felt some pride given that it was my brother that everyone came to see and to hear. He was always a blessing in our household in my eyes so I should not have fear that he has gained entrance into so many hearts and minds that stand in eagerness—reverence—and gratitude that they were the ones who had received an invitation. I respect them all at the same time I question their motives. They do not stay away from me but I expect there is a greater distance between us then they expect. I know that I do not have pity for any of them because I do not think that they have done anything—so far away from them I stand here and I am glad that the children have been spared.

Throughout my life my brother shapes my way—so I know I owe him that much. Our life together before the critical moment where we both developed desire to go our own way as gentle a stream as the canal outside of this building. I care for my brother more than I care for even myself. When he addresses the crowd I see and hear before me a summary of all of the fired passion I had been exposed to for the majority of my life. As I listen perhaps haphazardly my cares of the outside world and all of its varied and troubled past of our doing business together has swirled out of an open window just as the strange smelling incense that waifs throughout this place. He is in the middle of his speech and all I can feel is the distance of the sun from this spot and the dimness of the skies through that same window. I do little to show remembrance of the last years or days that we lived together under another roof. I turn around and the people behind me never turn their gaze away from the man on the stage. It is very strange that they do not realize that I am staring right at them. I see no hint of recognition as I turn and then glance back one more time. There is a greater darkness in the place and I want to leave it. I look outside the window and it is already dark. My brother has been speaking for a very long time.

There is a moment when I can no longer hear what he is saying because I am listening to my heart. It is so disappointing that he has chosen to sit down and into what looks to be a throne. My lips are numb from biting them in grief. When I wipe my mouth with a tissue I find the first trickle of blood. Astonished I look around at the crown to see if they share my shock of the red contrasting against the bleached white tissues. The reaction is not swift, but a path is made for my hurried exit all the way into and across the hall, until I begin to slow down as I enter a courtyard. I am outside of the temple and inside of a courtyard. This is close enough to where I want to be; turning to where I should have been all along. I have to turn away when basket bearers make their way through this enormous crowd standing grimly in front of this audience until pockets and purses are emptied for the right to be witness to these faithless acts at the base of these hills. Do you remember where you are? This is not meant to be a profound question.

The speech has ended and another line of grim sentinels dressed oddly enough in white—the same shade as my tissues discarded—they make way through the crowds with piles of cakes and the people are eating all that they can grab; they swarm in for more and are pushing and positioning against each other to get to that next sweet morsel for all of their efforts. They have only had to stand and listen but they seem to think that there is more reward and they eat those cakes until they are tired of the taste.

The crowd exits homeward very slowly through several pairs of large wooden doorways and I can hear them discuss the highlighted parts of the speech. They echo those points verbatim to each other and receive supportive nods and happy slaps on shoulders and backs. What is the meaning of this, did they think that they receive some previously hidden knowledge? How could my brother be so cruel? The crows and large black ravens are active along the paths back to the guest houses and they are making much more sense. I can see the girl and she is shaking her head and smiling as she approaches me. When she asks how enjoyable the event was I just shake my head dolefully because I do not have any profound insights that I will be taking back with me tonight. There is only silence and then a pledge to take her swimming tomorrow morning.

In my brother's speech he tries to remind us of the writings of Confucius: We come to the path of sunrise or sunset and just as we look up something changes. I am looking up at the building at the base of the hill and the lights are being turned off bank after bank until most of the central house is darkened and driven further into the shadowed recesses of the night. I remind myself that while there are no shadows in a hot place, there is nothing but shadows when it gets colder. The curves of the roof of the main house look like the pointed beaks of an evil bird ready to take flight after some less fortunate prey. Perhaps the bird has already flown and has taken its meal and is now settling down with its wings still unfolded and airing from the stench of the kill. This sight brought me to an empty place inside of my heart. It that my brother that I see standing inside of a broad archway, watching out over tonight's survivors, and planning who will be his next victim tomorrow. I think I used to listen to every word this man had to say. He was after all my brother and we were a gift to my parents—twins. Who do I resemble now?

The next morning is lost to because of some other tragedy. The girl has fallen off of the side of the canal and has taken a hard plunge into the swifter than normal currents. Another child said that Li-Li hits her head several times on the way down and is pulled under the torrents. I want to jump in well after the accident. I return to the very spot three times and cry out her name, slipping myself into the frigid waters. I want to blame the designers of the canal, and the fool who opened the flood gates up stream too far that morning. I feel that I could grab this fool and drown him in return. But instead I have slipped and my legs are wet when several people come to my side and pull me out. I want to blame them as well, but this is all due to my poor judgment. I brought the girl here with me. For some reasoning I cannot say at this time—I so wanted to not be lonely among this crowd.

The large towels are tightly wrapped around me by another group who are concerned for my safety even though I am pleading for someone to go down stream, following the sides of that canal and look for this little girl. I screamed that it was my responsibility and implored them to let me go. How can I only be wet? I want to be injured—the only thing that can justify my standing in this one spot and screaming out her name. I am supposed to be among (surrounded by) the associates of my brother but I sense that I am in a foreign land. Why do they not recognize who I am? My brother is suddenly at my side. He tells the crowd that he was watching the entire episode from the courtyard and was contacting the landscaper to shut down the flow to the canal. I protest his lateness but I cannot criticize his followers for being late. No, for them I will continue to be fitting mad by their ineptitude in surmising the situation and remaining by my side. I was only wet.

The following day the compound is holding a reception for another well know Chinese business leader. My brother spends his entire time with this man and a closer circle of business associates. There is a private feast in the main courtyard because it is a brilliantly sunny day. I am not invited because I am in morning. I do not choose to be close to my brother today. There is no joy for me to share around the massive table and the prepared feast. He tells me that everything is being done to retrieve the girl's small body by the local authorities but there is nothing else the can be done. It was an unfortunate accident. I do not attend knowing full well what would happen if I stood too close to him during his time of honoring this new guest and his party. There are nametags on all around the table; none of them have true meaning and no doubt things will be talked about that mean even less.

This visit ends with no good news.

The compound is far behind me and I continue to morn for the girl—the small and frail body that is never found. There are many explanations, but most are foolish wastes of time; the days that were passing made their execution even less reliable unless by chance. The search is called off and I am told that there is no choice. There is always choice, but withholding it all together is no choice at all. I will always love the girl. That is a choice. And then I will allow part of my life to be left grayer. When the next star streaks across the sky, tethered or not by gravity, I will visualize this girl holding on to its tail and having the ride of her lifetime. It is then that I will smile again, and once again it will be by my choice. One look onto my face and you will know when I am serious. It will be a while before I feel the joy I used to feel when I started or ended my next day.

My brother and I have lives which are inter-twined together. Distance does not always tell the true story. He calls me more frequently now and he wants me to join him at his compound soon.  He asks me if I still love him and I quickly tell him that I do.  There is no driving need for hesitation and there is no need for my sorrow to drive a wedge further between us.  I am holding off on my reply to his request to visit him for a much longer stay, however.  All though I have loved him throughout all of my years I cannot sit at his table just yet.  Does he really remember me?  Does he recall how I like to conduct my life?  In the beginning of time someone took a chisel and carved a paired figure into the trunk of a log to celebrate our birth.  They say it was done by my father.  It was said that it was done by another man who cherished my mother.  My brother and I never really got to the truth of this well talked about event, but I did have a preference in the ending.

This morning I reached out of my window to touch the sun.  I wanted to know if nature was willing to share rich knowledge with me and cheer up my heavy heart, because I use the rays to gain my daily strength.  If it were not for the sun I would not see my day begun or ended—so I am always tracking the annual weather to the growth cycles of my orchard.  But today I have to remind myself that I had given all of that up.  What am I to give up next?  My brother's insistence that I visit him is having a much stronger pull and I am running short of excuses as to why I should not go.  Perhaps I am starting to change my mind, even if it is to visit the spot where I lost my youngest friend—a little sister.  I am jealous that she was dragged under the water and not me.  I do not have a lot left since giving up the business. I am not living a life of prudence, having no new income to carry me forward; I spend all that I can.

There is a softer haze coming in through the window that I had thoughtfully opened the night before.  It is no great surprise that I am living on my brother's compound. My brother was surprised just how much he had to spend to move me up to this place. I am like a black omen when I first arrive—broke and still insisting on visiting that spot at the canal. There is a soft side to my brother. He smiles and he take me there if anything just to get the event out of the way. But it is not too soft because when he finds me weeping he does not offer a sweetly expected condolence. Instead he calls out that he will be in his study when I am done.

When I am done I will not seek him out and speak out to please him until called to dinner. I will glare at him instead across a ridiculously long dinner table and offer him follow up to some previous gossip about why is not running our farm. The conversation is never fierce but there are long passages of silence following loud stamps of goblets on the table and plates being pushed noisily away. I am too strong willed he says and he tells me that there is an iron gate between us that needs to be torn down. He is wearing glasses now and it is humorous to watch him constantly adjusting them when they slip down. I begin to laugh and the conversation becomes ripe with politeness and the sorrow is all but gone. There is digging down deep by both of us by the end of the evening and soon we have nothing to talk about but the markets. A transition has taken place and it pleases him and then it pleases me.

I have been living in my brother's house for over one year and there has been so much gossip across the compound. Men and women peer in through open doors and windows to catch a glimpse of whatever they can stumble upon: brother and sister or lovers. All the while I can hear the water rushing through the canal at greater length because it is now a source of additional income for our business. We have traveled far from our origins operating orchards to simply supplying water for a different kind of growth industry. We are providing a necessary resource for the expanding grape industry which in turn is providing a rich liquid for wine makers who have graduated from running technology companies. Although the money pours in so literally, it has been very troublesome to see the once rich rice industry turn their soils under in hopes of attracting the vast wealth of enterprising silicon agents into wine merchants.

The canal that runs through the length of our property runs over from time to time simply because there are periods when the demand is so great, and we have become less concerned with the changing landscape all around us. This is not desecration of the lands it is simply digging at them in a different manner in order to serve a demand in the marketplace. We are witness to vineyards that are now growing up onto the hillsides and when I listen at night I can hear sprinkler systems more often that the calls of coyotes or the mating calls of nesting birds of prey. I listen at night only with an open mind because I am aware of the contribution that I am making to this always changing enterprise.

With the seasons changing more rapidly I cannot remember if the nights are long and warm or shorter and much colder these days. We are so busy that we have lost track of the changing seasons and what they used to represent to us when we operated almond orchards.

I look out of my second story bedroom window and the three-quarter moon is casting enough light on the property below, allowing me to witness a group of coyotes chasing tonight's supper. I cannot stand for longer periods on my private terrace because we are operating with a full house with respect to our other business. We are the keeps of a vast amount of information—data—that culminates all things that can be known about Chinese immigrants into this part of the country. There are frequent groups of participants moving about just below and I step into the recesses because I do not want them to know I am above. It is my task to oversee and to overhear. Along the path below I can the voices of two women talking in a native language that I have had to retrain to understand. This seems so strange to me because it is a dialect that I was born into, but now have to concentrate on so carefully. My brother tells me that every utterance counts.

I am starting to seriously starting to question my brother's motives with regard to the keepers of this side of the business. For some reason still unclear to me everyone has shaved their heads and spending an inordinate amount of time just with each other. It seems we are never to be left completely alone and I cannot remember the last time I was able to just sit and contemplate my life outside of others. We drink tea together, stand in semi-formations, walk hand-in-hand and attend an unending series of formula presentations and talks all reinforcing the messages that appear above all doorways at the temple and at the start of each row of housing. There are now locked gates that one has to pass through to gain entrance to the main property, and to those gardens away from the main house. I have given up on my daily hikes up and along the trailheads running near the hills because someone is always hiking right behind my next footstep. As soon as I turn, they turn. I assume this is not by accident. The only one who seems to be able to be alone on the compound is my brother. And he rarely chooses to be alone, while I crave for a moment of complete solitude.

It has become certain that we cannot continue to accommodate all of the people who gain access to the property. Each week I see new tents and open as well as closed pagodas erected on lawn, patches of dirt and gravel, and now there is a series of long canvas overhangs extending from the sides of the guest houses, and parallel to the main access roads. One day my brother tells us that there are over one thousand guests expected for next summer. Send us a man or a woman so long as they are Chinese. The demands for my time are becoming less and less. It is though I am a walking ghost across the compound. People freely pass me but there are too many that never come to know me and this grows worse each season. I no longer have to hide behind the tall bamboo forests that stand in between the guest houses, because not on would recognize me anyway. I just see and I listen to their conversation and many of them are starting to talk alike. When there is so little to differentiate one conversation from the next my brother appears happier with this result.

One day I am handed a piece of paper by a complete stranger. It reads: *Wisdom exists only inside this place. Happiness will only come to those of you who wait inside and are patient.* At first these words mean nothing to me. Later on in the day I hear numerous conversations on my daily walks and it is being recited repeatedly and has become sort of a mantra. What has happened to this place happened in very slow motion and I feel remorse because I refrained from paying more attention so long as we were able to sustain our lifestyle.

Are we honorable business people? When we sold our almonds our marketplace was our only means of feedback. Was this even a market? Yes, I understand the value of our water supply to the region but I do not claim to understand anything beyond that, and I do not push my brother for answers in kind. Our bills are paid and this does not seem to be a place where people are being made uncomfortable. My brother has accepted a title of Doctor, and I make no mention that this is a mistake. I have come to accept it as well. His speech has become so eloquent and he seems to have an unending supply of knowledge and accompanying wisdom—enough to satisfy all—especially me. Even I am in such awe at his solemn looks during his opening dialogs on the morning grass still wet with dew. Are hands and our butts are never dry and we give him carefully orchestrated looks at the conclusion of each mastered train of thought shared for our uniform benefit.

Today I am happy but I do not think this is healthy. My brother has become a dragon and his clawed hands never relinquish their tight grip on any of us. Yet we smile and pass each other knowing nods of a long life and coming wealth. It is a promise we are told if we are patient, so we are beholding to my brother. There is a golden path laid out to his doorway and we sit patiently along this path in chairs of hope and prosperity and glad to be free from the encumbrances of the outside world. We chant together for direction, and this man who gives our lives such meaning. And then we listen closely for my brother to chant and for signs that we have heard the right words not just by chance. It is his reach and his hold that make me so fearful at times. What about the others?

There is a point in my life where I will refuse to live in darkness.  It is well illuminated outside even though it is in the middle of the night here at the compound.  The full moon and clear skies make this so that I am fortunate enough to see details of grain and sand on the terrace.  I have taken the time to draw my lifeline in the silky sand and I am please with the control I have over this horizontal canvas.   I am adding things that are so symbolic that even I have to stop from time-to-time to remind myself why I have chosen to do so.  I am not an artist I remind myself, and I am certainly lacking the wisdom to leave this place in the middle of the night when everyone is sleeping including my brother.   I wonder if the hills to the east would give me a suitable place to find my freedom.   But finally, I stop to ask myself what is it I want to be free from?  Is what I am supposed to do here so much a price to pay to stay out of harm's way from the other elements that pass through this place?  My brother has always been the bearer of fine gifts. Perhaps this is just another one.  The night air has a smell that is so sweet and it is providing me strength to have this conversation with myself.  It is a song that is resting on my lips, so much the better that I am here on the terrace alone.   I am not dressed appropriately for company—naked as the breeze—and less shameful than I might have been one decade ago.

The shame of it all is that it is the beginning of a fine spring and I am inside and sick with a fever.  The world around me is slower than usual and for most of the morning and early afternoon I see very little activity at the temple or on the grounds.  I have this horrible taste in my mouth from the medicine I took the prior night and the residue is has left on my morning tongue.  My senses are keenly aware of all of the signs of spring—so

I just wish I could taste it—too frightened to go out for a walk I sulk in my room all day. My hair did not grow back this time and I stare into a mirror and forget who is looking back. I am dressed in a thin and flowing gown and I want to believe that if I shed it I will be as beautiful at the butterfly I watch hovering just outside of my window. I do so—such is the time I last felt comfortable in clothes. I have become sort of a nudist. I hope that I am never too old to be so exposed. This causes me much laughter as I look at my reflection in the muted window panes and I think this might be part of the cure. Can this only be understood by a woman and a brother who loves to be near by her—not at all a desire as much as a comfort zone? I do like that phrase: comfort zone. It is a humbling thing that no matter how small the shelter when I understand it I am amazed how large it feels. There is nothing about this room that I want to exchange. It is my comfort zone and it is not so small after all.

In the middle of spring my brother summons me through one of his assistants. I can no longer tell if they are male or female when they first arrive because they all wear white flowing robes with thin hoods to cover their bald heads on colder days. I sometimes wait until the light hits them just right and penetrates the robes just enough to indicate the truth; is there one at any given time other than the one moment when I blush with my find. This one is a small girl and she has asked me to join my brother for tea. Fortunately for her she did not have to guess about me when she knocked and politely entered with a slight bow. She is so young and she is not used to seeing someone of my history so openly revealed. I have my feet set far apart and I am exercising when she enters. I notice that she does not turn her head away that is customary under such circumstances. Instead she stands over my legs with her polite bowing motion and she smiles at me without any discretion at all. It is all I can do to restrain myself from bringing a more appropriate gesture to par. Instead I simply insist that I will require another moment in regard to my posture. With that she stoops downward and whispers something that I wanted to hear, and then turns and leaves me to my activities. I enter the temple for tea long after that exchange. What is the worst that can happen? So I was late for tea. I remind myself that I do have freedoms.

I do not want to discount all that my brother conveys to me at the day or remarkable transition, but I made a choice to tell him of my strong reservations with regard to staying with him on the compound. I have seen him take too many followers under his protective wings, both men and women, and although I am not part of that inner circle I hear things from time to time. I really did try to swallow my pride that afternoon and share with him all of what I had been thinking about lately. I tell him what I know and that I no longer recognize what it is that this place represents to these people; shaven heads, and flowing robes that are discarded more often as each day passes and the sun is right and it is a vision that competes with my own sensibilities. Does his nature pretend that one shared with all under one rooftop is a good beginning or end? And just when I think that I have paid him suitable honor he admonishes me for those things that I refuse to engage and participate openly. I am confused almost every day and cry most nights until I fall asleep.

Tonight I break from my cycle of despair and sit on my terrace and stare up at a clear ski and witness the asteroid showers into the early hours of the next day. I am content for a brief moment and I compare my life thus far to that of particles still streaking across the skies. Each streak arches onward in a brocade of silver, orange and gold and this give me comfort because I now understand what beauty is all about. I am older and I do not measure up to the small and very slender bodies of the people who walk from vantage point to higher point up on the hill across from my terrace. I am dressed reasonably but when they look up at me they exhibit a look of confusion seemingly saying "look down, we are all undressed appropriately for nature's calling."

Some of them are embraced in intimate pose down below and I can hear their excited screams while I scream silently with my eyes closed. I do not consider myself above the masses but I do recall less casual encounters do nothing for me at all. They are engaged in simple occupancy and I wonder if the understand just how small their beauty really is without inclusion of that thing we seek out called love. This report is too fleeting to my brother when I reveal it over tea.

This morning there is severe wailing in another courtyard. I can see the gardeners and other laborers gathering around a growing crowd of guests until the crew head pushes his way through the crowd. I can see the body of a small woman in bounded feet and hands stretched out along the ground and she is not moving. She is not wearing clothing and her staid body no longer embraces the morning sun. My head and my heart are aching because I allowed myself to eavesdrop earlier in the morning to another loud conversation that was laced with anger, but was confined indoors. It was difficult enough to stand by and listen and now I understand how my dispassion for involvement has contributed to this act of cruelty. She is not moving and will not move again. There are people all around her sharing tears and unwrapping her bindings but there is little showing of anger. Something was permitted to happen and now it seems so cold that even I do not budge from my viewpoint until I see one of my brother's associates give guidance to the head of the grounds crew. All is cleared now and the motion and sway of this crowd is oddly arithmetic—an oddly predictable curve exists around that cottage until the end of that week.

Another morning comes warmly through my open window and I am sipping tea in my robe. These are not the first rays of the day but they might be cast by some oracle in that they temper the remains of my stay. My brother has made a personal visit to my cottage— something he rarely does—as he usually bacons for my appearance. When he enters I can sense something so grave that I carry an advanced look of astonishment making him less balanced. Wearily he staggers and sits down into a close and comfortable chair. His face is full of puzzlement and it is ridiculous when it is I who reaches out with a stronger hand. For the first time I am above my brother since he became rich beyond any real need. He is before me for consultation and I do not know if my input will make him happy or mad. But I do indeed react to his stated perplexities and will all due patience I vow to stand by his every decision for what is best for the both of us. Tonight he says in return—just tonight.

My brother and I have packed just what we will need to flee this compound and that traitorous temple. He does not know who have betrayed him but he understands the need for fast and deliberate action. There is money in a safe place—he does not want me to be alarmed.

We will not care to look back and listen to all of the gossip that must have been shared across that compound the next day. There is enough distance that it would have been nothing more than a barely audible whisper even if carried by the strongest winds to these new walls. After driving for two and one half days we are making way up a very narrow and winding road with the most beautiful vistas I have even seen. For as far as I can experience while driving to this place, there are numerous islands to my west, while my brother slumbers to my east.

This is the place where we are supposed to arrive; it was colder than I had expected and I am certain I will grow used to the climate change over time. We are entering into this new world and these granite and sandstone walls lurk just outside of our house.

I am ambivalent about the size of this new place and its monstrously large structure; I explore all of the possibilities. I will note all of the surreal details on his return from his many trips across the border to the north; wondering how close or how far we are from where we are supposed to be. I will engage with him—we are here my brother. It is just as you said we would be. I am so lost and wonder where we would go next.

**The Day's Closing Rests Assured**

There is a defined streak of clouds contrasting against an otherwise blue sky and look up to see the faces etched in the sloped sides of this mountain so caused by the erosion which continued after clear cutting its top. I am no longer certain that this bothers me as I sit adjusting against the hard and rocky perch I choose to sit on reading this journal. The deciduous trees are showing signs of a summer ending and their yellow and brown leaves are more abundant on the ground as they are in the sickly branches which sway even in the slight breeze. The hilltop in front of me is sparse other than the dried out brush that still provides cover to small lizards, and the insects they chase from hidden positions out onto the sun soaked ground.

Life continues in every direction with the exception of the one I am holding in my hands. This one was stopped; not before the right amount of time. Would I have read another paragraph or a page if that were not the case? It is not at all clear just when the last journal entry was made, but I know it was entered in just the right amount of time. I hold the entire story in this one book as I get up with several other potential endings racing through my mind.

I do not want to be so philosophical now on top of my mountain and I just want to listen to that water rush over small boulders and into the next bank on the way down off of the next hill. I am certain enough that I will not project another chapter of Yuecan's life no more than I can push this creek uphill or in another direction all together. The sun is closer to the next ridgeline and it will dip below soon enough for me to finish this one last thought. I want to share this woman's life with at least one other than myself, just to make sure I get it right.

But I sense there is still one part missing. I know it may come someday and I wonder just how much of a surprise it will be when it is upon me. I have even attempted to create this one part on my own.

Michael O'Connor

# Participate in Consideration

Fortuitous Event

# Chapter Twenty-two

## *Traders Beware*

I BEGIN MY DAY WITH EARNEST and then I am learning toward trepidation when I pick up a copy of the daily news while visiting a favorite breakfast place. I have just started in on fresh bread and a large tea as I skim the headlines and moved quickly past the introductory paragraph. I am at the table alone but for some reason I feel that all eyes are on me. It is just a feeling—I'll get over it soon enough—skipping down to the center of the news article. There is a little voice inside of my head giving me a number of choice interpretations of the text in front of me; paper flat against the tabletop, listening to the sounds of the street and of the rain and a chance to be refreshed.

There is an announcement by the Lummi Indian College in conjunction with Western Washing University to move forward on a joint development of a genealogy database of indigenous people to the regions near and around the Salish Sea. The announcement describes that they have co-developed a new software approach for genealogy database development and that they have received the go ahead on a provisional patent. The plans are also accompanied by a full endowment from the Federal government to go to the next level of development provided that the resulting data is made available to the general public.

There is a sense of understatement, or is it the movements inside of my head. My food and drink are in front of me and it is all I can do to reach out. I am quite certain that neither Julia nor I did cleanse that the entire data set—we thought what we provided was clean enough. It was our initial understanding that this code would be used to explore and evolve over time, at the College, and would probably go no further than localized use. Now it has national attention and is straddled across the two campuses for all to access and glean from it more than a sense of the past. If someone outside of our smaller circle looked deep under the hood—so to speak—they would no doubt discover its original use. Was this a good thing or a bad thing; I was not as sure as I ate and drank slowly staring off occasionally at the steadied stream of occupants to this cafe.

I did know that I would have to do just a bit of damage assessment with my counterpart. So would I contact her at home while I ate breakfast out on the sidewalk and away from the clamor of the crowd inside? It is raining lightly and I am partially protected by the awning up above and I am dialing some numbers on my hand held, between another bite and then another sip of hot tea.

It is ringing. I swallow hard hoping I have time to clear my throat before she answers.

"Julia, it's me." I do not wait for her counter greeting—if one was coming at all. "Have you read the local news this morning?   Yes, take your time.   I can hear the shower running."

There is nothing more surreal than listening to a phone conversation on speaker mode while the other party showers.   Here I am sitting in the moderate rain outside of a place that has gotten busier and now I do not have the option of moving back inside.   This is not the fine breakfast I had in mind.   I am wet.

"I had a look on line before stepping in."   Julia was relating the summation of the article she read on line on her new hands free tablet—hopefully before stepping into her stall.   There was an inviting and descriptive tone in her voice.

I jumped the gun and started in again before she finished her reply.   I swallowed hard and let another truth come forward.

"Look, this goes beyond our original deal with the College, but I will take ownership for the mess.   I let this thing go literally for months without a follow up.   The damage is done.   I do understand why they had to move so fast.   The relationship, as it turns out was already in the works.   Our software just accelerated the whole business.   We put them on the fast track to this announcement."

I was putting all of my cards on the table—so literally.   I was spreading out my contacts across the small café tabletop but I could not find our friends business card anywhere.   I could not conference him in.

"I do not have his number with me.   I'll have to make that call later on in the day."   I was somewhat frustrated by this shortcoming but was soon made to forget the business at hand. There was this other little voice—not so recognizable, just different.

The sounds I was hearing from the other side of the conversation were stimulating. Julia was busy with her shower and was making noises that would distract anyone within earshot. The outpourings of this tempest in the stall made me want to dash out into the rain in refrain. It changed my mood as I listened into the speaker of my hand set. Julia was engaged in much more than just a morning wash.

"Oh, this feels so good," she moaned in pantomime thinking that she had a fully attentive audience. My thoughts were on the image I had conjured up and projected into the space in front of me—so enjoining us.

There were several groups of people attempting to scamper out of the much harder downpour and into the eaves and entrances of several businesses around me. Across the street an older couple cut across a parking lot in front of a big delivery truck that almost did not stop in time. By the time this driver let loose with a stream of displeasures out of his open window, the couple rushed across the street and headed right past me at a speed not expected from anyone close to their age. I watched the truck go by and noted its message on the back side: *How is my driving?*

It was like watching a cartoon—feet never touching the ground until they reached a safe sanctuary. The traffic that pulls away; the warm food and drinks for all who sit here now, watching for the next fretful encounter.

"Well how did you like my show?" The voice pulled me from my private cartoon and back into reality.

"What were you doing in there besides lathering up, repeatedly?" I had asked this out of interest, while expressing a ventured guess. The rain was letting up a bit and the traffic had cleared away.

"I was enjoying my shower and a morning routine." Julia was laughing when she said this, further mocking my voiced concern. But there was something else.

"So this is a daily event?" I immediately regretted the inquiry. It was none of my business; I heard this retort well in advance.

"Hey, when I am alone for too long I have to make do with the tools I have around me. If you were here you would have gotten a ring side seat. Perhaps we would have asked for audience participation." She was still laughing—this made my day change appropriately— having centered around the use of the word 'we'.

"What did you think of the article?" I would have to force the exchange still thinking about the other.

"Oh, I do not think that this is the end of the world. If they find other data I do not care. It will no doubt be in fragments. It would take them far too long to figure it all out. By that time we will have moved the bulk of it."

I could not disagree with my partner but there was this little voice that suggests that something else existed just under the surface. The voice always proved to be right in the past. I would not let this go, but then again, I could not let this interfere with our closest prospect. Go with the flow; let this issue settle a bit before jumping right in—exacerbating a thing that was not quite a problem yet. I hated reaction rather than pro-action and kept this to myself.

"You know, I never told you the outcome of reading Yuecan's journal."

It was time. I wanted to share the outcome and Julia was the most likely choice outside of George, my friend just over the border, who so kindly translated the reams in a manner in which I could appreciate. George was also a photographer and collector and I gave him several boxes of photographs that must have spanned three-quarters of Zhao and Yuecan's life together. George had made a parallel passage from China to here, and he could more than relate to the content of this journal. It occurs to me he could have been one of the followers at the compound.

I am moved from that strain of thought. Julia's voice has penetrated the air forcing me to concentrate on the present. It occurs to me this was a useful transition to get invited to her house. I was still going with the overwhelming perceptions and sensations which occurred during the in shower call; hearing that other voice again brought me closer to a clear conscience.

"Well, it will have to wait I am afraid. I am heading out for lunch and some shopping with a girlfriend. Perhaps we can get together tomorrow?"

"Was that a knock on the door?' I had to probe because it was driving me crazy—that last piece I had to fit in.

"No, she is already here. Call me tomorrow. We can catch up then."

I had started out my day with trepidation and now it was returning to haunt me again. I am walking down the street and I could no longer care that it had started pouring rain. I probably walked six more blocks before I circled back to my automobile. There were so many other images swirling around in my head and I did have to remind myself that this wasn't even a hint of a relationship. Was it a partnership instead?

Several days ago I relished the thought. Now I just wanted the images to go way. There was more to this partnership but it would have to be kept at bay for the here and now. I spent the remainder of the day running errands and then ended up pushing my paddleboard well out into the bay to shake it all off. Fortunately for me the Bay was emptied of all of the usual boat traffic and I enjoyed paddling without out having to look back or around my sides as I sized up the next incoming series of four foot rollers that headed my way.

This was my escape. I am forced to think of what's before me.

Easing over the first volley I gulped in and then sputtered out a mouthful of sea water and enjoyed its punishing taste. It is the exposure to the extreme forces of nature that reinforced my belief in going this alone. Having survived the next two series of varying sized waves I pushed on until I was well into the next major channel and reminded myself that I was seven miles off shore when I felt the strong pull of the center currents. From this position the city skyline looked so miniscule and the dark forces of the rain filled cloud banks up above the city looked as though they would keep things drenched for the remainder of the afternoon. It was wet on the outside and I am wet on the inside. The tightness of my wetsuit keeps me from freezing and my muscles strain and generate enough heat to keep me on a heading out to the archipelago mass that lie ahead.

It was a dark mass that hovered above and then again inside my head. There are several dark masses in front of me and to my side. I felt the need to being alone but at the same time I relive the anguish that was expressed by Yuecan in her last journal entries: *I am not so lost but wondered where I would go next.*

I paddled out to what lie ahead and hoped that I would never get there instead. I paddled like crazy and blasted my way through the next sets of waves. Was it a relationship or a partnership? Could I ask the same with respect to Zhao and Yuecan? Parts of her journal lead me in different ways. What was the focus—could be the focus.

The next incoming series of waves engulfed me completely and I was under water for only for a brief moment. But when I resurfaced and climbed back on top of my board I could see the clear set of running lights heading right toward me. The shape of the eighty foot cruiser and its distinguished markings would be on me in the next fifteen minutes. There was no place I could go. When I paddled left they corrected their heading. And when I went right they were doing the same. It was a lost cause; my life was ever changing with each new set of incoming waves. It was a case of dead reckoning and it was on me.

The Coast Guard cruiser was coming here, right now, along my side. It was remarkable that they were able to spot this pinpoint in the rough waters. They created a greater wake with their presence and I could hear someone topside shouting to wait and let the waves settle down around my position in the swirling and foaming water. It was full stop ahead for all of us so many miles from any shoreline, and in a troublesome and swift moving channel.

"What the hell are you doing out here in these conditions. There are small boat warnings out. Are you not paying attention at all?"

I hated being yelled at by this very young officer but she did have a point. Small boats aside, this was no place for a fourteen foot paddle board. But I was not ready to back down and I steadied myself on the board as the waves lifted me up and then dropped me far below the waterline painted on this ship.

"I come out her all the time in these conditions and worse. Your wake is more harmful than these waves." I was shouting this up above in oblivion to the conditions or the authority topside.

"Well I won't tell you how to live your life. But be assured that we have no intension on circling back after you. There are reports of seven foot swells heading inward between the islands to the south. Why don't you do us a favor and at least start heading in."

"Yes Officer, I will turn in. Thank you for the head's up."

I was going to have to hold my thoughts for the moment. They had the right to pull me out and I could end up with a citation if I fight it. I paddled backwards away from the stern of the cruiser as it lurched forward and put a fair distance between us. The black belch of the twin stacks signaled that they were well under way.

The officer topside had reluctantly waived me off after she checked out if I was carrying the requisite safety equipment required even for paddle boards. The PFD was obvious, and his request that I show her my signaling devices was assured: one whistle and one small signal light. I continued to paddle backwards and was not countered in any way.

The cruiser and its crew are well under way and there was now a quarter mile between us and I was heading to shore as promised. I had wanted to deviate once I was out of line of sights, but then I thought about the other electronic surveillance gear they must have on board. If they did double back it would have been to pull my butt out of the water and to arrest me. I waited until they were at least one mile further north before I let up.

And then I cut in. I would be good to myself today.

Once inside of the cove to the east I cut north again against a firm but forgiving wind and made my way back up the coast. The waters were rougher here because of the reflection of the incoming waves against the sandstone cliffs and the pushed outward again. It was like paddling in a very busy wash cycle. But it gave me time to think about those highly anticipated next steps.

Yuecan was right in mind and spirit in the last entries she had attempted to convey if only to herself. It is good to have the time to think about it all, before taking that next step into my own future, and examining the possibility that I would share this with a widening circle.

# Chapter Twenty-three

## *Year of the Rabbit*

CATCH ME IF YOU CAN was the first thing I thought of when I woke up this morning. There was a strange sensation that had come over me and it took most of the morning to figure it all out. I had woken up completely sober; stranger truths befit us all.

Being completely straight and narrow was not an unusual first step for the first of the year. It is a new year after all and I had spent it at home alone, after attending a requisite neighborhood party which we lovingly referred to as an orphan's fiesta. A party aptly named in part because it was an annual tradition of those of us who deplore the usual strain of X-mass and New Year's Eve parties. We are the odd person out—so be it we are alone, we are alone together.

The beauty of attending the orphan's fiesta is that there are none of the usual rules of end of the year engagement. No one receives the lampshade of the year award, and if one plans on being moody and alone, but not exactly alone, this is one place you can pull it off year end after year end. This was my forth year at the end of time party—so my own personal twist—and I did not have one single drop of alcohol on purpose; not with purpose by any sense of the word.

This New Year day seems as promising as I logged on and scoured the planet earth for all of its New Year news. It is the year of the rabbit—a Chinese pronouncement—and one that attests to the fact that this year is dedicated to one of the most favorable animals in the Chinese twelve animal cycle. As rabbits are to nature I started to think about all of those attributes that I would carry forward with me throughout the year. I was already off to a good start by being alone and slightly aloof by not answering the non stop ringing of my phones, and I was also dodging emails and updates to a blog that I had created for friends years ago. And when I heard my doorbell ring twice, followed by a loud rap at the door I scurried into the hole of mid house waiting out the New Year carolers that sang on my front porch.

Why does this neighborhood have carolers in the first place bothered me to no end. It was a strange enough occurrence leading up to that obviously stated tradition, but this group also did the same on Halloween, New Year's Day, and on Columbus Day of all things to commemorate the fact that so many cultures actually took credit for the first discovery of this northern continent called the New World. They repeated a brotherhood-sisterhood series of songs each year, and I hid in mid house each time, just like I am doing on this year of the rabbit; as I do now. The song is diminishing and they are walking back out of my enclosed garden and onto the sidewalk heading to the next victim.

My day has begun as I swing into the safety of my kitchen and prepare the first meal of the day and of the same year. I spend a few moments rationalizing that I am not anti-social and that my behavior was simply one of self rescue. Self rescue was a staid tradition in my life. It was another one of those life's lessons I picked up from my dad. One I did understand at the time as much as I am cognizant of it now. But it did not go as easy initially.

When I was young I woke up on New Year's Day like any other completely sober. I was a kid; it was a natural act. One this particular New Year's Day my dad walked into my room without knocking—a usual event—and pulled the covers away from my bed before I could even wipe the sleepy state off of my face. The unfortunate aspect of this particular morning, however, was the other initial fact that I had been using the earliest part of my day for boyhood experimentation. My father's face caught the remnants of this early morning behavior and initially his jaw dropped. But then a rather strange thing happened. He turned away and suggested that I get up, shower, get something to eat and then join him outside at the care. Apparently we were off to another one of those sometimes appealing road trips where we would talk and hash out life's little or major quirks.

It took some time to drive out across the Golden Gate Bridge that morning more due to the dense fog rather than to traffic. The roads were pretty much empty as one might expect on the first day of the New Year. Most people would be just putting one foot after another on cold floors and scrambling out toward the coffee maker to push that pounding sensation well out of their heads, while contemplating how they would live through the antics of their previous night's folly. We were on an empty highway battling the fog, while not in a personal one. My dad told me that he had not had a single libation the night before this drive over one of the most beautiful bays on the planet, heading past the Marin Headlands and turning north onto the coastal road and through the dense tree line of Muir Woods.

It was one hour later that we drove into the tall redwood forest and into an area that paralleled and chased the winding path of the Russian River that emptied into the Pacific Ocean. We were traveling well in and away from the coast as I had originally suspected. This was very familiar territory as it was because this was where we had taken so many summer vacations as a young family. The tree lines were mostly recognizable that year because of the burnt and scoured marks left on their branches by the previous year's forest fire.

Although it was a minor one by comparison to the fires that sometimes plague the California landscape, it had a more memorable effect because it was one of the times I had wandered off from a family camping site. I was lost and in the middle of a smoke covered valley and I had found out there were several dozen adults looking throughout the forest for me, even though I had wandered back into our campsite and ate—simply waiting it all out until someone older than me had returned.

My dad and I reminisced about that event on our way up to the site where we would pull over and park. We were at the graveled edged of a large beach that usually was packed with families had this been in the middle of the summer. But we were her on the first day of the year and there was only the most modest gathering of mostly young adults who no doubt used this as an excuse to exit out of their own households of sleeping it off adults.

That day my dad took me for a marathon swim. My dad was an accomplished swimmer and typically took to the water to do things like stroking across the entire opening of the San Francisco Bay, well under the shadows cast by the Golden Gate Bridge. He was also actively participating with a group in an annual and ritualized swim out to and around Alcatraz Island just for the sport of it; there is no prize more important than the single contest, one-on-one competition, against all odds.

Today we were to accomplish the same. The winter currents of the Russian River were known well enough. But was not known to me at the time was the pleasure my dad took from swimming against this monstrously strong torrent of water as it screamed its way eventually out to the Pacific Ocean. That would have been enough for most people, but not my dad. At midpoint of this 'up against and then turn into its flow challenge' there was a dam with overflow which usually looked small during the summer but now raged with a roar as the might of this river pushed against its concrete and steel gates. And that was all part of this New Year plan.

It seemed to take forever to make any headway against the oncoming waters of the river, but I was determined to keep up with my dad. As we reached a far eastern curve that denotes our point to turn around I know that my dad has deliberately slowed his own strokes to match that of my own, giving me renewed strength and stamina to go it alone back down stream. The goal was to swim again with the rush of the current until we reached the cusp of the small bay which was cut out literally by this river on its way out to breach the Pacific Ocean. The next demarcation I was to look for was the dam and to prepare for my launch over the limited protection of the mid gate.

My aim was straight so far. I would already hear the roar of the overcastting waterfall that was made by river over concrete and steel. The current seemed to be picking up as I swam closer to this point and steadied my approach to the center of the river and thus towards the middle gate. The water seemed a whole lot colder as it grew deeper. At this point I was fighting the unforgiving cold and the nerve racking scream of the inner voice that begged me to forego this life lesson and swim to one shore or another before it was too late. The scoured trees flew by. The beaches on both sides of me were blurred beyond recognition.

It was too late. I was heading into the stronger pull of mid river and there was no backing off from the inevitable. I was soaring so literally over the top of the middle gate in a torrent pull of water that engulfed me and I knew well enough not to try to breathe as I felt my body being launched straight up and over its edge until I was plunged well onto the other side.

I was under water in a strongly rolling and sucking current and being pulled down repeatedly to the rocky and graveled bottom just on the other side of the dam gates. It was like a strong vacuum and I was not making headway even on my third try kicking off of the gate and attempting to launch myself away from this watery entrapment. This time I would push away from the bottom with all of my might in hope for breaching the surface. I made it and I fill my aching lungs with fresh air and copious amounts of fresh water instead, before feeling myself being sucked down to the bottom again.

This is a not too unexpected turn of events. I have been through this before, only while being pulled under and tossed by enormous waves in the ocean. What did I do before? I recalled suddenly enough and made my way to the bottom after my second breach and masterfully executed intake of fresh air this time. I had enough air for this planned task.

While pinned to the bottom this time I scoured around is barely visible whitewash and found what I had been looking for. It was a round and suitable enough weighted boulder and I picked it up at this watery depth and cradled it into my arms. And then I stood up and felt my head break water to air.

Excitement was torn between being lifted up and out of the water to my shoulder line and while hugging my prized boulder. I had managed to look up and saw my dad holding onto his son by only a handful of hair. He was at full stretch from the other side of the dam and the look on his face suggested he was not going to let go. My dad had come to my rescue but the look on his face when I kicked frantically away and back down to the troublesome bottom of the river told it all. My son is insane and must have a death wish. Why did he pull away?

I pulled away first and foremost because having head and body suspended by the roots of one's own hairline against the strength of the current of a raging river was much more than I could take at the time. Secondly, I was already in the middle of a self rescue and I wanted to take the disaster and the exit into my own hands. He was the one that got me into this whole mess, and I wanted to be the one that got me out. I was thinking this as I crawled and then stepped lively along the graveled footing of the bottom of the Russian River and I made my way downstream holding on to this sufficiently heavy boulder.

At long last I could see the ascending slope of the bottom and I climbed it until I broke through its surface and gingerly dropped my safety boulder to the silt bottom without crushing my toes. I was head and shoulder out of the dangerous grasp of the softening currents and stepped onto higher ground and turned around to signal my dad that I had self rescued. He was on top of the dam and bridge by then and was waving back before he tore over the side and plunged into the river to swim to my side well downstream. It was a happier reunion as I was able to get off the first salvo of screams, telling him what I had in mind at the time. And there it was finally, that look of pride.

The lesson of the day was taken in hand and I led for the first time and I felt that I had left part of my precious childhood far behind. We did eventually make our way to the place where the river empties into the awaiting arms of the ocean and fresh water mixes with the cold and salty currents. We spent most of the afternoon body surfing in the currents and waves and later on we drove to a favorite spot and gorged on barbecue oysters and an ample amount of crusty French bread. The sun was starting to set as ever as we retraced out steps along that coastal highway, before cutting in between a pacific mountain range and headed for home.

The last words of my dad broke the quiet spell of the drive back. "Please don't tell your mother."

# Chapter Twenty-four

## *2nd Chance Generation*

NO ONE CAN COMPLETELY PREPARE you for all the things that come with life, even within a family unit. It is not enough to say that to expect surprises is part of the planning process, but when we plan for surprises that is just doing good business. So when I say I wanted a good outcome from my latest project it appeared.

The initial reaction to Julia's very early morning phone call was one of grand surprise not only for the nature of the call but in part due to its timing. It was all too early and I felt that I was still in a dream state. I really thought I was that is, until I zoomed in on the headline news. Yuecan had someone to carry on her legacy.

Perhaps the more interesting point to be made for how the call wrapped up was the part about Yuecan not ever knowing this little jewel in this vast field of genealogy logic. Of all things to be missing from one of the most comprehensive bodies of data covering the whole of Chinese immigration to this West Coast was the apparent fact that the key designer and developer forgot a relatively point of input. She had a daughter.

Now the real surprise aspect of this knowledge was the fact that her brother would ultimately be known as the biological father of said offspring. That face was actually insinuated in Yuecan's journal, so this might not be especially surprising. It is not some cleverly disguised point of family history given the text that I had poured through, had translated, and then summarized for point-by-point analysis. I really did want to know.

"Make no mistake, Julia, I really did want to know."

My feedback to my longer than expected (term) project partner was truthful enough, however, there was still a part of me that wanted a more legitimate outcome. Now a clever disclaimer at this point might be apropos. I am not condoning siblings carrying that generational thing too far. I do think that some of the safeguards that civilizations created to protect their populous do in fact make sense. When things do go astray, as the often do, I do think that there is a tendency to overreact where the principal target—that offspring—takes the brunt of the whole conflict that often results after discovery.

Julia was exiting her automobile with her passenger and was heading toward my door. In tow was this kind of middle-aged woman who not only had a striking resemblance to Yuecan, but she was twice a rewarded with stunning physical beauty and prowess as an added bonus. Her graceful and determined walk up the pathway said it all. There was a blatant obviousness to her walk, and when I greeted them at the door her grasp of the situation and self control was immediately known to us all.

"Good morning, I am pleased to make your acquaintance. I am Lucy—Zhao's daughter. My friends call me Li-Li, by the way."

So the stun of my surprise, as it turns out, would be less so with the actual introduction of a coveted secret daughter, and more deliberately so with the apparent nickname that used now. It took me a moment to connect these dots with the journal entries. Once I did I became just as graceful a host.

"It is very nice to meet you, Li-Li. Please do come in. Julia, it is good to see you as always. Do come in and make yourself at home."

I did not know whose smile was more genuinely more absurd at the time—Julia's or mine. I closed the door behind and ushered my guests into my kitchen. We ate, drank, and then shared a multitude of interesting stories as we established the ground rules to moving this all forward quickly.

The pot of tea I made satisfied even the most discerning palettes within this happy trio. We made pot after pot of hot beverages and before long four hours had passed. I certainly did not want to interrupt the marvelous train of thoughts that were passed around my kitchen table so I excused myself and made several hurried phone calls, cancelling an equal number of prearranged business meetings. Each time I returned to the busy room I was brought up to date as though the interruptions were not apparent. And they were, of course.

"How did the calls go," Julia had inquired when our guest retired to the bathroom to freshen up. "Was there any concern on their part?"

I smiled back and gave her the short synopsis: "We are fine for the time being. There is no need to disrupt this new chapter. I think that this is much more important, yes?"

"Oh, without a doubt we have stumbled into something of a unique opportunity. I would like to offer a quick proposal: How about we turn this whole bloody mess over to the daughter and simple walk away."

Wow another surprise I may have not planned for in rapid succession. I was thus stunned again and did not have a handy retort in time. Our honored guest was making her way back down the hallway. This would be a tough one to work around. I could tell that there was no wiggle room left between my partner and I. Our engagement was over as quickly as Li-Li entered the room.

"Would it be possible to mix a bit of business into this more than pleasurable afternoon?" I would head this impending thing off at the pass, so to speak.

"Sure, I am open to a change of venue." Li-Li's reply was genuine enough. She bowed her upper torso only slightly to both of us and signaled that she might have anticipated the move well in advance.

I looked at Julia's face. Yes, she was as unnerved as I so we continued on kind of on the fly. I started back in on my off the cuff proposal.

"Your father and mother were maintaining a very interesting database with regard to your family lineage. It covers lot of families for that matter. And we thought that you might want to inherit everything up to the final entries. Perhaps it will more properly explain what Julia and I had discovered and how extensive the detail were—so are?"

"Please continue, I will just pour us another cup of tea."

This woman was as graceful as her parents were—for this there is no further doubt. It was very appealing and I tried my best to regain my focused intent—successive approximation to a desired goal. She was bowing again and the tradition is continued.

I spelled out the details we had garnered through our own research thus far. Julia added in some very spot on details, but I could see that something was troubling the woman. Her arms were crossed and she had a bewildered look—not quite stern—on her face. I reached out and touched her had at long last and begged her to share her thoughts on the matter. I had to as we were running out of tea. Time was of the essence with respect to this social turned all business gathering.

"I have to tell you something but I will need your promise not to overreact to its disclosure. I am not quite sure that I should even be talking about this at this time and place."

Another surprise was well within range and I shot Julia a knowing look to be ready for just about anything possible—within the normal range of pre knowledge—and its ramifications. I hoped the scant glance would have been enough.

Li-Li was about to drop the next succinct statement that would evidently be by design: controlling, with thoughtful intent of aim, and unbelievably earth shattering news. It would definitely be one of those things that would clearly through us off our game plan.

"I have a daughter as well as a son. This is one of the reasons I am here at this time. My daughter is stationed here in Bellingham. She is an officer in the Coast Guard. She is an Engineering Officer and has second command of a Coast Guard Cruiser."

Let me say now that there are times when one hopes that another cell phone will ring right in the middle of a conversation. Li-Li expresses a great sorrow but she must react to the name that has obviously appeared on the small LCD screen of her all too compact mobile phone. We nod in acknowledgement as quickly and she excuses herself from our round table and makes way out into my back garden. All present things aside we are unsure of her need for absolute privacy and scramble to clear the table before us in hopes of gaining a closer position to my wide and wonderfully open kitchen window. Some things can be preplanned, even when unintentionally executed. I would take this as a sign of meeting a necessary middle ground.

Julia and I listen in and we are happy to hear an endearing call between mother and son. The details are not as important to reveal.

"Thank you." Li-Li sings this out as she rejoins us at the table. "That was my son. He is able to come north today and will need to be picked up at the airport. I am afraid that I will have to leave soon. Please forgive me."

"What business in your son in, if I may ask?" This came from Julia.

"I am very please to say that he is a member of the State's Attorney Office. Both my daughter and my son have many accomplishments. I'm sorry if I am bragging; I am very proud of them both."

"Well it is a mother's right to be proud. Do you have any pictures of them?" It was my turn, yes.

Li-Li is walking with us down the hallway and then into a well lit front door entrance. The pictures she shows us in part fill in another piece of the upcoming puzzle that we will both have to anticipate well in advance, as well as plan for, now. The young female Officer is a picture perfect capture of the face that yelled down at me from the Cruiser I cross paths with earlier on. My heart is beating a bit faster now and it is not because of the inherited beauty of the woman portrayed in the photo in khaki uniform. It is because of the fact that the snapshot was taken in front of the local berthing pier and in front of the actual ship.

Full circle is now at hand and I am hoping this woman's departure is enough to shake me out of my stupor. In the beginning of my day no one could have completely prepare me for all the things that come with life, especially within the family unit. It is not enough to say that to expect surprises is part of the preplanning process no more than it would for post planning. So when I say: Now I want a good outcome from my latest project, it has a whole new meaning.

Julia and I would spend the remainder of that evening reworking all of our earlier views with respect to what we now planned to off load. And just who we would off load to was still up in the air, so to speak, and a very long night indeed. Julia slept over, again.

It is the dawn of a new day that I wake and fully expect my morning to begin without pressing questions. I do not want to be nagged so early in the morning—especially by me. There was some unfinished business about the sudden appearance of this mystery sibling. How was it possible that she found us on her own?

"Wow, that hurts," I suddenly exclaimed just to myself as I mustered up the strength to deal with this new reality.

Julia must have pushed this relationship. Did she do this on her own? I was not yet ready to accept this troublesome judgment and chastised myself for projecting a breach of trust. But it came back all the same to the expanding circle of friends this mystery was binding. Her friend on the island was the expert on hand. This is how Li-Li came to our door.

Suddenly I was more in tune with the little voice inside of my head screaming: "Her friend is an Investigative Genealogist, you dolt."

I was developing a sense of interest in this interesting sounding profession. But just how far back did this other woman become involved?

# Chapter Twenty-five

## *Mocking Accusation*

SO WELCOME TO MY WORLD I might add cleverly enough. I just finish up a call with a business associate overseas who is interested in taking my story to script. Well I suppose I cannot really say this is my story as it had innumerous contributors over a longer period of time as one can fathom. It turns out these data archives are not as uncommon, and we had originally came to a similar conclusion. But my associate is in the business of scripting interesting happenings and when I say the look on his face during that last Skype call I knew we had stumbled into something that would transition altogether, once again.

I begged and I whine for as long as I feel necessary and Julia has started to come on board. She wants to head in an opposite direction and let this thing quietly segue into something of a family matter. The daughter has shown interest in taking this on, but I am still reluctant when I hear that her own offspring won't use this matter as some kind of trap. To be on the safe side I have chosen to have this particular aspect so reviewed—my due diligence path to prolonged happiness.

"Well without having looked at the actual data, it appears that you have broken no laws—nationally or internationally. You were provided this data by its owners in good faith, although the methods used to gather the information over so many decades is still in that gray area. Any you say that you were not at all involved in its compilation?"

"As it is an intimate and very detailed genealogy study of Chinese immigrants over several family generations, and the fact that I am from a purely Irish vein, I can say straightforward that this is not my work in any shape or form." My mind was that clear on the matter at hand, but I did stand in disbelief that the question was even put to me that way.

"I do not think that this will be a legal issue for you. However, that said, it might be in your best interest to steer yourself away from any other interactions with that series of undersea cables. We still have not been able to ascertain who owns what."

I really do like working with legal entities. They always seem to be dealing with the straight and narrow on the surface, but deep down one suspects that there was almost a challenge being made just under the surface of this conversation. The truth of the matter is that the cables ownership is very well known, but those specific entities so thoroughly disclaim and connections so as to not incur the cost of cleanup. That said, and duly scrutinized by the legal bank sitting across the large table, I walked out of the conference room with a much clearer picture of this link which lay at the bottom of a murky Salish Sea.

It was kind enough of them to let me leave when I did— those fees were killing me financially. As I drove off I pulled the car over in a parking lot around the corner and provided Julia with an update, leaving out the part of the journal making its way to Europe for additional treatment.

"On the surface of it all, I do not think that anyone will come after the family. The review leaned toward her being a rightful owner of this property given her family connection. How she proves that to any court at a later date; given the issue of her biological parents is a strange one; is another legal entanglement all together. Perhaps you might want to stay clear of that. What do you think her offspring would make of that—with regard to their grandparents and family legacy?"

"I do not want to know the answer to that part, thank you very much." I could hear the smile on Julia's face during our conversation across towns. But then she signaled me that she had another incoming call so we would pick up this conversation at another time. "Sorry, but I do have to take this call. I will talk to you by the end of the week. Bye".

Asked and answered, as they say in the legal trade. I drove off and headed north. I had to see another friend across the border in Canada. It was kind of an unrelated yet still related matter in this expendable hour.

When I arrived at his house on the coast he was already outside waiting for me. He pretended to be playing with his dog but I knew all too well what this formal greeting meant to me. I was not going inside any time soon. So we strolled about his property and made some ilk of small talk as we commented for the third time about the weather.

"What are we avoiding?" I asked simply enough."

"My partner has been on the war path for hours on end, I am afraid to say. It appears that I may have strayed a bit out of the fold at a party last weekend. I am out here with the dog because anywhere else will put me in the line of his wrath. Would you care for a glass of wine?"

"So you cannot argue like any other couple outside? Yes, that is a cool and crisp white. What is it called?"

He was handing me the bottle as we sat down. We sipped the cold wine and looked over the side of the bluff and down to the large waterway that flowed between the Canadian mainland and that of the full length of Vancouver Island. To the north of our viewpoint was an enormous cluster of smaller islands and one could almost connect the dots using the enormous number of boats sailing and motoring between them. The bluff was clear of trees, but the stumps were still standing and were used to host large potted plants of any sort that could tolerate this regions varied weather.

"Normally I would avoid answering that sort of question. But the truth be told, we still reside in a segregated community with little toleration for First Nation fags—so their term not mine. Oh, don't fret so, we are used to it."

"It: this being the twenty-first century." I was cheerful with my less than guarded retort. I never learn those life's lessons: leave well enough alone.

"Hey, we still enjoy our traditions. Don't be a bad guest or I'll push you outside. It is complex to some, I suppose. It's just that we want the best of all worlds. Is there anything wrong with that?"

"That is not why I am here, by-the-by." I did need to change the subject sensing that the other would leave me in a dead end. We toasted out friendship and left the other alone, for the moment.

"Did you come across anything relevant to my earlier inquiry?"

"I did indeed. The software you brought to my attention is indeed on the market. And I must add that it has really taken off. I believe the appropriate phraseology is 'it's gone viral'. You are not going to reap anything soon, so I am going to advise you not to pursue this to any rightful end. It had already spread too far."

"Well that is good advice. I will take it with all due consideration. Thank you for looking into to it on our behalf."

"Oh, on our behalf: Is this where I am to be led to think, that you are some large and ominous organization? I think that we are larger and have more resources to throw at this than you think. It has already drawn the interest of the First Nations Council. They think this is the best thing since the dugout canoe."

My friend and wise business associate is laughing coarsely by this supposedly insider joke. I guess I only got half of it and stood by for the remaining explanation when his partner showed up with another bottle of wine and a third glass.

"I come with a peace offering. May I join you? Harry, don't laugh like that. You know you will hurt your throat and we have recital tomorrow." The maiden thus arrived at our side.

My friends partner—significant other for a longer period of time than I could muster—was a muscular presence and had a commanding enough voice of his own, sans the whispery finish.  The three of us drank and talked forward past the subject of my specific interest and reason for being here n the first place.  And as soon as he dominated our conversation I was being asked to stay for dinner among friends.

"I would love to stay.  Is this a small or large dinner?"  I did know well enough to ask.

The answer was as murky as the white capped water below.  The wind had come up and the three of us headed inside, swaying to the tune of wind and three bottle of wine downed between us.  Like fellows in a cartoon we attempted the double doorway simultaneously and then broke into long fits of laughter.

I thought the door jamb scene was ridiculous enough but the chores continue for a long time after.  If it were not for the knowing glances that they exchanged with each other I would never have guessed that I was the center of their joke not too long afterwards.  Perhaps it was then that I saw the banner stretched out between the two columns in the front living room, announcing someone's birthday—it wasn't mine.

No, I was not the guest of honor at this evening affair but I did have to dress a part.  As was typical with this entertaining couple this was to be a theme party for their intended guest of honor.  I am not suggesting in any way, shape or form that I felt particularly out of place at this predominately gay bash, but what they made me wear was embarrassing.  The theme was along the guidelines of ushering in the formal New Year for Asian and Middle Eastern cultures, and I was dressed in Alibaba garb. I looked positively ridiculous in my all the way out there transparent wraps and sash. The only thing crazier was the over-sized ceremonial sword that I must maintain by my side for the entire night of festivities. So there stands the one straight line in the already zigzagging crowd around midnight. It was here we were about to merge this no opting out party into a more formal tradition. Everyone chooses a partner for the first quarter, mandatory midnight kiss.

There is no disclaimer required at this moment in time. I simply had to fit into the crowd or be shown the way out by no less than my own timid sense of embarrassment. So when the gentleman to my left put his taught arms around me I allowed myself to be put to the test of friendship. I did not stand out at least for the next hour. And later on, after counting a sea of empty wine bottles and helping with some of the debris, I helped my friend and business associate with taking out the trash somewhere around six o'clock in the morning.

"So who was that I ended up with at midnight?" I explored all of the possibilities on my won during the early hours but met a dead end. My half in half out escort snuck out of the front door with another man around two hours earlier.

"Oh, come on, it was only a kiss. Get over it—you didn't melt, did you."

"No you know that was not my point. There was something more official about his manner; that kind of sensed formality like he was scanning the crowd for something else entirely. Am I making this up?"

"Not on your life, I'm afraid. He is an officer in the Tribal Coast Watch. His jurisdiction spreads all around the far edges of the nearby reservations."

"Like the Canadian Coast Guard?" I was startled on several fronts. I tried to recall everything that we had talked about across over one and one half hours.

"Yes, a lot of people noticed that you do not like to dance. You stayed on the sidelines for almost all of the night. But I understand why?"

"Is it because I suck at dancing?" We were both laughing at this inside joke.

"Yea, that's it my friend. It's because you suck at dancing. Hey, no one expected you to engage in make out sessions, but you did appear a bit stuck."

"You have no idea. He asked me to go up to one of the bedrooms at one point, and in another moment he attempted to squeeze into the bath room with me a share more than a pee. Yes, I was taken a bit off of my game—thanks for noticing."

"But did you enjoy the party?"

"I did indeed. Thank you for having me over for the extended stay. And please thank your partner." It was a good save.

"Does he know about the software and the databases?" Yes, I really did need to jump back into business at hand. I was not sure I had everything before leaving.

"Yes and no. He has heard about how fast its use spread up and down this coast, but I do not think he understands the origin. On the other hand he did let it slip out that the under seas cable network does lie at the bottom of Canadian waters. I asked him about this discretely, of course. Interestingly enough he was taken aback by the fact that more people have not heard about its extensiveness. My word, this whole thing has really started to get interesting. I think that may be why he singled you out. I did let on about your waterborne interests and where you hailed from."

"You did not." I was alarmed by this disclosure and I showed it too soon. My friend was attempting to change the subject.

"Well if it is any help at all, I will keep an eye on this for you, and let you know of any further developments from this end. In the mean time, don't frown so my friend. It will all work out, as it usually does. Perhaps you can count on this as yet another fortuitous event."

It was not long after this conversation that some of his other remaining guests strayed to life and down the stairs to join us in the expansive kitchen. Everyone grabbed hold of a bit of party goods and paraphernalia and dumped them into the trash before lining up for coffee and breakfast goods that were spread out along the longer countertops. There was a whole lot of bare skin across this crowd and I felt unusually overdressed in blue jeans and a t-shirt. Most were still coming back to life as my friend walked out to my vehicle with me.

As I started it up he leaned in and gave me a little kiss on my unshaven cheek. There was a sweet squint in his eyes and I knew well enough not to prolong the other subject. I did believe that he would carefully look into the subject at a later time and I felt comforted that I did not step over the line on so many levels. We signaled our goodbyes and forty minutes later I was crossing back into the United States and zooming short of seventy miles per hour back to my home town just as the rain started.

This had been a good visit; that much I can say. But I had just realized how interconnected this whole genealogy thing was across families, cultures and borders. It was a stupid transition but now I had that Disney song rolling around inside of my head: *"It's a Small World After All."*

My entry into the rain soaked afternoon was doomed after all. I could not shake that song and I could not sit out on my back porch and watch the sun set. The Pacific Northwest; you just never know.

# Chapter Twenty-six

## *There on Your Own*

IT IS SAID THAT WE FIRST encounter ourselves through our parent's eyes. We do this continually when we are young enough to not know any better and therefore all the better. The customs that I still keep are classical enough, but in their own right they become unique enough so that I can recognize this thing called self and how I see my world without over sterilization. I want to hang on to some of my past, as others do, but I do not want to be controlled or guided by it overzealously by label alone. I do not have a tribe. I compare and contrast this to my friends who do, as if by rite of passage, against the two who raised me to explore this world on my own, evidently. Alas, the lessons of my dad become my own over time. I am the proud and very independent son.

I am fascinated by the last several days and attempt to think of them as dispassionately as humanly possible. There are known linkages and tears in the fabric of who I became as well as the offspring of other families I met along the way. I am fascinated by to such a degree that I have taken a chance and had this journal purposely refashioned into a script by my very dutiful and skillful associate in Germany.

Yuecan's words are moving from strong rhythms of harmonic value—melodies line after line that blend and complement each other parasitically—to those of counterpoint. I received an update just today. It is a rare gift my friend has and in the next four days he has moved the entire journal into this new form so that I barely recognize it from the original.

Several weeks after the rewrites I am in Munich, Germany and sitting in front of an audience of varied origin, in a dark but warm tavern that doubles as a venue for improvisational theatre. A bank of monitors comes to life and then music fills the crowded hall and we witness the writings of Yuecan's journal in their stark original cast against so many high resolution monitors that act as a video wall for the audience to become overwhelmed to.

There are additional rows of even larger monitors that spring forth with the colored heads against black backgrounds as they reinvent the one and only character in as many languages. They are simultaneously translated—in as close to real time as possible—across this small and private network of digital equipment. The audience is astonished by this media overload.

No one is talking now, with the exception of the heads moving about the wall of digital displays. Death had sprung back to life in this trippy script.

Yet, the underscore of this production is a real analog life, come to life in a virtual world proposition. This is another obvious counterpoint. Yuecan's reproduction has taken on so many personalities as is depicted ahead of me and to both sides of this packed audience.

I can hear those voices and they all begin to sound the same—so like this elder woman that influences the later part of my life—now this crowd's life. Yes, like another parent she projects every feeling I have been exposed to in her presence over the last episodes of her life. It is uncanny and a magnificent performance—this suite. I can just make out the imposed Chinese accent as though she were sitting or standing here in Germany.

I sit with hushed anticipation of the crescendo finish and scan this crowd for immediate and receive intimate feedback across the board. They are thus moved. And there it is at the end of the final act: our last meeting together has been relived through the audience members who jump up toward this mock stage and hug the monitors, full of excitement to meet someone other than who they first hand expected. It is the magic of the theatre that grabs us and holds us all when we are forced to confront us—face to face.

I wish that I could save this moment and play it back along side of Yuecan's last written conversation for intimate friends that couldn't be here. I know who is at the top of my guest list. I think about the last physical meeting which included Julia; who wanted to be here for this inaugural presentation, but could not get away from her duties back home.

I wished to relive that last utterance before she took her own life; too long before seeing a daughter that became only several paragraphs in a lifelong diary. And I wonder if Yuecan could see herself in the eyes, temperament and personalities of two offspring she never knew she had—this final stroke of bitterness.

This multi-media play would serve to project these final meetings from another point of view. Was this so indifferent to the real one that never had occurred? We all invent aspects of our lives, and project aspects of others into our lives, on screen and off screen. Were the faces on the screens just something of news created for the sake of explanation? Could it be a final sense of closure? Or, was it a means—away—to express some of the compassion we feel for those who we met and regarded them well. My friend—the associate—is a brilliant artist.

I came out of the theater thinking that this was pulled off with better vision than I had anticipated in the beginning. It was also the product of a very generous and supportive friend who took on the project without having ever met this brother and sister. The audience was as enthusiastic with Yuecan and her haunting recollections of being a visitor to a land that she never felt quite at home. Her loss became gain because it was carried forward. Some call this legacy.

We do regret the loss of those that impact us most. If we can keep at least one part of them going, then we are very privileged to have met them in the first place. We will not forget this loss entirely. This interpretive theater piece was a means of allowing us to be compassionate. It was taken and given a serious enough set of implications: the examination of pleasure, a composition of change, and to participate with all due consideration.

I kept my stay in Germany long enough to capture a series of reviews. Yes it was mixed, but all-in-all it was favorable. Now there was talk of extending it to other venues including Helsinki, Finland. The show was named Cross Remainder. It was all inspiring even though I spent more of my time thinking about going home and clearing up the misunderstanding that was brewing between my counterpart and the far offspring of Yuecan and Zhao.

As they say in the business: *"Let the Show Begin"*.

In this case I did go home and monitored its progress virtually at best. The escalation caused by the grandchildren was starting to get a whole lot louder.

This thing was starting to garner a lot more clout.

Fortuitous Event

# Chapter Twenty-seven

## *Who's Credible Witness*

IT HAD BEEN A WHILE since I thought back to the entrance to their estate, which was indeed a fortress in its time. The world of Zhao and Yuecan had been under surveillance for a countless number of decades, and I am sure the new owners have inherited some of this need to sneak a peek at what goes on inside of those monstrous gates and walls. To live in a place surrounded by surveillance cameras yielded what secrets that would still have any meaning left to explore? Had I been a more credible witness I might not have been left with the still remaining missing pieces. I was trying to stall, but the persistent requests by the grand daughter to call her back could not be put off any longer.

When we eventually met it had been at a designated place and time of her choice. Although she showed up to the reunion dressed more casually than expected, I could not shake the assumption that this was still somewhat of an official interaction. I stood so infused with the sense of urgency implied by her last voice message that it made me kind of stagger as I reached forward to accept the extended hand. I was kind of off my game.

"I know it's quite insane actually, but your last message seemed angry. I was not sure what to expect."

It was kind of a rambling appearance on my part, but was I any more relaxed when she put forward that the meeting was more social than not. My guard is up anyway—it just maintains the mood for the duration over lunch. I was living in the moment too.

""So please let me continue," she was enjoying a glass of wine while talking. This had to be a good sign. "I am a bit concerned that most of my family's life is now on public display. This is the principle reason for our meeting, by the way. This is not official in any capacity."

Did she just play her hand, or was this a lie that could be told for the health and wellbeing of the country. There was more to this presented front than meets the eye, so to speak. I sipped my wine in return and just listened for other more subtle indicators. We had been at this for half an hour and it seemed that we were still stuck in introductions. Where was the heft of this thing?

The main course arrives—yes, still lunch—and we pretend to be fascinated with its preparation and the wonderful scenery around the marina. At this point I have become kind of bored and watch the first hour tick by before we decide to share one dessert. It is chocolate mousse and it becomes the tie breaker between us. It is always chocolate for me—this truth serum—and I began to talk more freely.

"So how exactly did you catch what was going on in Europe?"

"I am not sure I remember. Something in the media one supposes. We are so barraged by information these days. But at the same time it sticks and I looked for more with regard to this journal play that was going on in Munich." She takes another big bite of mousse. It will be a race from here on out.

At first I am pleased that she did not volunteer any knowledge with regard to Helsinki. That would have been too weird, given that the project was still warming the hearts of the financial backers. This is such a small production. What on earth could she have stumbled on that brought us here today? The play itself was successful in Germany—but now this? I was simply stumped for any answer that did not lead me to believe that the surveillance was continued, and was encompassing all parties who had come in direct contact. Wow, what would I tell my partner in Munich?

"Oops, sorry, but we are running late. Can you walk me back to my car? There are still some details I need to follow up on. Would you mind?"

We walked along the waterfront path around the marina from the restaurant to the parking lot. It was strange that she drove given that the Coast Guard Station was only one half mile away. This continued to put me off, but this time the reasoning was trivial. Some people are just too lazy to walk. On the other hand she may be rushing off to a meeting at the other end of the city where two eighty foot cruisers are berthed. I went with the later explanation for the good of the conversation. But then again, after closing my eyes to the visuals before us I reflected back to the securely fenced in docks at that location. If it was one thing that I could remember about the installation was that it had little to no place to park at all. The mind soars.

"What else did you want to talk about?" I asked to get to what I hoped was the real point of this get together. The wind was picking up as we entered the parking lot in question.

It's odd the things we notice out of scant attention. My mind was wandering around the expansive parking lot and all I could focus on was the large white van that was parked toward our end. It seemed to be staring back at us. It was only a feeling. But then there was the fact that it had a big bay window carefully pointed in our direction, and then there was the odd cleanliness of the vehicle. It had no markings at all. There was nothing to lock onto. What are the odds?

"Can we get back to the subject at hand?" This time I implored her to continue. I was nervous enough to pretend not to be staring at the vehicle in question.

"Your friend Julia mentioned something about your finding under water cables leading in and out of my grandparent's property. Did you ever find out what they were?"

At least we were getting somewhere. We stopped for a moment as I grabbed a magazine from the stack of a yacht broker's facility. There was a scene of Desolation Pass on the front cover. Perhaps it was an omen of things to come. I had been there far too many times. What rock did they scan down to watch my journeys? I have also paddled in that area and around the North Sound and San Juan Islands on a fairly regular basis.

Yes, I had come across sightings of the Cruisers on as many occasions but always thought it to be coincidental. Would I be patient at all now, or would I wait to see how this latest incident plays out. The van was starting to drive away. I cannot make out the license plates from this distance, but I do have the markings all the same. There was something on the back of the van.

"So what do I know about those cables. Well it seems that they are fairly public knowledge—at least from where the commercial fishermen are concerned. Most everyone I have spoken to have a story to tell. I assume many if not most are simple folklore. It is interesting at best." I would not play the Lummi hand.

"It is quite a mess actually. It seems that we are always receiving a call for assistance by some fishing vessel that has caught some piece of equipment around these cables. They are heavy and do not come free easily. We often have to send a diver down to free thing up."

Oh, good, now she is providing a whole lot of information. So why did she ask me? At the risk of sounding obnoxious I ventured about.

"You seem to have the answer—so why ask me?" Did I just sound like a prick?

She was taken back—this much I could read in the expression on her face. I had gone too far. But then again this is not an area of expertise. Perhaps graphic is better than leaving well enough alone. I smiled and used body language to explain my less than courteous pronouncement.

"Look, I thought I made this clear from the beginning. I am not here in an official capacity. Why don't you relax? Are my questions really that far out of line?"

Yes, there was some sort of pout. It was declarative enough, or I am just a sap for relating to this sad, non verbal communication. We both tried to smile.

"At lunch there was a couple standing by the retaining wall near the entrance to the docks. And just now, there is a clearly unmarked van in the parking lot that just happens to take off when I stare for too long. That is what I am reacting to—so not your tone after all."

We both stand in silence for a longer than expected time. I do not even look at her but I can sense that she glances over to me several times and then shakes her head. I catch a glance at the digital read out on her dashboard. It is now three o'clock. Our lunch and meeting has spanned two hours. I expect this may not be typical for a military officer with mid day duties to attend to. She did say that she was in a hurry to get to another scheduled meeting. That was now thirty minutes ago. We are standing in complete silence. No one even clears their throat. This is strange.

At long last she turns to me and she is not smiling. This is not a quick goodbye conversation that she is about to start.

"It's me they are looking after. I want to tell you something and I hope you can be as discreet as I need you to be at this time. I am being processed out. I have some baggage that they do not want to deal with and they keep looking for substantive evidence that will make their case."

"And we were under surveillance still?" I had to ask. I had a meeting I needed to be attending and I did not want to bring an audience with me. I needed a clever way out.

"No, that was the last of it; I'm quite sure. They make every attempt to be obvious. This is nothing like you watch on television. This approach is much more in your face. There is no attempt on their part to remain covert."

"Look, I really liked our talk. But this whole thing with your grandparents—I understand why someone or some party would want to take the matter in hand. I have to say that Julia and me; well we are only in it for the sheer pleasure of meeting someone as different as Yuecan and Zhao were—so still are. It is a story to tell. It is what we do."

"But I am trying to tell you that this is not at the heart of the matter. I wanted to ask you if I could see your notes with regard to the journal; that other thing is a whole different matter. Then again, perhaps it is not."

"Do tell." It was getting late and I would have to blow off my other meeting for now. This was a story I wanted to follow, more importantly to relate to Julia and what she had found about the brother. This was starting to get interesting.

"As it turns out I have a life style that is not entirely compatible with that of the Coast Guard's mandate for Officers of a certain rank. Because I am in second command of a ship, and of the ship's personnel, I am under more scrutiny than most. As a result of their ongoing investigations my time in the Guard is limited. I can no longer advance. I am at a dead end, and this is one place that you do not want to be at a dead end."

"It is an all too common story." I connected some dots.

"You were in the military?"

I was stunned by the question. This was some indication that I was not the target of surveillance. I would venture forward with this notion in mind. I assumed neither of us was off to another meeting at this juncture.

"Yes, I was in the Navy some time back. Are you asking me to weigh in?"

"Will you?"

"It was never important then, although I do remember one member of the crew being moved to base before one of our deployments. He told me he was under arrest at the time. None of us every heard about it from then on. There was a good amount of turnover in those days."

"Is it important now?" She wanted a more definitive answer, now that it was a more public media discussion.

"It still does not matter for me personally. However, that said, I do think that the issue has already passed and it is the media attention alone that prolongs it. It is just an opinion. I have many more."

"Well I can say that I am not astonished by your answer. Many crew members weighed in as well; to continue your vein of thought. Most did not—do not care."

She looked bewildered and at the same time adjusting to her own internal calm. It was at that moment that she reached out and touched my arm.

"Oh, there were one or two crew members that could not let it go. I suppose this was my own undoing. I was not as careful as I thought I wanted to be. It was bound to get out, that I was out. Enough said?"

Her eyes were kind and considerate even though I did not take a more definitive stand. I was thinking just then that I should have not had to—this was not my time. My time was in regard to her opening up to discuss that other matter. What did she need my journal note for—given that Julia had turned the original over to the daughter. There was something else going on and I could not get there fast enough.

We were walking once again. There was this draw to the water's edge to monitor the impending sun set and the changing colors of the sky and horizon behind Lummi and Orcas Islands. Mount Constitution, interestingly enough, became the forefront in this display.

"I want to see your notes. Is that a reasonable request? That is why I am here. I may have to leave the area if they continue. My formal review will be held at another location. It is not clear that I will ever return if I am processed out. Too many friends and associates living in the area, I'm afraid."

"Did Julia mention that the original was returned to your mother?" Asked and answered I think.

"She only provided my brother and me a summary of its contents. I was hoping there might be clues in my family history with regard to my current dilemma."

"Fair enough," I started to say as this new light shed another view.

But was it enough to disclose an all together different beginning. Certainly this new disclosure might push her over the edge. I tended to it carefully. We had rounded another turn on the path and took a seat on a long and private enough park bench. It was already dark given the sun's cast light was far below our visible horizon. We continued our exchange in the dark and I considered this to be a vantage point.

"I am not sure that I can be a credible witness to all that occurred during the life and times of your grandparents. One of the findings, on the other hand, was so clearly indicated by the journal. This is going to be quite difficult."

"Oh, that is a nice touch. Are you going to throw me into a state of panic? Is that the approach? Well let me tell you that I have been through quite a lot over the last several years of my own life. I think that I can handle about anything at this juncture."

She looked pleased with her declaration of readiness. So I volleyed back and gave her the not so usual news.

"Shit, I was not ready for that. Oh my word, that is not what I was expecting at all. My grandparents—brother and sister—are my mother's birth parents? I was not ready for that at all. I am already too exposed; now this"

And she began crying. I just sat there in silence, dwelling in this particularly sparse reconstruction of the woman's past, and in context of her present and impending future. So this is what now looks like.

Ok, it would have been righteous move if I would have leaned forward and told her that I understood. It would, on the other hand, never be enough of brightening moment, was it to occur at all, at this time and place looking over the darkened waterfront. For the moment all I could do was listen to the beat of my own heart. It was all resounding enough—this place I occupied; standing so stoic and remembering any other detail that I could have left out. If a particular memory of the journal serves any purpose it includes retaining and then playing back this nightmare intact, from the original author's point of view. This was Yuecan and Zhao's story. It was not for me to rewrite it for this woman weeping by my side.

For another moment it was all I could wonder as to how I would take this chapter if it was my life. It was shocking enough to read second hand. To understand its full impact I could no more stand in her place as she could stand in mine. And now she was stepping back and looking at me as though I have disclosed something else entirely.

"I wonder if you could drive me home. I do not think that I am in any condition to handle my vehicle. Would you do that for me, now?"

We drove out of that parking lot and only shared small talk between us. This was an inverse of set of problems that she had to explore for solutions with a much closer friend. The center of her universe would not allow me in, and her friends would not be my way out.

A final disclaimer is warranted here. My way out of any redress of life's complexities is to simply head out for a good paddle. Being on or under the water refreshes my body and spirit. It was not what I could offer her at all.

Perhaps with Julia we could share our thoughts within a similar same framework. Julia's life was in transition as well—so to compare and contrast where we can go. My friends across the nearest border shared a similar chapter, but on a different plane all together. And to deal with it appropriately they simply chased me out and across the border.

This thing was not about to involve Helsinki any time soon, or the other matter at all. But I knew that they were all somehow connected through spreading and shadowed cast of the journal. For a time I thought I could step out of it; I am dragged back in. And when her friend came running out of the house and out into her arms in the driveway it was instantaneously reinforced that this matter was far deeper than I ever expected.

Her friend was rather attractive; they made a good match. Yes, I am assuming all of this from one picture perfect moment at the edges of a driveway.

I drove off and left them to each other in the safety of the dark driveway. As I sped along I flipped open my cell phone and left a message for my counterpart. Yes, it was cryptic enough, though the message would be clear to the intended receiver. No telling how many people I had looking into the chapters of my life at this particular moment in time.

Michael O'Connor

Fortuitous Event

# Chapter Twenty-eight

## *Ahead of that Next Fall*

THE PROBLEM WITH USING cryptic messages
sometimes is the sender can often get too inventive with
regard to the sent and received message stream. In my
case I was simply too clever in my mix. Not only did my
beloved receiver not understand the intent of the stream
that ended up in her voice mailbox she was outright
incensed. Here I want to emphasize the intent, and the
unforeseen consequences of misinterpretation to all that
was read into this message. But the outcome—well I
am sorry that I got this so wrong. There was nowhere to
go now but down; down an inevitable period of time in
which I ashamed to admit: I was not clever enough.

Julia was not returning my phone calls. At first glance I
thought there was ample time to reinitiate the intended
message. That of course only made me the ultimate
fool. There was no getting around the fact that I had
sent off a cascade of loosely yet intertwined scenarios
which could not be stopped in the time. I never got
around to providing an explanation. It was like there
was momentum behind this cascade that was so
invisible that only its final outcome could be measured.

Too many parties were listening in on the conversation—this I could assume. An explanation at this juncture was no longer self evident. The thing built up speed and split off into so many direction at once that I did not even have time to inspect which strand to follow first. I sat in a dark room in the center of my house and watched another friend from my past go to work on part of the problem.

It does not matter why she likes to work in the dark. She just does. I could let this go because she was really good at what she does. Another mystifying aspect of her approach is she does not like to be watched by anyone beyond the locus of her control. So when she found just how many different entities have been creeping around my network she took this so personally that the veins in her neck and forearms pulsed with noticeable intensity.

"Why did you let this get so far?" It was accusatory enough but I was cool enough to let this go because it was part of her somewhat unabashed personality.

"The usual answer might be that I thought I could figure this one out on my own. Hey, I did get most of it, you recall, before I contacted you. Your roommate said that you were on vacation. You never take time off—so what gives?"

"Oh that is just stuff she makes up on the fly. You might never get a straight answer from her unless you know where to pry. Come over here; just look at all of this stuff, please."

Roxanne's intent was certainly clear enough when she ordered me to sit by her side. This might be really important or she was unsettled by my constant pacing behind her and then to each side. I was trying to get a look at the trio of monitors, but she placed that at such an extreme angle, as though enveloping herself in a strange spread of luminosity. Had I had my camera and tripod I would have attempted to capture this to use later. It reminded me of the war room on the ships I served on. Everything was aglow except of the steps one had to take to get to one side of the compartment to the other: on the ship and not so much in this centering environment. I stood closer and peered over her shoulders.

"That would be a total of seventeen ports that were opened. How many can be traced back?" I was not surprised and the tone in my voice was quite flat.

"That's the funny thing about official agencies. No one attempts to leer out from behind a wall or bounce across the globe. Most of these could be considered a straight line where I am concerned. Look at this one. This one leads straight back to a coastal watch server. We know who owns this one already—don't we."

I did feel a little better by this playful verbalization because it dealt with the obvious. Who else would want to know at this point? But then again that should have been a statement of fact rather than a question at hand. I had gotten clumsy in my approach. I could have gone further before calling in the next favor.

"Oh, get over yourself. We all miss the obvious on occasion." She was reacting to the look on my face and my hunched body position. "You missed a few more that even I would have expected, but then again we have not been in touch for a really long time."

There was the crux of the matter. If I wanted out now it would be far too late. She had that look on her face—so illuminated by the glow of the trio of screens and the traces of text that streamed by into as many logs. I am not so devout a friend. I only call when I need something, and almost never when they need to be reached out to and touched. Get over it I did when I spread open and embraced her from behind with a measure of good faith. This of course causing her to grab me by the shirt and pull me into one monitor in particular, almost rubbing my nose in the display surface.

"Look at this—do you see it now?" Her intensions and my receptors were a bit off.

"Fuck me running. There are a whole bunch of people looking at this. Why are they still here?"

"You tell me. What is it exactly you were looking into?"

Roxanne: she was so clever at time that it really made me angry and envious all the same. She had guessed her way into a part of my recent past. It was one I thought was buried deep enough.

Leave no trail and certainly leave no one body unopposed. It was her mantra and she was deploying onto me now. It was just a look. It was all it was going to take.

I explained the network of under seas cables to her and then by force of a more tortured day I let her know about the software we traded with friends at Lummi College and the further adoption by friends at Simon Frasier University. And then for the final disclosure I explained the girth of the genealogy database that Julia and I had turned over to yet another party. I stopped for a moment and caught my breath. And then I kind of casually mentioned the antiquities we had found in the undersea cave.

Her smile turned into a frown. Would she tie this to the sculpture? She did—immediately so. I could see it in her facial expression.

"Well busy boy someone loaded something into your network. Guess who?"

"Really—tell me it's not so?" I was so stunned.

As it turns out nine of the remaining sixteen traces all went back to the same place. It was like my life had been emptied into a clearing house. I was really that stunned.

"How could you not see that coming?" She was mocking. I was astonished.

The truth is told it was long expected. I have distanced myself for too long from this circle of friends. My only salvation was to allow them back in through one carefully placed invitation. They would help me survive.

"Will you help me back it out? Please be ever so gently, if at all humanly possible." It was a genuine plea.

"Oh, I am already in, and you can count on some of the others. Look, they made this easy for us. You came across it in the first place; as mentioned earlier don't feel so bad. This isn't as difficult as you think. We just back this thing up to its beginning and move away."

"Thank goodness these are kids on the other end."

"No, it's more like thank goodness they get bored so easily." Roxanne did not look away from the screen and kept trapping the message streams.

"It's the legacy that they never took the time to flesh out. It is only the latest and greatest that catches their attention for any span of time. We knew that back then, didn't we."

"Let's not stop to take any bows just yet. We have a bit of work to do. Here you take this board and start back tracking. You do think that it was your friend Julia that started this thing, yes?"

"I do now. I have had my head in the clouds too long."

"You still do. But keep it there for a while. It will come in handy."

For the next several hours we were able to back out most of the troublesome area. I had left the room and ordered a pizza and fetched a picture of tea from the kitchen. When I returned she was still on line with another pal. Her energy and pace were essential, and at the same time I was happy to see that she was also reaching out to our once tight knit group for an additional assist. I suppose she was getting quite a burst of feedback in regard to my status in all of this, and why she should have left me out on my own. My moving away was not some mystery that needed the layers peeled back to most. They knew that I had gotten bored with it all and to some it stung all the same. They were knee deep, so to speak, and I had managed to get away—even if just for a little while.

"You said that you did a sweep?"

"That was the easy part. Yes, and then again just before you arrived. Why—we spoke of this earlier—are you uncertain?"

"Paul says hello." She took a glass from my hand and looked up at me while I poured her some iced tea. Another old friend had joined on line and was having a look at the results. I liked to swear a lot.

"Your counterpart—do you not hear the loud whine?" I tapped my earlobe and she echoed my behavior.

"He is a constant worry wart. You of all people should know that. Is the pizza on the way? I am fracking hungry"

Cryptic enough; echoing a really bad show. This always made me laugh. Her skills at mimicry were hauntingly accurate.

She had this way about her. I had forgotten why I got close to her in the beginning. The pizza was not going to arrive for at least forty-five minutes—they were so backed up on Friday night in this University town.

That would be time enough. We pushed off of each other and headed to the bedroom. I think a stream of clothes littering the way throughout would help us find our way back.

This was such a cliché. It made me laugh again.

It was a long time before I had her shape outlined by my fingertips but a far shorter time to recall all of those noises which emanated from Roxanne in the same span. She sweetly tasted me from one end to the other and our return to a more playful time in this on and off again relationship came to an inevitable and oft repeated climax. It was cheerfully exhausting and we lay side by side under one soft lamp and continued to rehash why we had drifted apart.

It was not my chief meaning to monitor the digital read out of my alarm clock. But I did recall that she was always hungry after such a moment of intimacy. I was hoping there were some things that did not change. I was hungry as well. Five more minutes of holding onto and looking at the resilient past would have to be good enough. The front door bell rang out twice. We froze, and then we yelled.

"You know we might want to consider what that sounded like the other end." I was the first to get up because I could not appear at the door in this state.

I dressed and she sat up in my bed and shot me a look that brought back another row of entries from my past. I was not sure if it was the way in which I was dressing but it did occur to me that she was going through a similar set of reviews. Disappearing into the hallway did not help. The look was burned into my mind and I felt a wave—perhaps a flood—of rekindled passion. Would this be the right time to go back in and plea for forgiveness? Perhaps not—I was opening the door.

The pizza delivery guy asked me if everything was ok. He did hear our yells. I gave him an extra tip as I received the pizza. He got there.

As I stepped back inside I thought about the last time I heard from Roxanne, when she initiated the contact.

She and her significant other married around one year after I moved away. I was invited to the weeding but unfortunately I played out a very lame excuse and went kayaking instead. It was not that I wanted to dodge what I had left behind; no matter how painful the memories were at the time. These memories were still the same as I carried the pizza into the kitchen and began to assemble the meal onto the plates. I was still being a coward; never wanting to go back there in the first place. Now it was in fast forward.

This was to be another rite of passage. Only this one was the rite before the next fall. I was going to earn this one and wear it out in the open if there was any chance of counting on her continued assistance, and that of my remaining circle of friends.

After all, I knew full well that it was not a well intentioned greeting that she had passed along. She was telling me that some friends were imploring her to pass on this support, and let me drift into the dark recesses of whatever rock I had just crawled out from.

She would have been that incensed if I remembered anything at all. And I did acknowledge that it was all too warranted. She and I had strayed into a rebound before. Oh, who said this thing was the only thing that we had to backtrack and unravel.

This reunion and I found a middle ground as we sat close to each other and had a fine meal of pizza and tea. This was not so informal an occurrence as one might have been led to initially. She disclosed that this was something that had floated to the top in her world when she and her significant other decided to cool their own relationship. I came to find out that they in turn had become closer friends than ever; this avenue of separation brought them together.

Was I willing to do the same? She ate and I talked.

"Since we are taking a bit of a break from our other business, can we go there now?" I was certain that this would change the overemphasized appearance of fair game that was stubbornly caught between us.

"I thought we were doing just fine. Why ruin that—we will be just fine. On the other hand: if you think there will be anything left of your relationship with your other partner you are delusional."

Her pointing things out with regard to Julia and me steered a tad redundant in the conversation. I was already going through the stages of relationship change: alert, unclad, and gone away. Julia set a trap for me. How and why she did this was of less interest at this point. Right now all I was interested in what sat across from me and what it was supposed to mean. The other was simply an issue of damage control.

"What I meant was how we will react when they react to our walking this thing backwards. Certainly someone will notice." I decided to pursue the easy path first.

"Well, let's not underestimate ego on their end. My team will knock it back into place, but yours will have to put up a retaining wall. They will be back at it with a vengeance. But because they were not attentive to legacy, their efforts will flop. And that will be followed by boredom and coupled to budgetary constraints and restrains in further resource utilization. Sorry to break this to you pal: you are simply not that interesting to what they are trying to resolve."

She jabs and I feign to dodge. I remember the game well enough. We both have a good laugh. She can be so direct yet pleasant at the same time.

"I understand what you are suggesting. I am tripping over those things that have already have been discovered. But what about those things I make that much more apparent?"

She smiled because she remembers it first.

"So you are on your game. What do you have in mind? But before you get started, let's revisit the bedroom scene, shall we. Did you like it? Was it as good as the past?"

She leaned in and kissed me and stroked my arm right as I was attempting to swallow everything including the last bit of the pizza. As I did my best she was kind of laughing and kissing. This must have reminded her of something else.

"The first time we were intimate we had been drinking champagne. Do you remember? We were making out and all of a sudden you had to bolt into the bathroom for something."

This was a dare to return to it. It was also kind of sad.

"The bubbly caused a bout of back up. I fled the scene to fetch a Tums, if you remember anything of the truth at all."

Sad or mad, it no longer mattered. She was bracing and so was I.

It was a different look she held. So was mine. And we made ready for the battle that brewed.

"You said I always seemed to be running away from something. Would it have killed you to come to our wedding? What were you running from?"

She was so angered by my less than suppressed reaction that it impacted the remained of the conversation. This was supposed to be a sort of celebration of our lives moving forward again. But because of my not wanting to let go entirely, it became another barrier to entry.

She thinks you will do this again. I think that she is right.

I could tell that she was really mad over sad with this last non verbal communication. We held our ground, respectively. I kind of paralleled our other matter; in that it dealt with the painful obviousness of unveiling what had already been so obvious. There was nothing new to reveal. But she uses this motion so I would do my part in keeping the subject afloat.

I needed her in so many ways I was losing track. Did she feel something of the same?

It was a reasonable peaceful evening we continued to prolong. It was best not to test the industrial strength of a (past) relationship before one understands the full ramifications of pulling it forward. If it breaks at the wrong place at the wrong time it means impending and unavoidable disaster. It was enough that we both wanted to peek under the covers. We went to bed together, and then slept together until the first rays of the sun penetrated through the curtains of my windows.

It was the night to be remembered because it was so in tune with everything we had entrusted to each other before. I sometimes ask myself if there is any benefit to walking backwards.

In the morning we engaged in intimate play as we were accustomed to before. It was well into the late morning, and then into the early afternoon when we pulled each other out of bed and took a shower. It was one hour later that we were dried off and in the kitchen and eating a mid day lunch. And it was later on in the evening that we peered on line to witness the efforts of our extended circle of friends who were left to do the heavy lifting in the background while we rekindled our past.

I felt a tiny pang of the guilty as we saw that everything was back in place. It was a thing of beauty.

"Oh, that is truly a thing of beauty. It will keep them scratching their collective heads for some days to come."

We paused and we smiled. And it was just about then that we hugged for a longer time than expected. Was all forgiven in this short span of time?

"Want to go out for a celebratory nightcap?"

It was all we could do to keep ourselves from boasting about all of our fine efforts. Yes, we understood what was done and what would stay done, on the behalf of our friendship. But we could take some pleasure in the manner in which started this all off: successive approximation to a desired goal. It was an odd and often referred to bumper sticker of our past. If you lived through it you would already know what it means.

"What do you think Julia will say the next time you cross paths?" Roxanne was finishing her second drink and there was a hint of giddiness in her tone. It was for my reaction; I would guess—close enough to the real thing.

"I think that I have her angry in so many directions that she will not know where to start. I do have reservation about the other woman, as discussed. This means our troubles are still growing."

"Oh, you mean the open ends of this multi-faceted question. I think that she would have done fair had you not opened her to the fact that she is the troubled owner of this new plan. Or is this about the other thing with the two offspring?

Roxanne was good at summing things up. I sipped my second drink in silence and pondered her latest body position. How much of this I had to read into was entirely up to her.

"Did it ever occur to you that what you uncovered will have a good turn? The venture in Europe is successful because you sparked this thing in your buddy. Your friends and associates on the reservation—on both sides of the border—seem to be pleased. The brother and sister provided you with hints of wonderful omission on so many levels, that there will certainly be some interest to their difficult history, in respect to your own. So what gives; where is this tremor coming from. Let's start there."

"It is in the compare and contrast to my own life, I suppose. Most parents seem to have this instinct as to where to lean into their offspring's lives. I can only reflect on this at a distance."

"Most history is told at a distance. Why did you think it would be any different? Think of my own. Look at how that got us here."

Roxanne signaled the waitress for another round and then moved her chair closer.

"Look, if you follow most film and television shows they always circle back and put key characters right into the path of the story. It all ultimately becomes about them. It is this very odd strain of reality video that seems to explain this best. Our generation provided the means— the infrastructure—for this heightened exposure, but then again we are the most surprised by its content and utilization. What did we think would happen?"

"And your point is?"

We sipped our next round of drinks in polite silence and noted the resplendent array of activities all around us. It was the surrounding noise level grew at so many octaves that we really did have to lean in close to hear one another's thoughts. I was close to an answer. And Roxanne was close to a question.

There was no reason to let this moment slip away again, so I squeezed closer to let her know. Most of the people acting out and drinking around us were two generations back. I suppose I kept my thoughts to myself because what was in front of us was a reminder of what time was misspent between us yesterday. It was time to live in the moment and I was certain that she was managing to do the same. The other details were missed due to our self realignment.

It was strange to be suddenly caught up in the middle of this thing with Li-Li's daughter and friend sitting off to the left of us, and seeing Julia walking off hurriedly in the far distance to our right. It was a funny kind of reminder that things did not always seem as they appear just on the surface. Was this some kind of bizarre coincidence?

Things did converge indeed that night. But it would be a matter of more time to witness what was beyond the next fall in the morrow. This was still a small town. It could have happened well on its own. In the mean time we just had so much catching up to do that we did not care.

"Yea, that was, is, pretty strange. Never a dull moment in a university town is there? Do you want to dance or wander home?"

It was not a tough question. We wandered home followed by our own shadows thereafter.

# Chapter Twenty-nine

## *Back to the Pool*

I THINK ABOUT LIFE A LOT MORE now that I have time on my hands. This seems like such a pat statement on the surface but it is with resilient regard that I get there at long last. A brilliant exit plan was hatched and put into play as immediately: every good boy deserves a good deed, and every well thought out plan needs a good place to restart.

The impetus became 'why not now'.

At the most probable moment I became focused on what I needed was an earnest talk with me alone and in another place where I could not be easily found. There was this rush to early spring; my winter was already proving to be far too crowded and impossibly cold.

Many guests come and go this winter and although I embraced them with a heartfelt hello; I wish them a steadied goodbye at long last. The winter snow was extraordinarily light this year but it was quite cold. Even my last guest noticed this is not a holding hand and headed back south, to seek out the sun in the hope of start of a very promising early spring.

I was all the more ready for that gravitational pull toward change and a more temperate entry into nothingness. I wanted that reconnection with my roots, sparking a deep and lasting plunge into the pool of life at the deep end.

This is the harsh reality of being too caught up in this evolving soar opera, and therefore I knew bailing would bring me the necessary relief. Would it be sudden yes, but I knew deep down inside that the reward of change is change itself. Whatever else is needed at this time could be simply put off, or pushed aside altogether—a reward in its own right—to reflect on the universal essence of 'art imitates life'.

The rewards of this kind of lifestyle are sufficient, and might even be construed by others in my life as 'this is what he always does'. He simply bolts. But excessive consideration of bolting was all I had to do, to look for the new clues and report in summary that I'll be on my way to a new chapter in my life soon enough.

If I was right, as so it mattered, that no one simply steps into my path as the door is closed behind and the key fits the ignition to take me far away from this hopefully less than epic journey. Goodbye Pacific Northwest, so long to Bellingham Bay and the archipelago stretch in the Salish Sea. I am self employed so what would it matter if I simply stepped away? Would there be sufficient payoff if I simply operated with no plan at all?

The payoff, if any, would be thinking about the looks of astonishment on the faces of my last encounters from a really long distance. Did he really do this again? Of course he did—it's in his blood. Repetition sometimes pays off.

The payoff will keep me happy and solvent for the next several quarters and provide a means of rewarding myself with several new toys along the way. I am happily employed—so self employed and keeping my own hours and playing in an environment I probably would have been in had I any more free time at this time in my life. I leave this enlightening play land in stark contrast for something else. It is in this compared and contrast to my own life, I suppose that I only meant to move on if only for the next six months. I do this if anything by instinct alone—who needs a damn plan after all. Some others might argue, as they typically do: "we never saw this coming." Well I did and my reaction was to simply push off and reflect on all of this from a greater distance as if by instinct alone.

*Wait for what they say*

*"We did not see this coming".*

*Propagate that next*

Most parents seem to have this instinct as to where to lean into their offspring's lives. I can only reflect on this at a distance since I have none of my own. But for a lingering moment I became crushed by the weight of an extended family: the immigrating brother and sister, the by complete surprise daughter, and the invasive next generation brother and sister who wanted to get to the bottom of where it all of this the biology starts. A childless existence is one of life's little rewards.

This is no to say that I am the first to understand this. I go back in deep history and I can hear the Socratic Dialogue that *"a life without examination is not a life worth living."* I take this to also mean minimizing those distractions which get in the way of examining what it is in life you were looking for in the first place. In this case it was the drive for solitude.

I drive south and take in all of the pleasurable signs of an impending early spring. When I drive across the bridge separating Washington from Oregon I sense that the air coming in through the window is warmer at first touch and I can even taste the changing environment on my tongue. The sky seem a deeper cobalt blue as I listen to the sound of my truck tires go from hollow to solid ground. I am on land again and when I look below I see asphalt segue to sand. It is much finer sand that ever can be found on the rock and graveled beaches of the entire coastline of Washington. So here is the first transition that causes me to stop when I head west and away from Astoria. I am stopping just short of the coast but far enough away from the rush of fresh water that spills into the salty sea from the mouth of the Columbia River. It is churning at the outer edges of this blending liquid and I cannot wait to get into the water.

My kayak is fully loaded and I am smartly dressed in seven millimeters of tight warmth and crash through the first volley of incoming waves. This is a place I kept coming back to in mind alone when I sped through all of the islands north in the Salish Sea. That was a place that was far too mellow and I wanted another triumph under my belt. I was heading the bow of my sixteen foot and thirty-eight inch wide kayak right into the rough and was slammed by both air and sea. This was a brilliant idea—taking me back—to the roots which drive me further out to what I had wanted: nothingness.

As I bobbed and remained floating in reasonably active seas the swells carried me about like a ball batted between ten to twelve foot paddles. However it is not as bad as it sounds as there is a tremendous amount of time between volleys. There are times when I paddle down into enormous troughs and seem to be able to ride them forever. And just when I begin to think about vectoring my next landmark a wave surges in and carries me right to its top so that I can clearly see how far I have now drifted from land. By my best assessment I am anywhere from twelve to twenty miles out at sea. But I don't care, because I have been there before.

Another one of the lessons I learned from my dad that self reliance does not come without blood, sweat and tears. He and my uncle had taken me out to sea to do a bit of deep sea fishing. We were powering one minute in a twenty-two foot cabin cruiser under the splendor of the Golden Gate Bridge, and in the next recollection we were estimated to be twenty seven miles off of the coast of California just beyond the Farallon Islands. Our goal that day was to fish for rock cod off of the rocky shores of this place that had once upon a time been used as an egg hatchery for the San Francisco Bay Area. No, not chickens, but sea birds. There were lots and lots of sea birds hatching on these rocks seemingly out in the middle of nothingness. We were comfortable.

I remember my father and uncle were engaged in a very lively discussion after a clear morning of sun and soft breezes. I was in my mid teens and at that age I kept mostly to myself, sans the fact that we were all bobbing along in a twenty-two foot boat. Then it was all of sudden obvious that their discussion was about me. I was a teenager. It was always about me. I had been engaged in a string of not too well thought out exploits and this trip was a means of managing a rift that was spreading between me and my father. It would appear that a non partisan referee was warranted at this point in my life. My favorite uncle stood on the fantail of that boat and stared me down. He was a childless uncle and that was why I loved him the most. He screamed the life I want to lead. He did what he wanted, and when he wanted it most. And now he was deciding my fate.

I recall my father pleading with him to ratchet his plan down. But then they talked again in a small and huddled mass of two men with a plan to remedy a wayward boy. There was a shared smile and then a strangely ritualistic handshake followed by a hug. Apparently their plan came together before we would hit mid day.

The seas were eerily flat and the boat went from bob to sway. It was when my uncle came to my side with my father and cornered me to where I had no place to go. I listened to their proposal. It made me sick at first and I was thinking that I had gone over that far edge with regard to my dad. It was another of his life's lessons and he related the detail while sitting down on the edge of the boat's stern. The man took his time in reminding me that it was my insistence that we carry my long board along on the port side of this boat. Had I remember that I had pleaded with the two men that paddling around these islands was an important chapter in my life. And would I be willing now to hear their plan to carry an expanded version of that plan—in this suggestion of moving on to manhood.

My dad had been so right to assess that calm day that I had been somewhat of a disappointment as his son. I had showed strenuous disregard for his pleadings as an experience authority, and my teenage years had to change for the better for the both of us. It was a justified assessment as echoed by my uncle. Apparently he was already in the loop. I had been defined by my repeated defiance against all adults who appeared to stand in my way. Would I now be willing to prove myself in an independent act if that is what I really wanted? Did I want to appear independent, or did I want to relinquish that right of control.

I took a gamble as I pulled into my wet suit—head to toe—and then lowered my board into the smooth and translucent waters off of Farallon. Arc north and take a bearing. Then keep your eye on the coastline and paddle with the current until you see the Golden Gate Bridge and the opening of the Bay. When you are several miles off from this destination, paddle south and head in to Baker Beach. We will pick you up there. Those were my last instructions as I turned away and paddled for the shore. There were now only twenty-six miles to go.

It is in these smart moments that we pull in earnest to the far reaches of our world. Some people take on hermitage but I always reach that place far off shore. I am now an estimated twenty-two miles off of the coast of the exit point for the mighty Columbia River. There are limited similarities because it is dangerously rough out here on this particular outing and I am beginning to think this risk was too much. But whatever I could do to calm myself would prove to be its own self reward. My heartbeat was steadied as I reflected on that life lesson my day gave to me and I reflected back to the moments when I knew I would reach the Baker Beach shore.

Compare and contrast was my mantra. But I could not let go of the notion that I had pushed this idea too far.

The waves had grown to an average of fifteen feet and it was all I could do to hold onto my primary paddle and hope the next volley would carry me high enough to see the coastline of Oregon again. A second volley came, followed by a third and larger one. I went to deep trough to not high enough to do a proper dead reckoning.

There was nothing to vector off of this time. It was only the tip of the next series of waves and on this I could not realign myself to any hope of landfall. I murmured in quiet desperation. I had to; no one would ever hear the screams if ever if I could muster one that moment. My pleas were to myself.

I regarded myself ready for most conditions so there was nothing to complain about. I had ample food and water—bottled fresh—and I could look up at any time and observe the sea birds circling above. The question I now held in higher regard was do these flighty things have more of an interest in soaring forever, or are they in need of resting and drying their wings on solid land. I took the only gamble I was offered that day. I followed their trajectory and uplift on the next wind. I monitored the direction of the sea spray that danced above each wave, and then I put my paddle forward in smooth and consistent strokes. I was not about to let nature win this race today.

There were things we learn in life that include the necessity of understanding biofeedback. I listened to my labored breathing and felt the pounding of my heart through seven millimeters of outer skin. I felt the air around me in between the wash of the next towering wave just before it nearly engulfed me. I was right about some things, and I was not about to abandon those thoughts. Could I smell the landmass? Could I sense the sensation of my perceived spin? I could indeed.

I sensed something, but it was not mass I came to expect. I began to notice a large white object vectoring in a recognizable direction. It was heading on the bearing of me. Was it so smart to be in bright yellow kayak—one that must have looked like a man riding a big banana in the middle of the ocean so far from land?

Someone thought so and the ship became larger as its heading became more apparent with its countering actions. When I paddled left it did so as well. And when I took another heading it seemed to be anticipating my every motion and followed suit. I hoped this was not a game. And I was right. No one else would have used so much white paint with that telltale splash of invigorating red. It was the Coast Guard and they were making way dead ahead.

The fortunes of my life are many and all though I wanted to execute an about face I knew fairly well that they would pursue me at any cost. They knew that I knew that I should not have been out here in the first place. But that was not the readied answer I had in mind for the end of today. Who would bear the cost of this rescue if it wasn't a rescue in the first place? I had been steadied in my projection and I had the sense and sensibility of paddling about these choppy seas without restriction. Who other than I would acknowledge that the ocean is that last frontier in which we can entrust ourselves to the fate of the elements we so encounter? My plan was to go to the point of nothingness. Did they not get the memo?

The faces that came along side were so angry at first. I was receiving fired question after question about the regulations of operating in these waters. Did I have the required safety and back up equipment for self rescue if necessary. Well the answer was yes but I had to show them all the same. Did I have ample provisions for most unexpected anomalies? Again the answer was yes.

Did I know that I was heading into landfall? So again, yes. But I am smart enough to know that this was answer was a bit of a push. They in returned stood and nodded to each other that I really did appear to know.

Who was I? I relayed this plainly enough. But then there was a long and regulated pause. This information was obvious enough. Someone had called the information in and somehow I had a ready flag by my name on some database somewhere on dry land.

I was being told how my name came up. Someone else was looking for me while they simply came upon me by surprise. I was wanted back on land for further questioning. I was so order to board with my equipment intact, and would I comply?

"Of course I will." What else could I have served as an answer? They were not about to let me out of their sights.

On board safely, with my kayak and gear now on their fantail, I was brought below deck by a bevy of uniformed sailors not unlike myself. I was ushered into a stateroom and provided a welcome hot mug of tea, and then the flurry of questioning continued.

I went first. I really want to know.

"Do you consider this a rescue? I really did have a line of sight, and do not consider myself inexperienced in these types of seas." I sipped my hot tea and watched as their stern faces begin to soften.

"No, this will not go on record as a rescue. We were operating in these waters as a training operation for new members of the crew. When they spotted you it was up to them to apply themselves to this situational drill."

I remembered the terminology fondly. When I was in the Navy we were always executing situational drills. And when I was last paddling this far out in the water I remember the phraseology my dad and my uncle used as they bid me well on my quest and comparatively more simple situational drill. In that I thought about finally reaching Baker Beach and seeing the cabin cruiser with two men on board beaming on my arrival. Had I passed into manhood by their definition? Had I mustered well enough to their instilled drill to ready me for the life that was ahead?

I now sit before a far different audience who has assessed me as being of sane mind. We are sharing similar banter and life experience when we pull into their dock and a very forward senior officer comes on board to collect me and my sea worthy belongings. I am as quickly ushered off of this vessel as it is already pulling away from the dock as my escort gestures me into a military jeep.

From the docks we have a very short ride through a large bay door and well into a tall and solid building. There are personnel all about doing what they have been mustered to do during the preparation of day into night. My kayak and gear, I assume, have been loaded off in another direction and will be thoroughly searched. I do not like to be this fare away from my gear. I mention this, every so gingerly and their concerns are waiting on the arrival of two additional officers of rank.

"I am sure you are thinking that your being here is a grand mystery." It is the beginning of a dialog which is truthful enough.

"I was told that this was not considered a rescue. Is that still the case?"

"It is. You know they were about to turn about. But then something else came to our attention."

Oh, so that is why I am being detained. I waited patiently.

"As you may have come to expect, we have things that trigger alerts which warrant our immediate attention. This is an extremely busy point of entry and exit for a large number of passing ships and it is part of our job to keep their passage out of harm's way."

"So what did I trigger? I thought that I was paddling well outside of the shipping lanes." I was kind of on course.

"We have an automated operation in place. We leave nothing left to unplanned for routine. Needless to say we have also deployed several other parallel systems as a back up to automation by design. In short your ID came up on a daily print out. One of our up north counterparts has you flagged. Once flagged, you stay flagged for quite a while. But this is not why you were brought in."

I am surrounded by less than relaxed postures and ever penetrating looks. I am being scanned from three sides and they are watching for my next non verbal communication. I play my next hand and shift nervously in my already uncomfortable chair. I have been signed, sealed and delivered, but their collective temperaments suggest that they have no idea what to do with me. At long last someone new enters the room and bends closer to the senior officer in charge and whispers something in his ear. He barely maintains his poker face.

Papers are shuffled on the table for my benefit. The folder jacket is wide open and I can see my name listed in the text. I am supposed to see this, I assume.

There is a follow on pause and I take this as my cue to talk.

"So why have I been brought here?"

No, I am not being a smart ass, and there is no challenge in my voice. I simply want to know as much as they do. Ok, the people around this table are all smiling, including me. It is like some grand stand off and someone has to give. I was not planning on staying the night at this station, but I will if I need to. I had wanted to slip off into nothingness and this seems to be as appropriate a place as any other. My rig and trailer are safely parked, although many miles to the south. I find it interesting that no one seems to be interested in hearing how I got out there in the first place.

Another hour and one half passes by and my less than direct audience is in and out so many times that I have given up counting the intervals. I can see hints of the sky toward the ocean begin to grow darker. The sun has dipped below the Pacific horizon. All I can hope for now is an offer of a ride for my equipment and me to the State Park where everything else resides.

The offer is long coming. But then again the reappearance of at least two of the junior officers into the room smacks of closure, at least for the day.

"We would like to offer you an escort to wherever you are staying."

That is all that is said. I do not push for more and provide them with the necessary information in kind. Fifteen minutes later I am in front of a military truck that is already loaded with my kayak and my gear. Yes, I do inventory at least as a more than passing glance. For all intent and purpose all appears to be close to how I had originally packed it. But then I made plans to recheck it all later.

My ride to the State Park was mostly in coveted silence. The enlisted pair who brought me south was a sullen duo and only shared glances and small talk between each other. Apparently I was a non entity to these two. I held my pleasure close to my chest knowing someone at a much higher level was embarked on a virtual journey to find out why my appearance led to such a dead end, on all ends.

But then again, one can take greater pleasure in realizing just how helpful ones friends can be to make all of this fade away. There was another legacy starting that night and I wanted to enjoy all of it, alone—in my trailer I was alone for the remainder of the night.

Michael O'Connor

# Some Patterns Emerged

Fortuitous Event

# Chapter Thirty

## *Consensus is Difficult*

AS IT TURNED OUT it was appropriate that I spent the night alone to reflect on and make refinements to my approach to the entire matter. My desire is to accommodate everyone who had touched this moment. My aim is to use these successive events as a jumping off point. I felt that I no longer needed to maintain any sort of relationship with anyone in particular to go on my merry way. My only goal was to manage the operational integrity of my living off the grid for an appropriate amount of time even if it was in an empty side of a closed State Park along the coastline.

Sixteen, no maybe seventeen days I hung gingerly off of my every trace of existence electronically. I have not heard back from my friend yet but I was given a partial thumbs by the digital profile had come out of my latest experience with the Coast Guard. Now I just wanted to venture on. As appropriate enough as that may have seemed at the time, I could not help but think that it was last party of interrogators would opt to pursue why I was here in the first place. This is why I think I am still up to several voices chattering all at once in my own head. It was a matter of maintaining parity with all who like to listen and watch me more than I did myself. I just did not think that I was all that interesting outside of my small circle of friends. No, I was not losing it, but gaining it instead.

Some things did become clearer as my solo trial came closer to a deeper and more meaningful meditation on life. I was kind of tired of living in a twenty-five foot travel trailer for any longer period of time. I did however spend a great deal of time assembling my knowledge and experience of living off the grid from a varied if not enlightening perspective. It was kind of like a breath of fresh air.

Each new location afforded me the time alone to understand a small set of problems and how they stood to be tested away from other stakeholders. I was isolated, but would I start to go manic channeling the great but deceased monologist Spalding Gray? It was not the apparent comparison I wanted to endear.

Many people I knew got the significance of his act. To me was the only standard to compare myself against in front of my non existing campgrounds audience. I was a party of one apparently as I surveyed the area and saw no trace of anyone at all watching this pathetic theatre.

The only other aspect of my life, by comparison, might have been another enviable soloist named Lori Anderson. Her more memorable spurt of performance growth, by my regard, was her going back to the basics of 'high technology' and finding is useful to dissect its legacy in social life as entertainment rather than endearment. This is how I incorporated my own past into my future while I waited it all out. I simply drove it down to the basics—remaining legacies—and pulled them forward into what evolved into the performances I helped create for a friend overseas, and on the other side of the border to the north.

Things were a lot clearer now—so I tell myself out loud.

I understood that one standard of living does not equate to another's standard performance. Alone I could break this down for its useful and constituent parts: digging for the stronger remnant strains, selecting those with the most merit, and then applying methods of my own soloed innovations to hold up with greater regard. I suppose now this is not the best way to represent me. But on the simple vote of one, it became my most balanced view. True consensus was difficult. All I needed to move forward was to refine just one more point of view.

So what did I know so far? I know that Yuecan's journal had as many shadowed passages as it had clarifying insights. How different from my life was that alone?

The answer was not much. She lived at a distance within a crowd, at the infancy of a new way of keeping care of connections. I lived close to that digital umbilical cord we call 'on the grid'. I was, in a manner of speaking, born into the cusp of the grid, and I live forever on the grid—so awesomely connected I could not breathe on my own accord without my laptop or cell phone. Life was simpler with my notebook and pen.

Each chapter of my live was then and continued to be redistributable. I come from a time and place where every aspect of the big legacy stuff was pondered to the chip level, and inside of the chip, so microscopic it was just too small. Each instruction line of code was witnessed in its entirety before a more infant generation took over.  More specifically, we were the only ones who understand that even the back doors have back doors. We put them there because we were unsure of even ourselves.   And this all propagated forward as an underlying structure to the social networks they adore.

So, this is my compare and contrasts to the legacy that Yuecan and Zhao brought forward in the same way, only genealogically. This is how I came to understand our parallel paths.   Hopefully by being alone, for that measureable span of time, I can then become assured of how these two chief worlds converged, rather than collided.

## What Legacy Begot: Middle Ground

I can see my friends far off in the distance and they are coming back down after our staff meeting and collectively we are all hunched over with the weight of the world around us.  This place where I am standing seems so empty to me; it is like looking out of a window and seeing nothing.  I want to go back up stairs and seek out my saner friend but I cannot because she has warned me to stay away as her stand alone lover was perturbed by my sway.  But it is miserably cold in the first floor lobby and I want to feel the warmth of the sun on my face on the terrace just outside of her office.  It is a golden ball in the sky that I seek; it is brighter than I can remember than in my past and I will see that there are no shadows on the ground under its intensity.

I am stubbornly askew because I used to feel that the shadows on the ground could reach out to me.   They are soft and perhaps colder but they embraced the thoughts that were in my head and I can remember when they made me feel glad that I had someone to share my day with; these things that danced slowly across every living hour in my place of employment and varied silhouettes. Oddly enough all of this we call home, because we are rarely away from it walls and inner chambers. We are a new working elite playing inside something called an advanced technology domain. We never leave for long.

To begin with our new task at hand, as decreed by the leadership side of the house is to build something so inclusively memorable that little will avoid its stamped identification. We have started with a notion of what can be pronounced, gathered and then hidden, only to be retrieved another day. We start out with a mandate for human-powered diagnostics.

In the midterm playing field of standalone platforms we have been challenged to bring it to its downfall by exporting part of ourselves. This is my first comparison to the brother and sister who became one of China's chief exports at the time. We start with the notion of standardization and propagation arithmetically over networks, but we are left to decide where someone could hide. We did so with challenge.

As standards became more apparent we embedded our most guarded thoughts and aspirations. Every platform we projected had one, whether they were tethered physically or over the air. And like the goal of genealogy we initiated this task through a sequence of identification, presence and verification.

Our approach paralleled the efforts of Yuecan and Zhao in so many ways. They focused on a single train of thought, while we focused on cross compatibility. We built an endless stream of timelines, across our own

425

family trees and histories. Only ours promoted constant revisions.

Our cross compatibility is hidden well with a common denominator call bias. Not our first departure, certainly not our last contrast. This must be some kind of disclaimer.

At our time there was a massive fight across a spectrum of ideas and this became the early onslaught of systemic disillusionment. So we searched across and found comfort in the fact that we could look at all registers users for presence and verification. We capitalized on that. That was our way to straddle across as many generations as Yuecan and Zhao. We built run libraries that were redistributable that would check for the presence of those who did not know or care. This is where we could hide our collective existence. We also looked for what would become legacy of co-existence— that which propagates and lives on forever across, change, revision and time.

Over time Yuecan and Zhao's database collected, assessed, assigned and then marginalized most if not all attributes of the current and then follow on generations of immigrants from the motherland. We did the same across motherboards. And where they spanned their collective repository of family trees, we simply assisted in ushering in a new extension to socialization, which later spread its connections everywhere. It was by our common denominator.

Our favored paradigms were simple enough. Regard the legacy and place it in history. If it is on the grid it will check for prerequisites across all systems and platforms. If it is on the grid it will download those other things elements of society wants hidden in things which called out prerequisite knowledge.

But in the space and time continuum associated with genealogy it is very rare when someone goes off line permanently, rather than periodically, without someone noticing. Family legacy continues with the trust that someone else is always paying more attention. For all other matters within, what we collectively were entrusted to compose; being on the grid routinely ends up all around the world. Who would pay attention to that?

To cope with at least part of this dilemma we established routines that happened each time we revive ourselves. Embedded hidden attributes are present at all the time. The result of presence and validation are forever scrutinized when we come back on grid and our histories are written into not too hidden locations. Sit tight and wait, it will eventually come back full circle— onto the perpetual network of highly regarded attributes we are so inclined.

Yuecan and Zhao understood this with regard to people. They too go off line as they travel in between or across once sovereign domains: China and USA. We now refer to this as globalization. We placed special tags in genealogy databases to cross reference people's presence on all public and private networks to continue to build upon their respective and collective profiles. It is an easy and ongoing task to create profiles against the coded identities that surfaced every time presence is established or reestablished: library cards, driver's licenses, credit cards, and email accounts, public and private document tags, all the way through today's global currency including the social networks and global positioning algorithms ad nauseam.

If they surfaced on the moon today it would already be a crowded property. Where can they be placed beyond that?

Based on direct experience, Yuecan and Zhao's database was not unique by any means. Many talented groups of folks continue to peek under the hood: the environment has evolved beyond this ecological niche. Back in the day when it was rolled out as an imperative so vast and comprehensive that most governments would have fits of envy. The network of genealogical studies that is owned and operated in Salt Lake City far below the surface of the earth in an area that could be described in terms of many, many football fields in presence, is now a miner player at best.

Based on a bit of show and tell this environment has evolved with an appreciation for all points of origin. This is far beyond any holy grail.

In another parallel universe, the diagnostic work transcends beyond showy presence. There is always a word to describe such heartfelt pleasures. This one could be described as fuller integration. Wow, it was a wonder to not only predict but project direction for every insatiable call of introspective time. It was as simple as that to propagate it to higher layers until the entire legacy was well hidden inside and out of the way. This is the world in progress, we promise.

In a world more intimately connected it is no longer a rebirth, but rather presence and validation. To say the least there is no such thing as neutrality, nor any sovereign state. Who can be the keeper of something which doesn't include gates?

What standards portend scrutiny of any other party who knows about the backdoors, even they have backdoors. Around the world these things are well known. There is close to complete symmetry with regard to the number of people who know about this, to the number who have never heard about it at all. It is all done with great parity to compare and contrast this to what Yuecan and Zhao had gathered warrants a deeper understanding. They could not have relied on technologies which now have only come into play. So what is their specific secret? How well did they parlay their legacy at all and on what and who's grid?

## Coming to Grips with an Expanding Gene Pool

I stumble, twist and turn but I am starting to assemble a better understand of the China connection. As communication methods started to spread many technical considerations were simply left to lay dormant. New technologies emerged and were adopted and it is hardly worth saying that they are very much scrutinized in what lay ahead, leaving little to look behind.

Everything is connected today; let it be towers, notebooks, laptops or handhelds nothing is lost to the imagination. Even when Jules Verne wrote this in an end of the eighteenth century manuscript titled *"Paris in the Twentieth Century"*, there was never an end. Was this man was so well ahead of the time; so silly we have slight insights at all.

The key to understanding the passage of time is to understand the high vulnerability of connectedness—so monitor it, decipher it, assess it and play it all out on demand. I embedded myself back onto the grid with the same set of friends and rejoined with continuation what we use to laughingly refer to as Artificial Intelligence—the extension of us all. The withstanding joke was more due to the fact that geek designers were busily trying to unravel this mystery, when it should have been social scientists, biologists, chemists, and those later fellows collectively engrossed in a new thing called the genome project, followed by biosynthesis.

In short what artificial did was simply build a relationship, and then roll forward and backward with tidbits until a knowledge base is created. This is where I came in for my small but meaningful contribution. I simply assessed the variants with repeated measure, notwithstanding whether they are right or wrong. This thing led to the discovery and further assessment of 'this and that', and 'those' which were known to be persistent. And when I did I parked them in a hidden place.

Interestingly enough Yuecan and Zhao did pretty much the same thing with their database. And within this transition lies the most formidable contribution; investigative genealogy: Who is on the move and who hides out in all of those empty spaces. I am left to ponder this on a mass scale because this would be a doubling population in a shorter time span than some say. In the meantime I will have to think about moving again some other day.

It takes me a while to sort all of this out; all of this forward and backward chaining. But I got to that creative aha moment, not unlike the scientists we attempt to mind mirror over time. It was in an almost parallel intellectually spiked moment that I came to the realization of how Yuecan and Zhao were moving the data to China's mainland without submitting to the close scrutiny of folks who dwell in this expansive virtual world.

And the good chase was on. I was back on the grid with good intent.

Fortuitous Event

# Chapter Thirty-one

## *In with the Old*

I DID NOT MEAN TO DISAPPEAR completely, but sometimes these approaches work better than most assumed would under this specific set of circumstances. It would be somewhat meaningless to backtrack at this point. However, whatever my undoing would point back to I did not want it to include that I stuck around too long watching their surprise.

It was one thing to invent a complete persona and invest in the remarkable amount of time of nourishing it for such a long time, but that is exactly what Yuecan and Zhao did and nearly perfected the approach. Their undoing in the end was pretending to be too despondent over the loss of their true identities back in their homeland. And that is precisely what set this whole difference thing off. I would care less for culture.

My intent in the beginning was to show off a bit and tap back into the pigtail that I had attached to one of the undersea cables. The funny thing about new technology is that it habitually falls back to descriptors of the past to describe itself in the present. In this case what I had added was a vampire tap. The imagination soars even if one has not been exposed to the actual process in question. A quick visualization does ample service to quickly filling in the visual blanks. If more is needed a simple suggestion of a bite to the exposed neck will suffice. In this case however, given that the task is executed twelve to fifteen feet below the surface of the sea additional context was required.

When one blows off the flame from a candle sufficient displacement of oxygen passes over the target point to create a momentary drop in one of the three things necessary for a flame to burn: oxygen, fuel and heat. Remove any one of those aspects of a good burn and the flame's life is remedied null and void. In the case of a very old submerged and shielded coax cable there are necessary elements to survive as well. The task here inevitably includes not putting a stray signal onto the coax when disrupting or modifying its original intent: to carry information from a source toward a destination without undue distortion.

It was still dark out when I rolled off of my paddle board and slid into the water. I did not have to stifle my entrance into this watery world because no one was quite close enough to hear anything at this moment before the break of dawn and first light.

When working in a familiar environment great visualization is not as paramount in importance. As I submerged slowly using at least part of my negative buoyancy—holding some in reserve—the soft undulating current cradled me as though I was in a softly rocking hammock. At one point I was almost rocked into a sleepy temperament. This was not the most appropriate sensation even when a diver is in calm and relatively shallow waters: the fact that any false sense of security or calm can be your last. I alerted myself back to the task at hand and I would forego the meditative quality of my cold and richly saline environment.

When I hit bottom I pushed off a bit and felt around for the cable. By the second try I felt my fingers brush against a surface that was unnatural to my world at the bottom of this inlet. So finding this material meant that I would have an ample guideline to my next destination. I checked for the direction of the current and then moved along the length of the dense cable and its weighted mass in the general direction of my tap in near darkness. Any source of artificial illumination would have been cheating.

There is a bit of pride still, when one goes up against one's self. Where everyone else in this sometimes overly eager to compete society engages with obsession, I tend to stand apart and simply relay against myself. My last race, last crawl, climb and paddle are always a one person competition. It was a quality my dad instilled in me; my simply watching the feats he commanded for the simple pleasure of the self willed contest was lesson enough.

As a simple diversion to the task at hand I recalled a comment of a journalist in a local newspaper calling into question the feat of another kind of challenge. The individual competitor was making a claim that he was already "the standing champion" of the now world popular Iron Man marathon held in the Hawaiian Islands. What had occurred to the journalist had also occurred to me: What about all of those champions who did so outside of the purview of a watching world? Yes, the ones who never required anything close to the bevy of cameras and microphones to engage in such simple pleasures of an already common task. It was an amusing exercise to cure the ultimate boredom of this task at hand—following the lead set by others several decades ago.  My competition had to be against myself as the labors of those who laid down this heavy network were long gone and forgotten.

When I was serving in the Navy and in the Hawaiian Islands, bored friends invited me to step off base and head to the Big Island for what they concurred was a rousing good time.  These friends had been going to the Big Island for several years by now, and were joining some local athletes in a competitive journey of a one hundred and twenty nine mile bicycle ride, followed by a twenty six mile run, and capped by a very refreshing five mile swim in the ocean.  This was at the turn of the 1970s.  I joined in the fun in the fall of 1973.  It was not until well after I got out of active duty in the service that I even heard of this thing which evolved into this mass circus called the Iron Man—the World Class Race.

At long last I found what I had been looking for: my tap. My most immediate task was to add in an additional cable without upsetting anything going on with this line. It had been a while since I had last tested it, and for all I knew it was dead or had an even dozen listening in.  It was a large enough gamble that I was undertaking, by adding myself into a potential active party line.  I did so a long last, and without having to go over to my reserve tank.

I snaked my more flexible cable along the rocky bottom and then in and out of a rocky shore.  The shielded coax extension was as dark as the surrounding shoreline so it would be near impossible to spot from the edge of the twenty eight foot cliff that loomed above.  Since my whereabouts was nested in a pockmarked cliff line of sandstone, I was able to wind my way through a maze of wind-carved and water eroded caves until I relocated a suitable flat surface. It was here that I made my final assembly and fired up the battery operated equipment as the rising sun began to snake over to the sea. It was a lovely morning to be tapped into and I decided to take my time in coming on line to this older world of yesterday's technology.

The methods I employed on the lovely morning with soft winds barely rising above a steadied breeze included a time domain reflectometer. They have been around for decades and the first time I used one was with a very early stage start up that matched the event of the light shining over the cliff line and out across the waters of this bay. This method I was deploying was the most accurate way to ascertain what exactly this cable was being used for at this precise time of the day.

Time Domain Reflectometer—TDR—can be a most useful tool in identifying faults in the type of cable coax as I was exploring on the bottom of the sea. The primary task underhand was to take a bit of a census of just how many pieces of equipment were in place, and with the additional pieces of equipment I now had on line with regard to this network, and how many were still in use. The technology of the past was being deployed to assess the present, so that I could make a knowledgeable assessment of what was in store for the future—with regard to the task at hand, of course.

The principle of operation being staged was to place an unobtrusive pulse of energy onto the cable and use sensitive instruments to assess how long it takes to reflect from a source to a destination, and back again.

The equipment and programs I was using would then look into all of the subtle information which could be gleaned from the bounced signal. It was a distance reading under the best circumstances. Once I had this information I switched on my second piece of equipment in tandem and did a waveform signature match against any other ongoing reflections on the line, across the continuous length of the cable network. This resulted in a simplistic numeric readout which I captured as a stream and fed into to a database for comparison. Any similarities in the readout were used to match up to traditional types of waveforms that could be construed as anomalies or recognizable signal streams. And I had found my first match—with regard to pulse width and frequency, and velocity of propagation—I knew I had a good match. At least I thought I did at the time.

There were recognizable pulses of energy propagating repeatedly across this line. Through my network of working equipment I could begin to make it all out. It was transmitted information and at the fault of its sender for not paying careful enough attention, I could simply listen in and copy with the smallest margin of fault. But when I began to study this closer I came across something I could not easily explain. I would have to copy as much as possible, close my tap, and take all of this back for evaluation off line.

**Never Far off of that Grid**

By the time I got back to my new dwellings it was well into the night. The drive had been absolutely beautiful so this I did not mind at all. The splendid valley I had driven across cut between two high ridges of the North Cascades. Although it had been a clear day on the coast there were definite signs of dense overcast and a fine wet haze alone the highway I took back. I had to stop numerous times for the busy intersections cutting across parts of the highway to allow lumber carrying trucks pass across as if by rite of passage. It was an inconvenience but one could not help smiling back to the tips of their caps or friendly waves as they recognized the gesture.

The road I turned off onto was already wet from the now heavy mist from the clouds above. It was not quite like driving through a rainy downpour but it was thick enough to warrant the intermittent time beat of the windshield wipers. It was useless to turn on the radio in this densely tree lined area so I slipped one of my favorite composers into the truck's DVD player. The richly sounding renaissance blend of Spanish guitars in a modern composition brought a smile to my face. I was uncomfortable driving such a long distance wearing seven millimeters of only semi dry wetsuit, but I did have this soothing music in the company of a great deli sandwich and a tall bottle of iced, honey tea.

Perhaps I should forego the mention of the open and partially empty bag of potato chips, but I will be quick to call into attention that they are organic, low sodium and baked in olive oil. There is my next quick and equally important disclaimer before I arrived at home.

The hot shower was as rewarding as I toweled off and slowly dressed and listened to my phone messages. Two were short and one was long and all three were dialed into a wrong number. It was a wonderful way to show that when you go away so many others are still able to find you. Two of them were caller ID back to a survey. Would they really want to know what I was doing now?

By the time I return my friend's call it was well after midnight. She was in a rather good mood and this was my way in back onto her good side. I had done many wrongs in my past with regard to this good natured woman. Now I was wondering if she would still accept me for staying too far away.

"Well first of all I don't like it when anyone calls me between midnight and four o'clock in the morning. This is when I do my best work. You of all people should remember that." She was testy but friendly—so much I could tell by the sway of her voice. "What are you up to?"

I played a quick game of share between myself and my all too patient friend. It could almost be described as a contest. Usually I like to play this one alone, but she had duly challenged me and I felt compelled to comply with regard to her nature in the middle of the night. I slipped a cup of hot tea in front of me and took my time as I spilled it all out. Her being so patient was reward enough.

"So the most baffling aspect of this scenario is just how low the frequency was." I have never come across this; not at least for thirty or more years.

"It sounds like what you are dealing with is an extremely low frequency range of communication. What were you doing thirty years ago—remind me?"

"Well it was over thirty years ago, actually. Toward the end of my active duty in the Navy I had volunteered to do weekly maintenance on a pump circulation system at St. Francisco Point, down near San Diego."

"It was a pump circulation system for what?  You know how I get annoyed when you break things down into little chunks.  Don't do that."

"The Navy had dolphin tanks that required an enormous amount of sea water to be circulated through as well as properly filtered.  My task was to keep it running and well maintained including clearing out the filters on the weekends.  The tanks were populated with dolphins and I volunteered for the task because it included free diving with the local inhabitants.  It was a lot of work but it was also a lot of fun."

My friend had gotten quite by this time and I used this pause to enjoy my tea before it grew too cool.  It was a rich blend of green and mint teas and it was best enjoyed just below hot.  It oozed across the top of my tongue and the mint was always a pleasant surprise with each successive sip.

"So where does the ELF part come in?"  She was back on line—literally so.

"Did you just pee while we were talking?"  I was not surprised and pretended to be taken back.

"Now, let's get back to the ELF"  She was impertinent at times, but that is why I was attracted to her in the first place.  There was no rush to her statement of the obvious.

"The Navy was collaborating with UC San Diego for underwater hydrophone and speaker development.  During the study another group of scientists joined in with an analog computer to capture under seas noise, in conjunction with a signal generator to transmit noise and measure the results."

"This was in the seventies?" She wanted more chronological detail.

"Yes, and it also included another group in parallel who were attempting to communicate with dolphins."

"Why?" It was a detailed enough question. I knew the intent.

"Because it was interesting at the time," I fired back.

"Was it successful?" She shot to the point.

"Most of it was. They refined the existing hydrophone and underwater speaker design, and the analog computer was able to generate, capture and store a whole array of meaningful waveforms and store them into a database for later use."

And thus my well thought out counterpoint.

"And the whole point of this tale was that they did so using extremely low frequency." She had never wanted the last word before.

"As a result of the high electrical conductivity of sea water, signals are attenuated as they propagate through it. This also depends on frequency. The lower the frequency of the generated signals the 'more' deeper the signal can be received."

There was another one of those supposedly important pauses and I could hear her fingers pounding a keyboard with intense fury. Her capability was on an opposite course of extremely high frequency of digital impact on plastic keys of an expectedly well worn out keyboard. I recalled that it was a rare moment indeed when anyone could make out the worn symbols that should have existed on the keyboard in her office on a much earlier campus. It became an inner circle joke, in fact, who had the worst for ware.

"Ok, your point of contention seems to be 'who' on earth is still using this technology outside of the military. Is that correct?"

She had really gotten to the point. I sat proud in my chair and sipped tea that was too cool to enjoy, but at the same time I no longer wanted hot.

"When can you have something for me.?"

"What are the useful coordinates? I presume you took some signal measurements and collected some recognizable data streams?"

"I did indeed. Where do you want me to park them?"

After another twenty minutes or so she said that she had to sign off to attend to a far different matter. Somewhere in her planetary circle of friends someone obviously had proposed something more interesting.

But at the same time I needed a few hours of sleep before I turned to an entirely different task at hand. We both agreed to link up again in four to six hours, before hanging up in more ways than one. I liked her still—I really do—but I could only be exposed to her for only so long. Too many memories were flooding back in, as they did before, and I needed the break and certainly the distance.

After I hung up I went to be to catch up on some highly regarded sleep. In a sense I had been running ragged in another kind of marathon. I was not the first, but I knew who was and I was planning to keep this to myself. What I needed from her was another point of confirmation. That could wait until another time in the day.

There was one more means of communication, however, that I had to engage in before my head could hit that pillow. I slid across the bare wood floor of my bedroom and speed dialed another number. It rang twice before anyone answered.

"Is there still a notable flurry of activity?" I spoke into the hand held in not quite a whisper.

"More than you can ever surmise. It is not often someone is able to back out completely from their system. I don't want to know how or even why. But are you sure this is how you want to play this all out?"

The voice on the other line had an old and very familiar sound. It took me back to another time in my life, and one that I had lost appreciation of. I could not only hear her, but now I could smell her and feel her all at the same time. I was calling in an awful lot of favors lately.

"Roxanne, I do want to thank you for everything that was done on your end."

"Well I want that in person." She was making a real enough point and I wanted to comply sooner than was possible. I could feel my body moan just thinking about a reunion.

"Well, if it is any consolation at all," I started in with good intention, "it will not be as long as before. This I do promise to you, now."

"Oh, sure, but I've learned not to hold my breath with you in mind. Yes, let's make lame plans to get together soon. Keep me in the loop when you can."

"I have evolved, after all. I can get through these great hurdles." Was I being sincere enough? We were not using Skype this time, so I could not see her face. "I am not afraid of heights if that is what you mean." I just lied.

"You may think of me as some Herculean task, but I am far from that. Think of the story you told me about your dad. That he was one of a hand full of people who deliberately dove off of the Golden Gate Bridge and survived. You can survive us in the same manner. You just have to work up the required nerve."

It was Roxanne's turn to hang up. She did so in no uncertain terms. Of all the challenges I had faced in my childhood, and pulled into adulthood, relationships were my greatest fear.

It was not about having them, but rather not tending to them as carefully as I would the great outdoors. This was a constant contest I was having with myself. I would have to revisit this very soon, and hoped I would not confront it too late.

Fortuitous Event

# Chapter Thirty-two

## *Just Wait for It*

ONE OF THE GOOD THINGS about getting older is that one can gain the necessary traction over that longer span of time to master patience. At least that should be the case. I was never good at that when I was younger and had this desire to get to the heart of matters without delay. Now there is a part of me that likes to think things out, with the added balance of not over thinking the issues of concern unless truly warranted. I do fret sometimes, but I am working on this all the time.

To strike a balance between the methodological approach of science and technology in a lab, and the spiritual aha moment that an artist might rely on in a studio, takes effort. Living in both worlds and straddling a very fine line is common enough, but only a small percentage of both populations get the balance so right with consistency in outcome. A long time ago Galileo Galilei wrote a manuscript titled *Dialogue Concerning the Two Chief World Systems*, which explored the notion of a helio-centric versus geo-centric existence. In a concluding treatment he comes to the conclusion that more likely it was a little bit of both. That is how I saw Roxanne.

I could clearly spell this out in my head, with regard to my impending approach: that I had spent most of the earlier part of my life getting in and out of relationships; that now I was attempting to completely back out, while asking for a hand out. I had surrounded myself with a multitude of associates who created all these back doors for all of these data things connected, but I could not fine my own.

I was not the first to think about subverting this dominate paradigm. Certainly there were those who did before. But how would you test for the validity of successes? Where was the detailed analysis of variance with repeated measures? And if so, could that be pulled off without garnering further attention if I needed another hand out again.

Could we survive successfully in these two chief world systems? Was this going to be a little bit of both, or was being both on and off the grid just a bit of hopeful 21C slang? I wanted to find out. Fully understanding all of the risks was of keen interest to my circle of friends as well. They made bets as to how well I would pull this off.

Yes, I am so sure I was going to get this one right (my next disclaimer). This would indeed be a full circle—a hermetic circle—as I devour myself for their collective amusement. Would this be a pinnacle of my life as I planned it, or just another moment of hopeless narcissism?

I had really wanted to think this thing through—my way. I went for a paddle. And on that day I really hit upon something far more contentious than cold and deep waters. I had an unexpected shadow.

Being a person of interest kind of sucks if it turns out it is for all of the wrong reasons. They made bets as to how well I would pull this off.

It was like the time my Dad took me on my first road trip into Mexico. After the sessions and arguments over how the Beats really would influence my life we piled so literally into that VW Bug and drove from San Francisco to Tijuana. It was a long but conversation full sojourn between a son and his dad—perhaps one of the more memorable.

The night before crossing the border was spent in a modestly priced motel along the coast. After pizza and cold drinks we walked on the beach and watched long boarders paddle out beyond the rock jetty and we discussed my future, of course. My Dad was glad about all of the things he had exposed me to and I reiterated each sense of appeal I had felt at the time. The successive journeys were so culturally crossed that one might be quite surprised just how center lined our relationship had become. He said he was conservative and I countered toward the liberal. But when the night air came upon us it was sufficiently clear that why we survived as we did was because we were both seeking the center of the universe.

We made this discovery and sat on the jetty, watching long boarders lay on their backs on their wood or fiberglass boards, bobbing in between sets of waves and watching the same flock of low flying pelicans as we did in earnest. We scanned the darkening skies for the train of silhouetted beauties soaring eighteen inches above the surface of the ocean looking for their next shimmering meal. And then the sun set far below the distant horizon and my dad and I made our way back into our motel room.

That night after we were well asleep with one on the bed and one on a comfortable pull out couch someone used an old pass key to enter the room and attempt to slide open the security chain. The noise woke us both. With a shout for me to stay put my dad rushes out across the parking lot in his boxers under the illumination of clear skies and an almost full moon. His pale skin is a delight as he rushes into the street with a custom lightweight gun held high in the air as he is being watched from the café across the street by two San Diego patrol vehicles.

That scene is properly set. They join in the chase but it is not as clear as to who is chasing who. But they are all running with intent. Given that all this will prove hilarious to all surviving parties I could not help but being both shocked and amused that some of the other patron of that motel joined me and they made bets as to how well any of the parties would pull this off. It was another of life's lessons no matter how strange it seemed at the time. There were as many cultures in play simultaneously as there were observers and actors pursuant to the scene. But it all wrapped up rather nicely within the next thirty to forty-five minutes and we would have yet another fortuitous event that ties this all together

At long last I finally understood the subtleties of genealogy and how they collectively become the greatest trail of clues with regard to our collective and very predictable futures.

Michael O'Connor

## Fixed in Post: *Language of Objects*

Language of objects

Navigating Salton Seas

First you must step out


Each day a baseline

No limits from this viewpoint

Which one could attain


Something greater now

Is still on par with nature

Daylight to shadows


Once North Puget Sound

That chance to witness unique

Creations take shape

Fortuitous Event

Open all year around

Welcome to this grand New Year

Discover your core


That world of objects

Is not so unfamiliar

Albeit reeling


Just glance around that Sound

Still life is just so spread out

Art without taut frames


No reproductions

This great work is always real

Avenues with trees


This path of art speaks

Therefore why not infinite

To make that certain

Michael O'Connor

Sunsets do detach

Precisely similar lines

Just sit down to watch


Alternative sides

In that break of space and time

You notice this now


That same line of thought

Comedy then tragedy

Now show likeliness


Passing on that spot

An act of fidelity

Makes one feel humble


Unwitting actors

Translated by their good looks

Recognize that bond

Fortuitous Event

Step through space and time

Like pavements of perspective

Fuel this new order

Michael O'Connor

Fortuitous Event

www.ingramcontent.com/pod-product-compliance
Lightning Source LLC
Chambersburg PA
CBHW062120280526
45788CB00001B/2